Commanding Grace

D1568239

Commanding Grace

Studies in Karl Barth's Ethics

Edited by

Daniel L. Migliore

WILLIAM B. EERDMANS PUBLISHING COMPANY

GRAND RAPIDS, MICHIGAN / CAMBRIDGE, U.K.

© 2010 Wm. B. Eerdmans Publishing Co.

Published 2010 by
Wm. B. Eerdmans Publishing Co.
2140 Oak Industrial Drive N.E., Grand Rapids, Michigan 49505 /
P.O. Box 163, Cambridge CB3 9PU U.K.

Printed in the United States of America

16 15 14 13 12 11 10   7 6 5 4 3 2 1

Library of Congress Cataloging-in-Publication Data

Commanding grace: studies in Karl Barth's ethics / edited by Daniel L. Migliore.
    p.   cm.
  Chiefly proceedings of a conference held June 22-25, 2008,
    at Princeton Theological Seminary.
  Includes bibliographical references.
  ISBN 978-0-8028-6570-0 (pbk.: alk. paper)
  1. Barth, Karl, 1886-1968. 2. Christian ethics — Reformed authors.
  I. Migliore, Daniel L., 1935-

BJ1251. C693 2010
241.092 — dc22

2010016206

www.eerdmans.com

Contents

Acknowledgments

Most of the essays in this volume were presented as lectures at the Third Annual Karl Barth Conference held June 22-25, 2008, at Princeton Theological Seminary. I want to express my thanks to the Karl Barth Center at Princeton for sponsoring this event; to Princeton Seminary for hosting it; to all the lecturers and their respondents for their stimulating leadership; and to the many conference attendees whose comments and questions sparked lively discussions during our days together. A special word of thanks is reserved for Matthew Puffer, my research assistant at the time and now a Ph.D. student at the University of Virginia, who provided indispensable help with every aspect of my editorial responsibilities. Thanks also to Dr. Clifford Anderson, Curator of Special Collections at the Princeton Seminary Libraries; to Amy Ehlin, Conference Coordinator; and to Christopher Terry-Nelson and Travis McMaken, student assistants for the conference. Finally, I am grateful to Tom Raabe and all the skilled staff of Eerdmans for their careful editorial work, and most especially to Bill Eerdmans and Jon Pott, editors extraordinaire, for their encouragement and support. I dedicate this book to Eberhard Busch, who has contributed so much to Barth studies over the past half century, not least in emphasizing the inseparability of theology and ethics in Barth's writings and practice.

Abbreviations

CD   Karl Barth, *Church Dogmatics* I/1–IV/4. Edited by G. W. Bromiley and T. F. Torrance. Edinburgh: T. & T. Clark, 1936-75.

CL   Karl Barth, *The Christian Life: Church Dogmatics* IV/4, *Lecture Fragments*. Translated by Geoffrey W. Bromiley. Grand Rapids: Eerdmans, 1981.

Contributors

NIGEL BIGGAR
Regius Professor of Moral and Pastoral Theology
   University of Oxford
   Oxford, United Kingdom

JOHN R. BOWLIN
Ruth and Rimmer DeVries Associate Professor of Reformed
   Theology and Public Life
Princeton Theological Seminary
Princeton, New Jersey

TODD V. CIOFFI
Assistant Professor of Congregational and Ministry Studies
Calvin College
Grand Rapids, Michigan

JESSE COUENHOVEN
Assistant Professor of Moral Theology
Villanova University
Villanova, Pennsylvania

TIMOTHY GORRINGE
St. Luke's Professor of Theological Studies
University of Exeter
Exeter, United Kingdom

Contributors

ERIC GREGORY
Professor of Religion
Princeton University
Princeton, New Jersey

DAVID HADDORFF
Associate Professor of Theology and Religious Studies
St. John's University
Staten Island, New York

CHRISTOPHER R. J. HOLMES
Senior Lecturer in Theology
University of Otago
Dunedin, New Zealand

DANIEL L. MIGLIORE
Emeritus Professor of Systematic Theology
Princeton Theological Seminary
Princeton, New Jersey

PAUL T. NIMMO
Meldrum Lecturer in Theology
New College
University of Edinburgh
Edinburgh, United Kingdom

KATHERINE SONDEREGGER
Professor of Theology
Virginia Theological Seminary
Alexandria, Virginia

KATHRYN TANNER
Dorothy Grant Maclear Professor of Theology
University of Chicago
Chicago, Illinois

WILLIAM WERPEHOWSKI
Professor of Christian Ethics and
Director of the Center for Peace and Justice Education
Villanova University
Villanova, Pennsylvania

1. Commanding Grace: Karl Barth's Theological Ethics

Daniel L. Migliore

Interest in Barth's theology continues to grow. Its consistently high quality, often stunning originality, remarkable comprehensiveness, and strong provocations to fresh theological reflection in both church and academy assure its place among the most influential theological writings of the modern era. Best known for its singular christocentric exposition of the core doctrines of Christian faith, Barth's theology is also notable for its contributions to the history of doctrine, to biblical exegesis, to the interface of theology and philosophy, and by no means least, to theological ethics, the topic that receives special attention in this volume. A number of the articles included here were presented at the conference "Karl Barth and Theological Ethics" held at Princeton Theological Seminary, June 22-25, 2008. Others were subsequently written by participants at the conference in response to the original presentations.

From the beginning, the project that we know as *Church Dogmatics* was also a project in the reconstruction of Christian ethics. In the current renaissance of Barth studies, the study of his theological ethics has an important place even if this aspect of his thought has not received as much attention as many of his doctrinal topics. That is reason enough for the present volume. One way of formulating the wider question that the volume attempts to address is: Can Barth the magisterial dogmatic theologian offer significant help to theology and church today in the area of Christian ethics, a discipline Oliver O'Donovan has succinctly defined as thinking "from truths of Christian faith to conclusions in Christian action"?[1]

---

1. Oliver O'Donovan, *Common Objects of Love: Moral Reflection and the Shaping of Community* (Grand Rapids: Eerdmans, 2002), p. 3.

Already in 1911, in a speech to members of a factory union in Safenwil, Barth explored the "inner connection" between the message and work of Jesus the incarnate Word of God and the values and aspirations of modern social democracy. In that address he advanced the blockbuster thesis that "Jesus *is* the movement for social justice, and the movement for social justice *is* Jesus in the present."[2] In later years, Barth would express himself quite differently; nevertheless, it is clear that for the Safenwil pastor Christology and ethics were already tightly intertwined.

As Barth would later explain, when WWI broke out, he was shocked to learn that ninety-three German intellectuals, including many of his revered teachers, had issued a manifesto supporting the war policy of the kaiser. He describes the impact of that event as "the twilight of the gods," a failure of the theology of his revered teachers in the face of the ideology of war, exposing the fact that religion and scholarship could be so easily changed into "intellectual 42 cm cannons."[3] By the end of WWI, in his famous Tambach lecture, "The Christian's Place in Society," Barth approached the question of the relationship between Christian faith and social responsibility much more critically than he had in his earlier lecture to Safenwil workers. He now distanced himself from an uncritical affiliation with Christian socialism even as in the intervening years he had taken leave of the theology and ethics of nineteenth-century liberal Protestant theology. The true Christian, Barth argued, is not any Christian, whether conservative or revolutionary; the true Christian is the Christ. The kingdom of God is not the kingdom we build but "the wholly other Kingdom which is God's."[4] Barth did not then, nor did he ever, understand this emphasis in a quietist or merely otherworldly sense. Toward the end of his life, in an exposition of the petition "Thy kingdom come," Barth wrote that Christians "not only wait but also hasten. . . . Their waiting takes place in the hastening. . . . [T]he petition 'Thy kingdom come' is not an indolent and despondent prayer but one that is zealous and brave."[5]

2. Karl Barth, "Jesus Christ and the Movement for Social Justice," in *Karl Barth and Radical Politics,* ed. George Hunsinger (Philadelphia: Westminster, 1976), p. 19.

3. Quoted by Eberhard Busch, *Karl Barth: His Life from Letters and Autobiographical Texts* (Philadelphia: Fortress, 1976), p. 81.

4. Karl Barth, "The Christian's Place in Society," in *The Word of God and the Word of Man,* trans. Douglas Horton (Gloucester, Mass.: Peter Smith, 1978), p. 321.

5. *CL,* p. 263.

It is not my task in this introductory essay to trace the continuities and discontinuities in the development of Barth's theological ethics. It is sufficient to make the point that, early and late, Barth saw dogmatics and ethics as inseparable. For him, when rightly understood, both are based on the living Word of God that announces a gift to be freely and joyfully received and that contains a command to be freely and joyfully obeyed. From the Romans commentary where Barth states that "The problem of ethics is identical with the problem of dogmatics: Soli Deo Gloria";[6] to the Münster *Ethics* of 1928 (repeated in Bonn in 1930-31), which he wrote as the necessary companion to his first two cycles of dogmatics in Göttingen and Münster, and in which he declared that "not just in general, but also in particular, the concern of ethics is a proper concern of dogmatics";[7] through the production of the *Church Dogmatics,* which is structured in such a way that extended treatments of ethics immediately follow the doctrines of God, creation, and reconciliation because "dogmatics has no option: it has to be ethics as well"[8] — through all the phases of his theological work, Barth viewed dogmatics and ethics as a seamless garment. Had Barth lived to complete his plan, he would surely have included a treatise on ethics in volume V, the projected doctrine of redemption. For Barth, from beginning to end, dogmatics and ethics belong together.

While the unity of dogmatics and ethics in Barth's thinking is clear enough, there is far less consensus in the assessment of this union. Why has Barth's theological ethics met with some considerable head-shaking, if not severe criticism, from the earliest period of his work to the present? Is it simply because in this area of his work, as in others, Barth is simply determined to swim against the current? Are the presuppositions and method of his ethical reflection those of an outsider to the guild who does not conform to established schools of ethical reflection such as deontological, teleological, or contextual ethics? Or is it because Barth's ethics, in making a 180-degree turn away from modernity's doctrine of unrestricted human autonomy, rides a pendulum swing to a view of divine heteronomy that supposedly has no place for free human agency? Or is it because, as numerous critics

---

6. Karl Barth, *The Epistle to the Romans,* trans. Edwyn C. Hoskyns (London: Oxford University Press, 1957), pp. 431-32.

7. Karl Barth, *Ethics,* trans. Geoffrey Bromiley (New York: Seabury Press, 1981), p. 16.

8. *CD* I/2, p. 793.

charge, Barth's ethics offers little concrete ethical guidance, little help
in everyday Christian decision making, save to refer to the living Word
of God addressing hearers in their concrete life situations by the power
of the Holy Spirit? Does Barth dismiss all rules and generalizations in
Christian ethics with the result that he is simply unable to say that in
every situation there are some things that are commanded and some
things that are forbidden? Or again, the critics ask, is Barth's ethics
able to make any significant contribution to public discussion of ethical issues in a pluralist society, or does he write ethics only for a
ghettoized Christian community? Such questions compel many
ethicists, even those with a high appreciation for Barth's work, to look
for a way beyond Barth, whether by a retrieval of natural law ethics (the
route taken early on by Emil Brunner), or by retrieval of Thomistic theology in which, as Fergus Kerr notes, the inseparability of dogmatics
and ethics is emphasized as strongly as by Barth,[9] or by an ethics of virtue and Christian character cultivated by church practices (the route
taken by Stanley Hauerwas and others).

As will become apparent from the essays in this volume, even
those who find much to approve of in Barth's ethics part company
with him at one point or another. We should not expect it to be otherwise. Barth intended his work in ethics, as in theology, not to close
down debate but to challenge long-established ways of thinking with
fresh attention to the voice of Scripture as it centrally attests God's
work of reconciliation in Christ. Our authors were chosen not because
they toe some inflexible party line in the interpretation of Barth's theological ethics but because they value the contributions he makes and
the challenges he poses in this area and are determined to think creatively with him and at times also beyond or even against him.

By way of preparing the reader unacquainted with Barth's ethics
for the essays that follow, I propose several basic questions that need to
be asked in reading and assessing his writings on ethics to measure the
extent to which his work may have continuing value for church and society today. First, what understanding of God, humanity, and their relationship forms the dogmatic context of Barth's theological ethics?
Second, how are grace and command, gift and task, gospel and law re-

9. See Fergus Kerr, *After Aquinas: Versions of Thomism* (Malden, Mass.: Blackwell,
2002). "Both Thomas and Barth composed ethics in the light of their understanding of
God and God's relationship to the world," p. 114.

4

lated in Barth's ethics? Third, what understanding of human freedom, maturity, and responsibility is at work in Barth's theological ethics? Fourth, is Barth's theological ethics able to provide any helpful guidance in the area of public policy, especially as it relates to such matters as systems of economy, the modern democratic state, and the exercise of state power? Barth's answers to these four questions might be summarized by the phrases "covenant of the triune God," "commanding grace and gracious command," "freedom to love," and "power in the service of just community."

The Covenantal Context of Barth's Theological Ethics

Barth sets ethics in a particular theological context. The word "context" can, of course, have a multitude of meanings. If used in relation to Barth's construal of the location of Christian ethics, it does not refer primarily to the psychological or religious situation of the individual Christian. Nor does it refer in the first place to the political, cultural, or economic context of the church at a particular place and time. The context in which Barth situates ethics is a distinctive theological depiction of the reality in which humans are called to live and act. More specifically, Barth's description of the context of theological ethics, far from being a vague theism, is unabashedly *Trinitarian*. That is, the context of ethics for Barth is the decision and activity of the triune God to establish in the life, death, and resurrection of Jesus Christ a covenant of free grace made present and imparted by the power of the Holy Spirit. The aim of the free grace of God the Creator, Reconciler, and Redeemer, "actualised and revealed in God's covenant with man, is the restoration of man to the divine likeness and therefore to fellowship with God in eternal life."[10] As attested in Scripture and proclaimed in the witness of the church, the covenant of God with the people of Israel confirmed and fulfilled in Jesus Christ for all humanity is the context of Barth's theological ethics.

John Webster, author of *Barth's Ethics of Reconciliation*, calls this covenantal context of Barth's ethics his "moral ontology," that is, "a depiction of the world of human action as it is enclosed and governed by the creative, redemptive, and sanctifying work of God in Christ, present

10. *CD* II/2, p. 566.

by the power of the Holy Spirit."[11] Nigel Biggar, a contributor to this volume and author of *The Hastening That Waits: Karl Barth's Ethics,* similarly describes the covenantal context of Barth's theological ethics as the activity of the triune God in which God is self-defined from all eternity as God for us and humanity is defined as humanity for God.[12] On this point Biggar and Webster are agreed: the covenantal activity of the triune God constitutes for Barth the real world in which Christian ethical reflection takes place. For Barth, then, the discipline of theological ethics does not exist in a vacuum. The perennial question of ethics: "What are we to do?" properly follows the questions of the identity and activity of God. "The command of the one God," Barth writes, "is centrally the command of the Lord of the covenant, in which the action of sinful man is determined, ordered, and limited by the free grace of the faithful God manifested and operative in Jesus Christ."[13]

The word and work of the triune God in which Barth's ethics is situated is not only particular; it is always also a living word and work, personally addressing particular human beings here and now. The God who as Creator, Reconciler, and Redeemer covenants with humanity in Jesus Christ is the living God. God's activity is not imprisoned in the past; it calls for faithful response of particular human beings in the concreteness of the present. If God is the living Lord, it follows that the divine command is a living command and cannot be reduced to a general rule or set of rules. This is the reason for Barth's well-known rejection of ethical "casuistry." As Barth defines the term, casuistry is any understanding of the divine command as "made up of biblical texts in which there are believed to be seen universally binding divine ordinances and directions, of certain propositions again presumed to be universally valid, of the natural moral law generally perceptible to human reason, and finally of particular norms which have been handed down historically in the tradition of Western Christianity and which lay claim to universal validity."[14] Note that in this passage Barth clearly disavows every ossification of the divine command even if it takes the form of a biblical text or set of texts. Leave aside for

11. John Webster, *Barth's Ethics of Reconciliation* (Cambridge: Cambridge University Press, 1995), p. 2.

12. Nigel Biggar, *The Hastening That Waits: Karl Barth's Ethics* (Oxford: Clarendon, 1993).

13. *CL,* p. 3.

14. *CD* III/4, p. 6.

the moment the debate whether Barth himself engages at times in some forms of casuistic reasoning. As Barth uses the term, casuistry is any form of ethical reflection that turns the living Word of God into abstract, general rules that supposedly govern Christian behavior in all circumstances. Casuistry for Barth, we might say, is the colonization of Christian ethics. It results, in his words, from "a lack of confidence in the Spirit (who is the Lord) as the Guide, Lawgiver and Judge in respect of Christian action."[15]

Barth's critique of what he calls casuistry, however, is only one side, and indeed only the negative side, of his advocacy of a responsible theological ethics. The idea that Barth's critique of casuistry reflects a disdain of careful reasoning in the work of theology and ethics is entirely mistaken. According to Barth, when one becomes open to the history of Jesus Christ as God's salvation history for the world, this does not mean that one "takes leave of his wits and starts raving. It means that he finally comes to himself, to rationality. . . . There is no more intimate friend of sound human understanding than the Holy Spirit."[16]

The other, positive side of Barth's critique of casuistry is his insistence that Christian ethics, when pursued in its proper context of the covenantal activity of the triune God, offers a "formed reference" for Christian ethical reflection.[17] Far from being empty or amorphous, the formed reference to the concrete divine-human encounter above all in Jesus Christ is such as to give substantive guidance and direction to Christian life and action. Christian ethics is informed, formed, and reformed by the covenant history of God the Creator, Reconciler, and Redeemer with humanity. In this history, God is the free and faithful God who remains ever true to Godself and God's gracious purposes, and the human creature is truly human as it freely and gladly corresponds in its action to the activity of God. In Barth's view, a concrete encounter of a particular human being with the divine command of the living Lord does not float freely on an ocean of indeterminacy. Instead, it is a moment in the concrete history of God with us in which God speaks and acts anew yet remains ever faithful to Godself and to God's creatures. God is "the living, eternally rich God" whose mercy is "new every moment," who never simply repeats himself, yet who is ever constant and

15. *CD* III/4, p. 7.
16. *CD* IV/4, p. 28.
17. *CD* IV/4, p. 18.

faithful.[18] Similarly, the particular human encountered by the specific command of God is not for Barth an abstraction, a humanity in general existing everywhere or nowhere. Instead, the real human being is the actual, concrete human creature who is ever and again called to free obedience to the command of the gracious God revealed in Jesus Christ. As Barth writes, "True man and his good action can be viewed only from the standpoint of the true and active God and His goodness. It is this connexion with dogmatics which guards ethics against arbitrary assertions, arguments or conclusions, and allows it to follow a secure path to fruitful judgments."[19]

If theological ethics for Barth is situated always in the context of the covenantal activity of the living and faithful God revealed in Jesus Christ, its task can be neither the compilation of a set of general rules nor the call for a leap in the dark. If on the one hand theological ethics must not be based on arbitrary divine commands, lacking in constancy and varying according to divine whim or capriciousness, on the other hand theological ethics must not be the reduction of the divine command to a set of universal rules that in effect replace God's living lordship with completely autonomous human decisions and actions. All this prompts the question among Barth's critics of whether Barth so emphasizes the actuality and particularity of the encounter between the gracious God who commands and the human creature who is called to faith and obedience that Barth is unable to give theological ethics any universally regulatory content.

This is, at least, the problem that Barth's ethics raises for, among others, the distinguished ethicist Robin Lovin. Lovin expresses his concern in a chapter of his widely read book *Christian Faith and Public Choices: The Social Ethics of Barth, Brunner, and Bonhoeffer.* Lovin knows that for Barth "God's action somehow sets the stage for human moral life."[20] The problem for Lovin is the "somehow." If Barth's highest priority is the preservation of God's freedom and initiative, Lovin wonders whether this must lead Barth both to marginalize human activity and to exclude from his actualist ontology all ethical generalizations of what must be done or not be done not only in a particular circum-

---

18. *CD* IV/4, p. 16.
19. *CD* III/4, p. 3.
20. Robin Lovin, *Christian Faith and Public Choices: The Social Ethics of Barth, Brunner, and Bonhoeffer* (Philadelphia: Fortress, 1984), p. 23.

stance but in every circumstance. Is Barth able to provide any specific moral guidance that is applicable outside a particular moment of encounter with the Word of God? Is not the effect of Barth's relentless stress on the specificity of the Word of God to every human situation "to call all rules into question"?[21] According to Lovin, even Barth's greater use of analogy in his later writings does not correct the deficiency of his ethics. Barth always begins his analogical reasoning with revelation, from the top down, so to speak, rather than, as Lovin prefers, also from the bottom up. Lovin's conclusion from his analysis runs as follows: "An ethical theory can only provide specific guidance if it includes some general propositions," and Barth rejects all generalizations about God's will because "that would reduce God to an object and restrict his freedom to act."[22]

The worry that Lovin expresses in this essay has been and continues to be a worry for many readers of Barth. Might this worry, however, arise from a failure to take with sufficient seriousness what Barth means by the "formed reference" of Christian ethics? If this formed reference is neglected, the predictable result will be the loss of the christocentric and Trinitarian history of the covenant of God with humanity that provides for Barth the essential context, norm, and direction of all Christian ethical reflection and action.

Gift and Command in Barth's Theological Ethics

Characteristic of Barth's theological ethics is not only its covenantal theological ontology but also its construal of ethics in terms of the divine "command." That is, ethics for Barth has to do with the real and objective command of the living God to his human creature who is summoned to concrete obedience. The command in question, however, is not just any command but the command of *God revealed in Jesus Christ,* and the obedience demanded is not just any obedience but the obedience *appropriate* to the command of God so revealed.

Because Barth uses the language of command so pervasively, some of his readers have judged that his ethics is largely determined by the ethics of Immanuel Kant. Now while there may be formal similari-

21. Lovin, *Christian Faith,* p. 23.
22. Lovin, *Christian Faith,* pp. 41-42.

ties between Barth and Kant, at a deeper level their ethics could not be further apart. The command of which Barth speaks is not the same as a universal moral awareness or categorical imperative. It is instead a command that comes not from ourselves but from outside us, from the God who is genuinely other. The divine command is not a regulative moral principle but the command of the living God. Moreover — and this is of decisive importance for a right understanding of Barth's ethics — the commanding God is the gracious God. If Barth refuses to posit the absolutely autonomous moral agent as the basis of his ethics, he equally rejects the idea of the arbitrary will of God as its basis. Far from being an abstract moral idea, or the will of a capricious or arbitrary tyrant, the God who commands is the gracious God who has chosen from all eternity to be God for humanity and has elected humanity to fellowship with God.

While it is certainly true that Barth makes frequent use of the language of divine command, it is important to determine in what sense he understands this language. In accordance with Barth's insistence that every word we use to speak of God gains its proper meaning from the identity and activity of God rather than from our common usage or assumed meanings of the word, the command of God is not to be subsumed under what is generally understood by the word "command." The command of God is the command of the gracious God made known in Jesus Christ. As Barth writes, "There is no prior time in which the commanding God was not the one he is in Jesus Christ, and no later time in which he will not be so."[23] Everywhere in Barth's theology and ethics, grace and command, gospel and law, gift and task are tightly interwoven. According to Barth, the law is embedded in the gospel and the gospel contains the law, as the tablets from Sinai were in the ark of the covenant, as Barth suggests in a vivid image.[24] Indeed, Barth's refusal to see law and gospel in opposition to each other, or to confuse one with the other, or to give priority to the law rather than to the gospel is a signature mark of his theology and ethics.

Barth's distinctive understanding of the relationship of gospel and law is pervasive in the *Church Dogmatics*. It is evident, to cite a few examples, in his treatment of the dialectic of the divine perfections —

23. *CL*, p. 13.
24. Karl Barth, "Gospel and Law," in *Community, State, and Church*, with a new introduction by David Haddorff (Eugene, Oreg.: Wipf and Stock, 2004), p. 80.

such as grace and holiness, and mercy and righteousness; in his discussion of the relationship of justification and sanctification; in his description of the being and mission of the church. There is a Chalcedon-like logic at work here: just as Jesus Christ is truly God and truly human, without confusion or separation, and just as the order of the relationship of the two natures is always asymmetrical, so gospel and law, gift and task are for Barth intimately united yet without confusion, and in such a way that the gospel or gift of God is always the primary, initiating factor while the law or command of God is always the included factor that calls for a free and appropriate response to the gift given. It is in this sense that the law or command of God is "contained" within the gospel of Jesus Christ as God's self-gift — the gift of forgiveness, reconciliation, and new life — and is misunderstood when seen apart from this gift. God's command is a gracious command and his grace a commanding grace.

I might add parenthetically that Barth's reading of the relationship of gospel and law makes him very suspicious indeed of any theology that marginalizes the Old Testament. This is part and parcel of his repudiation of every theology that separates the church from Israel. For Barth, gospel without the law leads to antinomianism; law without the gospel to legalism. Both of these "isms" are light-years away from the inseparability of divine grace and divine command that Barth finds in the witness of Old and New Testament alike.

The question nevertheless persists among some critics of Barth: Is Barth mistaken to employ the language of divine command in his theological ethics? Has he not undermined his own evangelical intention by retaining this category in his theological ethics? Chris Huebner has recently written an interesting article comparing John Milbank and Barth on the question of whether the language of command is appropriate in a theology and ethics where gift is the central category. Huebner begins his article by explaining that even if Barth did not know Milbank, and even if Milbank does not directly address Barth's writings at length, Milbank's theology of gift and his rejection of the language of command can nevertheless be viewed as posing a serious challenge to Barth's theological ethics. "Milbank's ontology of the gift," says Huebner, "constitutes an objection to even the so-called anti-Kantian interpretation of Barth. According to Milbank, any appeal to the notion of command is necessarily problematic, including Barth's attempt to re-narrate the notion of command in a specifically theological context of gift." Huebner concludes that "while Milbank agrees with Barth on the need for a specifically Christian ethics, he [would argue] that Barth himself failed to achieve this goal just to the extent that he retained the notion of command."[25]

If Huebner's reading is correct, for Milbank the language of command is inseparably bound at some level with the threat of violence. According to this view, the logic of command is utterly incompatible with the logic of gift. However, Barth speaks of the divine command as a "permission" rather than an obligation, let alone an instance of coercion.[26] He emphasizes that the appropriate human response to God's grace *(charis)* is action born not of duty or fear but of free thanksgiving *(eu-charistia)*. If violence belongs to some ways of thinking about the meaning of command, this is certainly not the case with Barth's understanding of the gracious command and commanding grace of God. To suggest that Barth's ethics of divine command traps him in a logic of violence would go against the grain of his entire theology: his doctrine of the Trinity that describes God as a God of peace and harmony; his doctrine of the eternal election of grace in Jesus Christ in which God determines to be our God from the foundations of the world; his doctrine of divine omnipotence as the omnipotence of love; his doctrine of Christ and his atoning work as a liberating and renewing gift *(Gabe)* prior to the task *(Aufgabe)* to which we are summoned; his doctrine of the distinctive activity of the Holy Spirit as like a light that illumines and energizes rather than like a force that compels and tramples. All this stands as the very opposite of threat and violence. The difference between Barth and Milbank most probably roots in their different theological methods. Barth's use of the language of command within the orbit of the grace of God derives from his method of attending rigorously to the history of the covenant of God with Israel fulfilled in Jesus Christ as God's decisive self-disclosure. Milbank's method is to construct an ontology of divine gift-giving that is indebted to but also relatively independent of the biblical narrative.

---

25. Chris K. Huebner, "Can a Gift Be Commanded? Theological Ethics without Theory by Way of Barth, Milbank, and Yoder," *Scottish Journal of Theology* 53, no. 4 (2000): 472-89, here p. 473.

26. *CD* II/2, pp. 593ff.

Barth's Theological Ethics as an Ethics of Freedom

I turn to a third set of questions: What is Barth's understanding of the relationship between divine agency and human agency, between divine freedom and human freedom? How does Barth's understanding of human moral agency before God differ both from the Enlightenment conception of moral agency as absolute autonomy on the one hand and from the mere submission of human agency to heteronomous divine authority on the other? How successful is Barth's description of human beings in the covenantal relationship established by the triune God as a description of genuinely free moral agents? Has Barth really offered a convincing third alternative to an ethics of casuistry on the one hand and an ethics of arbitrary divine authority on the other?

A helpful response to these questions is not possible unless it is understood that Barth's conception of freedom is radically different from the common conception of acting as you please without any constraints. He frequently uses the image of "Hercules at the crossroads" to portray this widespread view of freedom. Against this understanding, Barth contextualizes human freedom within the covenant of grace in which God's loving is free and God's freedom is loving. Properly understood, human freedom is not empty freedom, ever teetering on the edge of the choice between good and evil. Rather, it is freedom formed and directed by the activity of the freely gracious God of the covenant fulfilled in Jesus Christ. "In the covenant relationship . . . the initiative is wholly and exclusively on the side of God. But this initiative aims at a correspondingly free act, at genuine obedience as opposed to that of a puppet, on the part of the man with whom the covenant is made."[27] True human freedom is freedom for God and each other that corresponds to God's way of being and acting in loving freedom for the world. Human freedom is freedom to be who we truly are in Jesus Christ.

Barth's Trinitarian ethics of creation, reconciliation, and redemption is throughout an ethics of freedom. God as Creator commands us to be free for God and others as God in Jesus Christ is free for the world, to live and act as who we truly are by the grace of God, not grudgingly or in resignation but "freely and cheerfully."[28] God as Rec-

27. *CD* IV/2, p. 800.
28. *CD* III/4, p. 4.

onciler commands us to exercise the gift of new life in free obedience to the gracious will and work of God realized in the humanity of Jesus Christ, to pray for and wait on God's coming reign, and as we pray and wait, to hasten and to work on behalf of the weak and the poor and in the direction of greater justice and peace as witness to the coming reign of God. While Barth did not live to write of the command of God as Redeemer in the projected fifth volume of the *Church Dogmatics,* in my judgment he would surely have made much of the divine command to give thanks and, above all, to rejoice. No doubt already contemplating the shape of the unwritten final volume of the *Church Dogmatics,* Barth declares that by the grace of God human beings are "free supremely to rejoice. [They are] also free to become finally serious and thankful, to obey, to think and speak and act responsibly, to believe and love and hope, to serve God and man. But above all, in a way which is basic, decisive and normative for everything else, [they are] free to rejoice."[29]

Some recent commentators on Barth's ethics and his doctrine of the Christian life have been especially interested in the question of whether Barth offers an adequate description of how the new freedom in Christ, human moral agency as willed by God, is nurtured. I have in mind astute admirers and critics of Barth on this issue like Stanley Hauerwas, Reinhart Hütter, and Joseph Mangina, who find Barth's work powerful but ecclesiologically underdeveloped.[30] Among their concerns is that Barth fails to give sufficient attention to the formative practices of the church in which Christian character and moral agency are cultivated. Ecclesial practices are, in Mangina's words, an indispensable matrix of Christian life and Christian ethical reflection. A related concern of Hauerwas in particular is that authentic Christian witness is necessarily embedded in a new form of life. Concrete depiction of the lives of exemplary Christian witnesses would strengthen Barth's doctrine of the new life in Christ and the theological ethics it supports.

Regarding the first concern, I believe Barth does in fact say much more about the practices of the church and their part in Christian life

29. *CD* IV/3.1, p. 247.
30. See Stanley Hauerwas, *With the Grain of the Universe: The Church's Witness and Natural Theology* (Grand Rapids: Brazos, 2001); Joseph Mangina, "The Stranger as Sacrament: Karl Barth and the Ethics of Ecclesial Practice," *International Journal of Systematic Theology* 1, no. 3 (1999): 322-39; Reinhard Hütter, "Karl Barth's 'Dialectical Catholicity': *Sic et Non,*" *Modern Theology* 16, no. 2 (2000): 137-57.

than he is often given credit for saying. The ethics of reconciliation begins with a treatment of baptism, continues with an unfinished exposition of the Lord's Prayer, and was finally to conclude with a treatment of the Lord's Supper. Baptism, prayer, and Lord's Supper are not merely formal, organizational rubrics in Barth's ethical reflections. They belong for him to the very essence of the responsible Christian life. As every reader of Barth knows, his theology of the practice of prayer is pervasive. In the ethics of reconciliation he posits the practice of prayer as the practice that surrounds all Christian life under the command of God. "The life of Christians," he writes, "is to be understood in its totality as a life in invocation of God." Moreover, prayer for Barth is "the work of the community," and not only of Christians individually. "It is a movement in which Christians jointly and persistently engage."[31] Prayer for Barth is a free act, the epitome of human freedom before God.

True enough, Barth resists any simplistic identification of the free working of the Holy Spirit with church practices, however precisely they may be conducted according to canon law. Emphasis on the actuality of the living God in Barth's theology is evident in his treatment of the practices of Christian life as elsewhere. Ecclesial practices do not have the power to be effective by themselves but only as the ever new and gracious activity of God the Holy Spirit works through them.

As for the second concern — the ethical value of concrete depictions of lives of the saints — it should be said that Barth has a place for such models of Christian life. He speaks, briefly to be sure, of "singular saints," who provide "definite personal examples of Christian life and action." Barth continues by saying that while all who belong to the body of Christ are saints, "the Holy Spirit is not a friend of too doctrinaire democracy." "The community always needs and may point to the existence of specific individuals who, without leaving the multitude of believers . . . stand out as models or examples in their special calling and endowment, its witness being more clear and comprehensible and impressive in their persons and activity than in those of others." Barth even claims that the community would not be "healthy," or its witness "eloquent," if it did not have such "shining exceptions."[32] But, as we might expect, for Barth these "singular saints" or "models" of Chris-

31. *CD* IV/3.2, p. 882.
32. *CD* IV/3.2, pp. 887-89.

tian life are always distinguished by their service of Christ and the gospel, not in virtue of their own moral excellence.

Barth's worry here, of course, is that attention to exemplary Christian witnesses must not be allowed to compete with or even displace Jesus Christ as *the* Holy One and *the* true witness. In an excursus in *CD* IV/1, he expresses this worry in a response to Balthasar's theology of the saints. After reading Balthasar on this topic, Barth says he now understands what Balthasar meant in describing Barth's own Christocentrism as "constrictive."[33] For Barth, a true Christocentrism is not constrictive or exclusive, let alone "christomonistic." On the contrary, Barth's Christocentrism simply but relentlessly places Christ at the center of all Christian theology and all Christian life and witness. The centrality of Christ is not a matter of exclusion but of precedence.

Barth's Theological Ethics and the Public Domain

My final set of questions is as follows: Does Barth offer only an ecclesiastical ghetto ethics? Is his theological ethics able to provide any guidance to Christians as they participate in public policy discussions and decisions? These are questions often asked of Barth's ethics, and they are serious questions indeed. Beyond dispute, however, is the fact that for Barth Christian witness includes political responsibility.[34] While only God can bring God's kingdom, Christians must not adopt a hopeless or dismissive view of "penultimate developments" that point in the direction of greater justice and peace.[35] Christians are summoned to take an active role in looking and working for "correspondences," "analogies," "intimations," "parables" in history that are "kingdom-like" and thus in their own way bear witness to the great hope of God's coming reign.[36]

Of special interest is Barth's theology of the nature of the state, and in particular his understanding of appropriate use of state power. At the outset it is important to understand that Barth grounded his

33. *CD* IV/1, p. 768.
34. See William Werpehowski, "Karl Barth and Politics," in *The Cambridge Companion to Karl Barth,* ed. John Webster (Cambridge: Cambridge University Press, 2000), pp. 228-42.
35. *CD* IV/3.2, p. 936.
36. *CL,* pp. 265-66.

understanding of the state in the reconciling activity of God in Jesus Christ and not in a doctrine of "orders of creation" separated from this reconciling activity. But matters are more complex than this statement might suggest. Within the christological horizon of Barth's understanding of the state and its power, indeed even within the pages of the *Church Dogmatics,* one can find different emphases. On the one hand, he can speak, as he does in *CD* II/2, of "the secret purpose" of the political order as God's will to patiently grant time to the world and the church to receive grace. If God's wrath does not exist apart from his grace, it is also true that under the conditions of sin God's grace prevails at present in the form of a "graceless order." In other words, although the work of Jesus Christ has overcome and abolished sin, the still unredeemed world requires the order of the state to be an "order of the sword, compulsion and fear. . . . Where the grace of God is not yet known and exalted, has not yet found obedience, only the sword and compulsion and fear can reign."[37] Christians must not be ungrateful to God, who graciously provides for the graceless order of the state in order that they and the world might have time and opportunity to acknowledge and receive God's grace.

On the other hand, Barth can speak, as he does in *CD* III/4, of force as no "normal, fixed and in some sense necessary part" of the political order demanded by God. The exercise of state power does not constitute the essence of the state, its *opus proprium.* On the contrary, it belongs to the *opus alienum* of the state. Christian ethics "cannot assure the state that in the exercise of power either the state or its organs may do gaily and confidently whatever they think is right. In such cases it must always confront them with the question whether there is really any necessity for this exercise."[38]

The complexity of Barth's thinking on this topic has made for fascinating controversy. Some years ago, Paul Ramsey entered into vigorous debate with Barth's view of state power. The debate has recently been reviewed by Oliver O'Donovan.[39] According to Ramsey, "the use of power, and possibly the use of force" belong both to the *esse* and to the *bene esse* of the state. Ramsey considered those who thought otherwise

---

37. *CD* II/2, p. 722.
38. *CD* III/4, p. 456.
39. Oliver O'Donovan, "Karl Barth and Paul Ramsey's 'Uses of Power,'" in *Bonds of Imperfection: Christian Politics, Past and Present* (Grand Rapids: Eerdmans, 2004), pp. 246-75.

overly idealistic and even naive, in his view a chronic tendency of liberal-ism. It should be added, however, that Ramsey thought that Barth was actually closer to Ramsey's own view than were many who appealed to Barth to support their own "liberal" or quasi-pacifist positions.

The debate about state power widens out into reflection about the nature of true, life-giving power. As might be expected, Barth deals with this question in a number of places and always in strictly theologi-cal terms. In the section on the perfections of God in *CD* II/1, Barth has a lengthy discussion of divine omnipotence where he distinguishes be-tween *potentia* and *potestas*. *Potentia,* as Barth defines the term, is power in itself. It is abstract, absolute, raw power, having no limits or con-straints. According to Barth, this is precisely not the power of God, and it is not the power that God ordains for the state to exercise. "If power by itself were the omnipotence of God it would mean that God was evil, that He was the spirit of revolution and tyranny *par excellence.*"[40] In contrast to *potentia* understood as power in itself, true power is *potestas,* legitimate or moral power. God's power is grounded in itself, "in the love and freedom of the divine person. . . . God's *potentia* is in all cir-cumstances *potestas.* . . . [T]his power is God's power, and not merely any kind of power."[41]

Barth finds the basis for this understanding of divine power in the Trinitarian reality of God as this has been disclosed in the life, death, and resurrection of Jesus Christ. "God has the power, as Father, Son, and Holy Spirit, to be Himself and to live of and by Himself. This is His omnipotence. Everything else which He has the power to do, He has the power to do in virtue of this power. . . . [A]ll His activity consists simply in a recapitulation of His own being."[42]

A christocentric and Trinitarian understanding of the power of God provides the background for Barth's understanding of the exercise of power by the state. To be sure, the power of the state is far from iden-tical with the Trinitarian power of God. Indeed, it often stands in di-rect contradiction to the power of the crucified and risen Christ, the power that in weakness is stronger than all the powers of this world. Nevertheless, the power of the state under the Lordship of Christ is not properly understood as raw, unrestrained, coercive power. The primary,

40. *CD* II/1, p. 524.
41. *CD* II/1, p. 526.
42. *CD* II/1, p. 532.

normal, divinely ordained purpose of the state's exercise of power is to protect life, uphold justice, and secure peace. Its God-intended purpose is to promote human well-being. The exercise of force or compulsion can only be legitimate in truly "exceptional" cases.

As is well known, toward the end of his life Barth repudiated nuclear weaponry and nuclear war categorically. Was Barth a secret just war theorist, or was he a closet pacifist? Or is neither of these categories helpful in describing Barth's political theology? Does Barth's thinking on the power of the state and the Christian witness with regard to war lack coherence, or does it give evidence of a "powerful underlying consistency," as Rowan Williams suggests, a consistency that, as Williams also suggests, is constantly on the move and sensitive to new events and exigencies?[43]

Another aspect of Barth's theology of the state well worth exploring is his understanding of democracy and its relationship to the purposes of God. As in the question of the use of state power, one can find rather different statements of Barth regarding the pros and cons of various forms of government. On the one hand, he clearly refuses to canonize any particular form of government as necessarily God-ordained and inherently superior to all other forms of government. On the other hand, he is open to speaking of certain features of democratic government, when seen through the eyes of faith, as "parables" of the reconciling work and redemptive purposes of God made known in Jesus Christ.

How convincing are the reasons Barth gives for claiming that the Christian gospel favors a democratic society? How well developed is his understanding of the form Christian political responsibility should take in the public forum of a democratic, pluralistic society? While these are open questions, Barth clearly rejects the idea of a Christian state or a Christian political party. He firmly holds, however, that even if anonymously, Christians exercise their political responsibility by choosing those political possibilities open at any particular moment that most suggest "a correspondence to, an analogy and reflection of" the content of the gospel.[44]

---

43. Rowan Williams, "Barth, War and the State," in *Reckoning with Barth* (London: Mowbray, 1988), pp. 170-90.

44. Karl Barth, "The Christian Community and the Civil Community," in *Community, State, and Church*, p. 170.

Daniel L. Migliore

The Essays in This Volume

All these issues and many more that swirl around Barth's ethics are in play in the articles found in this volume. Nigel Biggar provides the lead article, "Karl Barth's Ethics Revisited." It involves a "revisiting" of Barth's ethics because earlier Biggar authored an outstanding introduction to Barth's ethical thought entitled *The Hastening That Waits: Karl Barth's Ethics*. In that book the author takes note of the "barrage" of criticism of Barth's theological ethics, including that of Robert Willis, James Gustafson, and Reinhold Niebuhr. While judging that these critics are "not entirely wide of the mark," Biggar concludes that they do not attend adequately to the affirmation of the faithfulness of the triune God that is a crucial element in what Barth calls the formed reference of Christian ethics. In his present essay, Biggar says his earlier work was a reconstruction "more expressive of where I thought Barth should have gone than of where he actually went." With a continuing appreciation of Barth's contribution to ethical discourse, and determined to retain some of its central elements, Biggar now indicates what he would leave behind, what he would keep, and what he would develop further.

In his response to Biggar's article, Eric Gregory writes "The Spirit and the Letter: Protestant Thomism and Nigel Biggar's 'Karl Barth's Ethics Revisited.'" Gregory is the author of *Politics and the Order of Love: An Augustinian Ethics of Democratic Citizenship*. He shares with Biggar and Oliver O'Donovan the desire that Christian ethics provide a "more systematic, more eudaimonist, more exegetical, and more realist account of Christian moral reasoning that does not abandon fundamental Barthian convictions." In the course of his essay, Gregory notes the intriguing fact that the recovery of a form of natural law ethics by revisionary Thomists is accompanied by the rise of a Protestant Thomism that sees the moral life as too fragile and too contingent for any "*excessively* legal approach." Gregory suggests that if Thomists have tended to read Barth with Thomas in mind, it may be time for Barthians to read Thomas with Barth in mind. One can hope that the essays of Biggar and Gregory will open up possibilities of a new and fruitful conversation among contemporary Protestant and Roman Catholic ethicists in which both sides may find surprising partners.

Four of the articles in this volume attend to the topics of war and democracy. William Werpehowski writes "Karl Barth and Just War" to help untangle the knots of the debate about the nature and use of state power in Barth's thinking. In particular, Werpehowski's question is to what extent Barth shares in the tradition of just war theory, that is, whether there are specifiable conditions under which going to war and waging war can be morally legitimate. Werpehowski, author of *American Protestant Ethics and the Legacy of H. Richard Niebuhr* and coeditor of the recently published *Oxford Handbook of Theological Ethics,* has long been a keen reader and expositor of Barth's ethics. In his essay in this volume, he contends that there is common ground between Barth and contemporary Roman Catholic interpreters of just war theory. For Barth and Catholic ethicists alike, it is imperative to recognize the "horror" of war and to "stigmatize" it without condemning it in every possible circumstance.

John Bowlin responds to Werpehowski in "Barth and Werpehowski on War, Presumption, and Exception." Author of *Contingency and Fortune in Aquinas's Ethics,* Bowlin finds that "lack of precision and consistency makes it difficult to determine what exactly Barth's remarks about war ultimately amount to even as I suspect that these local deficits have everything to do with Barth's struggle to remain faithful to his other theological commitments." Bowlin recommends continuing "in a slightly different vein the rehabilitation of Barth's reflections on war that Bill Werpehowski has already begun." That slightly different vein would take the form of working with concrete examples and cases of unjust aggression and legitimate political sovereignty and considering "examples of obedient witness to the God who at times commands war and yet always prohibits murder."

David Haddorff writes on "Barth and Democracy: Political Witness without Ideology." Haddorff is well equipped to take up this topic, having recently written an extensive introduction for the republication of three of Barth's essays in political theology under the title *Community, State, and Church.* According to Haddorff, "Barth prefers democracy because it limits power, protects individuals and communities, and encourages responsible participation by standing under a constitutional rule of law." At the same time, Barth resists "an ideology of democratism" that fails to recognize that there is no form of government, including Western democracies, that is "immune to the tendency to become at least a little Leviathan."

In "Karl Barth and the Varieties of Democracy," Todd Cioffi responds to Haddorff. Cioffi agrees with much of Haddorff's analysis

Daniel L. Migliore

but contends that Barth was never interested in democracy in the abstract, especially if it left out of consideration the economic and political conditions of the poor and the weak. Not democracy as such but "social democracy" or "democratic socialism" was the name Barth gave to the direction of his political theology. According to Cioffi, "Barth's concern is not a political system per se, but the mercy and compassion of God reflected in our political arrangements — God's justification of the sinner and the new life that springs from this divine act."

The next two articles by Timothy Gorringe and Katherine Sonderegger focus on the relationship of God's justice manifest in Christ to dominant theories of criminal justice in Western societies. In his book *God's Just Vengeance,* Gorringe calls for major reform in our penal justice systems in the direction of restoration rather than punishment as the proper goal of criminal justice. He charges the traditional penal substitutionary doctrine of atonement with providing theological support for a view of justice as punishment. In the article for this volume, "Crime, Punishment, and Atonement: Karl Barth on the Death of Christ," Gorringe revisits this topic, arguing that although Barth remains captive to an "unreconstructed understanding of punishment" as the meaning of the death of Christ, his wider reflections on the gospel in fact provide promising grounds for a "different and less alienating system of criminal justice." Commenting on Barth's fourfold discussion of "The Judge Judged in Our Place," Gorringe contends that Barth's description of the death of Christ as putting an end to self-righteousness and the violence it generates is "a more convincing way of understanding the New Testament reflection on the significance of Christ's death than maintaining a residual place for punishment."

Katherine Sonderegger, author of *That Jesus Christ Was Born a Jew: Karl Barth's "Doctrine of Israel,"* responds to Gorringe in her essay, "For Us and for Our Salvation: A Response to Timothy Gorringe." Offering a reading of Barth's doctrine of the atonement that differs from Gorringe's, Sonderegger notes that Barth does not have an exemplarist view of Christ's death. Instead, in his passion and death Christ "takes our place in a visceral and dynamic sense." While sharing Gorringe's outrage over abusive and cruel treatment of prisoners, Sonderegger finds the difference between Gorringe and Barth in that "[f]or Gorringe the carrying out of Christ's work lies ahead of us all," while for Barth Christ's death is "sufficient in itself." Sonderegger acknowledges that the task of tracing how the differences in the doctrines of atonement held by Gorringe and Barth might work themselves out concretely in practices of criminal justice is a highly complex matter and certainly not achievable in a brief essay. Her central point, however, is that Barth's understanding of the death of Christ, when properly understood, "gives rise to a Christian humanism" and in no way allows us to learn meanness at the foot of the cross.

The following two articles by Kathryn Tanner and Christopher Holmes look at Barth's approach to economic theory and practice. At a time when not only the future of the American economy but also that of the global economy is on every thoughtful person's mind, Professor Tanner's article, "Barth and the Economy of Grace," is highly pertinent. In her previous work, Tanner has creatively extended theological ethics and the doctrine of the gracious gift of God on which it is based into new areas. In *Jesus, Humanity, and the Trinity* and in her more recent book, *The Economy of Grace,* Tanner explores the difference between an economy of grace and an economy driven by the spirit of competition and possession. In the present volume, she explores what Barth called "a new and third way" beyond unfettered capitalism on the one hand and total state control of the economy on the other. Valuing Barth's work but also taking a step beyond it, Tanner argues that lodged in Christian dogmatics is "a very odd account of relations between owning and enjoyment by others — an alternative noncompetitive economy of sorts brought to its completion in Christ." With Christ as the key to God's ways with us and our history with God, "human fellowship as we know it should be thoroughly reworked" in the economic sphere no less than in other areas of our common life.

Holmes responds to Tanner in "Karl Barth on the Economy: In Dialogue with Kathryn Tanner." According to Holmes, an important reason why Barth does not offer the kinds of prescriptions that Tanner thinks necessary to render practical and realizable an economy of grace is because for Barth "[t]he witness Christians bear and the economic goals for which they work are never separate from the hearing and the hoping that is new every day and to which the Holy Spirit gives rise." Holmes fears that "the move toward principles and programs would lead to a domestication of the hope for 'wholly other things,' to an obscuring of the direction and line contained in the hope itself — Jesus Christ."

Rounding out the articles in this volume — and in a way returning us to the initial questions of the theological foundations of Barth's ethics — are essays by Paul Nimmo and Jesse Couenhoven. Author of a recent book on Barth's ethics entitled *Being in Action: The Theological Shape of Barth's Ethical Vision,* Nimmo writes here on "Barth and the Christian as Ethical Agent." Mapping the christological and Trinitarian grounding of Barth's understanding of the Christian as responsible human agent, Nimmo notes how Barth's thought is governed not by an "analogy of being" *(analogia entis)* but by an "analogy of relationship" *(analogia relationis).* There is an analogy of relationship between Father and Son in the eternal triune life, between God and Jesus Christ in time, and between Jesus Christ the true image of God and us. To be truly human is to act in freedom, love, and obedience in conformity with Jesus Christ, to "correspond by grace in our being and in our action to our election in Jesus Christ." This does not involve an "imitation of Christ" in the sense of a "formulaic repetition of the life of Christ," but rather a free and responsible human life that follows and reflects the "prominent lines" of the servant Lordship of God embodied and revealed in Jesus Christ.

In "Karl Barth's Conception(s) of Human and Divine Freedom(s)" Couenhoven examines the meaning of freedom, a prominent theme in Nimmo's essay. With what conception of freedom is Barth working when he speaks of some sort of analogy between human and divine freedom? Couenhoven distinguishes between an "incompatibilist" and a "compatibilist" understanding of freedom. According to the former, freedom means "self-initiated self-making" as one chooses between alternate possibilities. According to the latter, true freedom, normatively understood in the light of Christ, does not mean the power to choose between alternate possibilities ("Hercules at the crossroads," as Barth puts it); it means instead choosing and acting in line with God's own goodness. Couenhoven argues that only on the basis of a compatibilist understanding of divine freedom is it possible to discern an analogy between true human freedom disclosed in Christ and the freedom of God.

By way of conclusion, I offer two comments. First, if at times it appears that the discussions in this volume become overly theoretical and insufficiently practical, we would do well to remember a distinction made by Oliver O'Donovan, to whose work I have previously referred. O'Donovan distinguishes between "moral reflection" and "moral deliberation." He speaks of moral reflection as a necessary "taking stock of the world," a re-flection, a "turning back" to look on what is already there, an inquiry about who we are, "our placement in the world, our relationship to other realities." Moral deliberation, on the other hand, is "weighing up," "facing an alternative, looking at possible courses of action that have not yet occurred."[45] We should not be surprised if in the examination of Barth's theological ethics we find that while he certainly does not avoid "moral deliberation," he nevertheless insists repeatedly that we must always engage in rigorous "moral reflection," that is, turning back again and again to the questions of who God is and who we are as God's creatures, forgiven sinners, adopted children, and responsible and joyful partners. Only then are we prepared for the moral deliberation that moves toward specific decisions and concrete courses of action.

Second, it goes almost without saying that not every possible topic touching on Barth's theological ethics is addressed or perhaps even mentioned in the following essays. The specific issues docketed for discussion at the Princeton conference and retained in this volume have to do mostly with political theory, economy, war, and the justice system. This leaves largely unmentioned many topics like abortion, suicide, euthanasia, and same-sex marriage. Given the conference limitations of time and resources as well as the formidable range of Barth's thought, it could not be otherwise. Nevertheless, our hope is that the insights offered in the essays collected here will stimulate further discussion and inquiry not only in relation to the topics taken up in this volume but also to many other topics in Barth's theological ethics.

45. O'Donovan, *Common Objects of Love,* p. 13.

2. Karl Barth's Ethics Revisited

Nigel Biggar

I have long admired Karl Barth, but I have never quite been a devotee. From the early 1980s when I was a doctoral student until the publication of my book on Barth's ethics in the early 1990s,[1] I was a disciple. I sat at his feet and dwelt in his thought world, because I wanted to learn what a vision of moral life might look like that takes the living reality of God seriously, that assumes unequivocally that God wears the face of Jesus, and whose theological structuring is systematic rather than haphazard. Much of what I learned there I have carried with me ever since. Yet even before I had finished my book, I was aware that its interpretation of Barth's ethics had at certain important points become a reconstruction; it is clearer to me now than it was then that this reconstruction was more expressive of where I thought Barth should have gone than of where he actually went.

It is now over fifteen years since *The Hastening That Waits* was published, and since then I have written only two pieces on Barth, one a contribution to John Webster's *Cambridge Companion,* the other a chapter in a book on the natural law theory of Germain Grisez and John Finnis. Since the mid-1990s I have spent most of my time at the practical end of ethics, writing about moral issues raised by the task of dealing with the past after civil conflict (especially in Northern Ireland), by the invasions of Kosovo and Iraq, by proposals to make physician-assisted suicide and voluntary euthanasia legal, and by the demands of

---

1. Nigel Biggar, *The Hastening That Waits: Karl Barth's Ethics,* Oxford Studies in Theological Ethics (Oxford: Clarendon, 1993, 1995).

some political liberals that theology be banned from public discourse. Having spent most of the 1980s taking the measure of a comprehensive, systematic theological structuring of ethics, and thinking predominantly from the top downward, I felt that it was time to approach the ethical task from the opposite end, to get stuck into the messy complexity of practical issues, to attempt well-crafted judgments on them, and to track how and where Christian theology actually shapes those judgments. I also thought it was time to stop conversing only with fellow theologians and to start expressing a Christian intelligence in a wider public.

In the long term, however, my intention is to make the return journey. I intend to lift my eyes again from practical cases and to refocus on the moral import of believing in the God who wears the face of Jesus. For that reason in particular I welcome this opportunity to revisit the ethics of Karl Barth for the first time in almost a decade. I welcome the opportunity to take fresh stock of his comprehensive theological-ethical system in the light of what I have learned (or think I have learned) from trying to bring a Christian theological intelligence to bear on complex practical issues and awkward cases. And I welcome the opportunity to consider what from Barth I would take forward into my own account of how belief in the Christian God should shape moral vision.

My review of Barth's ethics will touch on the following points. First its spiritual focus; then the basic terms in which it is articulated — namely, those of God's commands; and third, its Trinitarian information. After that come comments on each of its three substantial dimensions: creation, reconciliation, and redemption (or, as I prefer to call it, sanctification). Finally, I will conclude with some methodological remarks on the relationship of theology to philosophy and empirical data.

The Spiritual Heart of Moral Life

I begin with what, for want of a better expression, I will call "spirituality," by which I mean the relationship between God and human creatures. It is one of the salient features of Barth's ethic that this lies at its heart, and it is for that reason that I have always thought it very apt of Stephen Sykes to suggest that we view him not only as a "formidable

Calvinist dogmatician," but also as "a spiritual writer."[2] At the very beginning of all that we ought to do — and remaining basic to it — is prayer. The importance of this is that prayer is the basic condition of human freedom and gladness — or what I call human "flourishing." When the human being acknowledges God the Creator, Reconciler, and Redeemer in prayer, she is freed from the intolerable burden of coping with her finitude by trying to shoulder divine responsibility; she is freed from guilt over past sins; and she is freed from anxiety about the future. In prayer to the triune God, the human being is freed to be a creature who has been graciously reconciled and who will be sanctified at the end. Through prayer she grows the virtues of humility, faith, gratitude, and hope, which enable her to flourish in the only way that a sinful creature can. Prayer is the first and the last thing that we should do. It is basic to an ethic that takes God seriously as a living reality to whom human beings can and should relate in a personal way. It is also basic to an ethic that recognizes that, before we turn to the business of deliberating about how we should conduct ourselves in the world, there is the prior task of contemplating what kind of beings we are in the first place, and what is the context in which we are set. Prayer embodies and confirms a theological view of the agent's self and of her location.

This feature of Barth's ethics has always seemed to me one of its greatest virtues — and it still does. It endows thinking about moral matters with an existential seriousness. The ethical task is not just — and not primarily — about our solving practical problems out there in the world. It is first and foremost about coming to terms with a true, theological, and soteriological description of our own creaturely nature and sinful condition, and of our standing before a benevolent, forgiving, and saving God. It is about adopting a posture and a set of dispositions appropriate to our nature and situation — on our knees, humble, grateful, hopeful, and glad.

Why Command Should Be Legislative before It Is Military

One way in which Barth seeks to keep the focus of ethics on the interpersonal relationship between God and the human individual — that

---

2. Stephen Sykes, ed., *Karl Barth: Centenary Essays* (Cambridge: Cambridge University Press, 1989), p. 83.

is, on the spiritual dimension — is to articulate it basically in terms of God's commands. A command is distinguished from a precept or a law by its interpersonal directness and by its definiteness: it is addressed by one person directly to another, and what it directs is concrete. In both his Münster-Bonn lectures of 1928-29 and his *Church Dogmatics,* Barth develops his ethics in chapters on the command of God generally, and then on the commands of God the Creator, the Reconciler, and the Redeemer specifically.

There is an ambiguity here, however. The word Barth uses is *Gebot.* While this is invariably translated into English as "command," its meaning actually ranges from an ad hominem "command" to a general "precept."[3] In *CD* II/2 (especially §38.2, "The Definiteness of the Divine Decision") Barth writes of God's *Gebot* addressing individuals with absolute definiteness. The command of God, he tells us, is "the specially relevant individual command for the decision which we have to make at this moment and in this situation. . . . The Law of God . . . is not merely a general rule but also a specific prescription and norm for each individual case. . . . A command . . . is a claim addressed to man in such a way that it is given integrally, so that he cannot control its content or decide its concrete implication. . . . It does not need any interpretation, for even to the smallest details it is self-interpreting [*selbst interpretiert*]."[4] It is clear, then, that Barth is using *Gebot* here to refer to something very much like a military order, which is addressed by a commanding officer directly to a subordinate and is ideally unequivocal and definite.[5]

Elsewhere, however, Barth tells us that by "hearing" a command of God he does not mean "direct and particular divine inspiration and guidance,"[6] and that subordination to God's Word does not mean that

---

3. It is true that the usual German word for "command" as in military "order" is *Befehl.* Nevertheless, the semantic scope of *Gebot* can overlap with that of *Befehl,* meaning a "command" as in "to be at somebody's command." I owe Gerald McKenny thanks for prompting me to reflect on this verbal distinction.

4. *CD* II/2, pp. 662, 663, 665.

5. I was alerted to the nature of military orders when, before the conference at which this essay was originally delivered, I visited the American Civil War battlefield of Antietam. There I learned that the commanding general of the Union forces, George McLellan, failed to rout the Confederates under Robert E. Lee partly because the orders he issued were equivocal, leaving room for different interpretations. However, even military orders will often leave some room for the recipient to use his discretion in carrying them out. They will be definite, but not absolutely determined.

6. *CD* III/4, p. 15.

we have "simply to abandon and forget our ideas, thoughts and convictions."[7] Further, in his exposition of the "special ethics" of the doctrines of creation and reconciliation in *CD* III/4 and IV/4 (that is, the 1959-60 lectures, "The Christian Life"), he himself offers an elaborate, systematic interpretation of the constant, general form of God's commanding. Here, then, *Gebot* looks much more like a general precept than a quasi-military command, and commanding a *Gebot* is more like promulgating a law than issuing orders.[8]

There is, I think, a major problem with conceiving God's commands in military rather than legislative terms: it implies that receiving or hearing a command of God takes the place of reflecting and reasoning — that it is a substitute for ethics. The human creature is put in the position of being less a moral agent than a servile subject, passively receiving absolutely definite instructions, which leave nothing further to be thought about. This does not imply a very dignified picture of human being — nor, arguably, a very biblical one. It also connotes a correlatively despotic picture of God. What is more, it postulates an event that barely finds a footing in the lived experience of faithful Christians. After all, when did *you* last hear an absolutely definite command of God?

It is true that the legislative and military kinds of divine commands can be reconciled. Hearing a command of God in the military sense can be construed as a moment of discerning an individual vocation *within the terms set* by ethical reflection and reasoning about the constant precepts or laws that God has laid down in creation and in the incarnation. Indeed, this is how I construed it in the very first chapter of *The Hastening That Waits*, which bears the indicative title "Ethics as an Aid to Hearing." Nevertheless, this construal involves a considerable measure of reconstruction, resolving tensions within Barth that he himself did not quite resolve, and pulling him in a direction that not all of him wants to go. In his recent book, David Clough is absolutely correct to say that my interpretation of Barth's understanding of hearing God's commands is "one-sided." He is less correct, I think, to say that my one-sided reconstruction deprives Barth's "vigorous and provocative ethical thought . . . of many of its most compelling qualities: the lion's roar becomes muted and the

---

7. *CD* I/1, p. 718.

8. That commanding can be legislative, and that Barth sometimes uses *Gebot* to denote this, was first suggested to me by John Bowlin in his article "Contemporary Protestant Thomism," in *Aquinas as Authority*, ed. Paul van Geest, Harm Goris, and Carlo Leget (Leuven: Peeters, 2002), pp. 235-51.

lion tame."[9] On the one hand, such criticism gives me pause, since I would be loath to think that I do not take seriously the divinity of God, and the creatureliness and sinfulness of human beings. God being God, and humans being creatures and sinners, one should expect the former to surprise, bewilder, wrong-foot, and amaze the latter. At least as far as Christians are concerned, the idea of a tame God is surely a contradiction in terms. On the other hand, there are different kinds of divine wildness, and I do not seek to tame them all. What I do seek to tame is the notion that God's will is entirely unpredictable, that it cannot be articulated in terms of principles or rules, that it cannot be reflected upon and interpreted rationally, and that it expresses itself in such a way that leaves no room for the responsible exercise of creaturely discretion. What I have no desire to tame is the stringency of the moral demand that God's principled will may make, or the tremendous impact of his holy presence upon self-satisfied creatures, or the wonderful rashness of his love when it reaches beyond the limits of what passes for prudence. In pressing for an understanding of God's commanding as primarily legislative and only secondarily military, and of his commands as general precepts or laws before they are individual orders or vocations, I do not think I offend against God's divinity — because I do not see the theological need to include in that sovereign divinity the freedom to confound every human attempt to understand and interpret the divine will.

In sum, I have no quarrel to pick with the notion that God commands general precepts or laws, insofar as this gives a theological account of the source of the moral order that we find in the nature of things. My quarrel is rather with the notion that we learn what is right (as distinct from what is our vocation) by hearing an absolutely definite set of divine orders.

Trinitarian Ethics: Economic Rather Than Immanent

The question of how we come to know what is right — the question to which "hearing a command of God" is, I think, the wrong answer — is an epistemological one. I move now from moral epistemology to the question of the structure of normative ethics.

---

9. David Clough, *Ethics in Crisis: Interpreting Barth's Ethics,* Barth Studies Series (Aldershot: Ashgate, 2005), p. 116.

It goes without saying nowadays that a Christian ethic should have a Trinitarian structure. In one way or another it should articulate itself with reference to God's acts as Creator, Reconciler, and Redeemer — or, better, Sanctifier. (I prefer to call the final act "sanctification," since that title expresses the nature of the act, namely, the growing of spiritually fitting and morally virtuous character on the basis of God's gracious offer of forgiveness-as-compassion and of its penitent acceptance by sinners. By contrast, "redemption" etymologically connotes a moment — the payment of ransom — rather than a development.) If Trinitarian structure is now a commonplace in contemporary Christian ethics, that of course is largely owing to Barth. Note, however, that what he pioneered was the material shaping of an ethic in terms of the economic Trinity rather than of the immanent one. This is because of his emphasis upon their unity, which is driven by a determination to take with utter seriousness God's incarnation in Jesus. What we see in the economy of God's saving work — which finds its focus in the Word made flesh — is what we get in God himself: "The reality of God which encounters us in His revelation is His reality in all the depths of eternity."[10] It is true that Barth does admit a distinction between the economic and immanent Trinities, but its function is formal rather than substantial, namely, to assert God's freedom, and in particular the freedom — the sheer gratuitousness — of his love. God exists before time and apart from creation. He enjoys fellowship within himself; he does not need it from human creatures: "He is this loving God without us as Father, Son and Holy Spirit, in the freedom of the Lord, who has His life from Himself."[11] The fact that God loves us, then, the fact that he generates an economy of salvation at all, is entirely due to his graceful decision to do so for our sake, and not for his own.

Nevertheless, it might seem that Barth derives some ethical content from the immanent Trinity. Within God himself, he tells us, there is "a co-existence, co-inherence and reciprocity,"[12] and this is the ground of God's eternal decision to be for humankind in Jesus. Jesus' being for humankind, his radical fellow-humanity, therefore "reflects the inner being or essence of God."[13] It is this that is God's image. It is also this

10. *CD* I/1, p. 479.
11. *CD* II/1, p. 257.
12. *CD* III/2, p. 218.
13. *CD* III/2, p. 219.

that is real or genuine or fulfilled humanity. And since "humanity" here implicitly refers to a set of virtuous dispositions toward other creatures, it is ethical and normative, and not merely ontic and descriptive. Human beings *ought* to regard other humans as their fellows, and to treat them out of concern for their own good. The question that concerns us here is whether this normative ethical content is supposed to be derived from the immanent Trinity or only confirmed by it. I believe that the latter is the case. The point at which we *see* God's radical solidarity with sinful creatures is Jesus. It is there that we behold the vision of real, normative cohumanity, and it is from there that we infer God's essential coexistence, coinherence, and reciprocity. Barth is clear: epistemologically we move from the economic to the immanent Trinity. We get our ethical content directly from the incarnation.

It is conceivable, however, that what the incarnation implies about the immanent Trinity might yield more anthropological and ethical content than the incarnation itself. It might be that what we conclude about the nature of God himself as a unity-in-plurality, and about the quality of interpersonal relations within the Trinity, yields original insight into the nature of human individuals as constituted by their relationships, into the properly egalitarian character of social and political arrangements, or into the proper nature of love.[14] It might be, but I am skeptical. One possibility is that the immanent Trinity, which establishes God's freedom, serves also to establish the utter gratuitousness of his love — and therefore a norm of gratuitousness for human love. Apart from the controversial question of whether such gratuitousness is possible or desirable for human love, however, there remains doubt as to whether it was really reflection on the immanent Trinity that first taught us about it. Did the cross of Christ not already show us it?

My strong suspicion is that what purports to have been read out of the immanent Trinity was first read into it. I suspect this partly because what we can reasonably claim to infer about God in his Trinitar-

---

14. For example, Charles Taylor appears to argue from the fact that "the fullness of divine life passes between persons" in the Trinity, through the creation of humans in the image of God, to the anthropological conclusion that what is important in human life is "what passes between us," and then to the ethical assertion of elements of human fulfillment that are "essentially together-goods" (*A Catholic Modernity?* [New York: Oxford University Press, 1999], pp. 113-14). I observe that Taylor makes this argument gingerly, and I suspect that he does so because he is half-aware that it was not by reflecting on the Trinity that he was first convinced of the essential relationality of human being.

ian self is too little and too abstract to generate much ethical content by itself. However, I also suspect it because some normative assertions that have been made by appeal to the immanent Trinity reek of romantic anarchistic political assumptions that I reckon mistaken. For example, while I have no quarrel with the claim that human beings should be regarded as equal in certain respects — say, before God and before the law — I disagree that such equality entails the repudiation of every kind of hierarchy.[15] For sure, hierarchies can entrench the privileges of some classes and involve the domination and oppression of others. On the other hand, hierarchies can be simply functional, distinguishing and ordering roles, and enabling a large body of people to cooperate smoothly. Saint Paul's famous metaphor of the church as the "body" of Christ does not do away with functionally "superior" and "inferior" roles, but it urges an equality of esteem.[16] The truth is that any sizable social body needs a hierarchy for the purpose of coordination. If the immanent Trinity can get along without one, that is only because the Godhead comprises three persons, and not three hundred.

The Ethical Dimension of Creation:
Explicating the Human Good[17]

So much for overall, Trinitarian structure; now I turn to each of the component dimensions. I begin with creation.

15. Thus in *God the Economist: The Doctrine of God and Political Economy* (Minneapolis: Fortress, 1989), M. Douglas Meeks argues that the divine *perichoresis* (the equal, mutual indwelling and cooperation of the three persons of the Trinity) is normative for relations between human beings and renders immoral any form of hierarchy, since it necessarily issues in domination and exclusion (e.g., p. 72).

16. 1 Cor. 12, especially vv. 24-25: "But God has so composed the body, giving the greater honor to the inferior part, that there may be no discord in the body, but that the members may have the same care for one another." It is relevant to note here that Barth does not shy away from talking about God the Son's "divine subordination" and God the Father's "divine superiority" (*CD* IV/1, p. 209). It follows that whatever the equality that characterizes relations between the persons of the Trinity, it includes, according to Barth, an element of some kind of hierarchy.

17. This section draws very heavily indeed on a part of my essay "Karl Barth and Germain Grisez on the Human Good: An Ecumenical *Rapprochement*," in *The Revival of Natural Law: Philosophical, Theological, and Ethical Responses to the Finnis-Grisez School*, ed. Nigel Biggar and Rufus Black (Aldershot: Ashgate, 2000), pp. 171-76.

A Christian ethic ought to explicate itself primarily in terms of the human good — that is, the good that is proper to the nature with which the Creator has endowed his *human* creatures. A deontological concept such as "command" is not self-explanatory. It naturally raises a question about the authority it claims: Why should it oblige me? Why should I obey it? And the answer to such questions, it seems to me, has to be given in teleological terms of what is good. The reason why I should heed a command is that what it commands will defend or promote the good — or, better because less abstract, the flourishing — of others and of myself. Even Kant, who is usually taken to be the patriarch of deontological ethics, can be found resorting to a basically teleological rationale: in the *Foundations of the Metaphysics of Morals* he implies that the moral law is generated by the dignity of rational beings, whom he describes as "ends-in-themselves"[18] — which is to say, that which is intrinsically valuable or good. Logically, then, the first word in any ethics should be "good," and the first word in a theological ethic, "the good that God wills." Whatever it is that God commands makes full sense only in terms of his benevolence.

This priority of the good to the right is not only logical, of course; it is also evangelical. After all, it was Jesus himself who said, "The sabbath was made for man, and not man for the sabbath" (Mark 2:27) — that is, the purpose of the law is to serve human flourishing, not to stifle it. This point was hardly lost on Barth, who ever since his work had acquired a christological focus, asserted the priority of the gospel to law. In his chapter "The Command of God" in the *Church Dogmatics,* therefore, he makes it plain that the command with which he is concerned is not simply heteronomous. Rather, it is that of the God who decided from eternity to be *for* humankind in Jesus Christ,

18. This is how I make sense of the following statements in the *Foundations:* "The practical necessity of acting according to this principle, i.e., duty, . . . rests merely on the relation of rational beings to one another, in which the will of a rational being must always be regarded as legislative, for otherwise it could not be thought of as an end in itself. Reason, therefore, relates every maxim of the will as giving universal laws to every other will and also to every action toward itself; it does so . . . from the idea of the dignity of a rational being. . . . [T]hat which constitutes the condition under which alone something can be an end in itself does not have mere relative worth, i.e., a price, but an intrinsic worth, i.e., dignity" (in A. I. Melden, *Ethical Theories: A Book of Readings,* 2nd ed. [Englewood Cliffs, N.J.: Prentice Hall, 1967], p. 348). That is to say, the will of a rational being is an end in itself or a good, because it has an intrinsic worth or dignity; it is this dignity that, commanding respect, generates moral law.

and is therefore the command of grace. Its intention is always benevolent — to achieve "a liberation and loosing."[19] It appears in the form of "an alien and imperious law" only because it is addressed to sinners and so contradicts "the foolish wishes of the old man."[20] It opposes us only "in so far as we are against ourselves,"[21] and only "for our own highest good."[22] In Barth's thought, then, God's command is subordinate to the human good as means are subordinate to their end.

Nevertheless, explicit references to the human good are rare in Barth's writing.[23] What this signifies is not that Barth denied that acting rightly is good for humans,[24] but that he resisted any focus upon the human good as the end of right human action. The reasons for this are several. One is his tendency, following Anders Nygren, to regard eros — the desire to realize one's natural, specific potential — as simply selfish, and therefore to suppose that the realization of one's own good cannot be a properly moral intention.[25] A second reason is his conviction that, partly because creaturely life "belongs to God" and partly because sinners can live "only in the power of His mercy,"

> it is obviously outside our power to try to discover unequivocally and conclusively what constitutes the real pleasure of our real life, and in what the fulfilments which summon us to gratitude actually consist. We think we should seek them here or there because this thing or that appears as light or alleviation, as warmth, benefit, refreshment, consolation and encouragement, promising us re-

19. *CD* II/2, p. 602.
20. *CD* II/2, p. 602.
21. *CD* II/2, p. 595.
22. *CD* II/2, p. 652.
23. When Barth does talk about "the good," he usually understands it in Kantian fashion as "the perfect correctness and therefore morality of human will and conduct, . . . the sum of all that is required and commanded" (*CD* II/2, pp. 665-66), and not — following Aristotle — as the ontological state of *eudaimonia* or flourishing. "The question of the good [is] the question what man should do" (*CD* II/2, p. 564) — not the question of what he should become. What Barth means by "good," I mean by "right."
24. Barth is in no doubt that what God intends through his commanding, and what is achieved through our obeying, is "man's welfare" (*CD* II/2, p. 709).
25. See *CD* IV/2, pp. 734-35 ("a grasping, taking, possessive love — self-love — . . . is the direct opposite of Christian love"). Barth's view of self-love, however, was more nuanced than Nygren's: see Gene Outka, *Agape: An Ethical Analysis* (New Haven and London: Yale University Press, 1972), pp. 221-29.

newal and the attainment of that which hovers before us as the true goal of all that we do and refrain from doing. But do we really know this true goal and therefore our true joy? God knows it. God decides it. But this means that our will for joy, our preparedness for it, must be wide open in this direction, in the direction of His unknown and even obscure disposing.[26]

A further reason for Barth's reluctance to focus on the human good is his conviction that the human good is realized only as a by-product of right relating to God, and that therefore the focus of our attention should not be on our own self-fulfillment as such, but upon the nature of God and upon appropriate human responses to him.[27]

However, although Barth is shy of explicit reference to the human good and its component goods, these are nevertheless present in his ethical system. In general, he characterizes the human good or human flourishing as "freedom" — the freedom of humans to act and to be in a manner befitting their status as sinful creatures whom God has reconciled to himself and whose redemption he is completing. In the first place this freedom is not negative; it is not the condition of lacking constraints. It is primarily the vital freedom of self-fulfillment or flourishing — as is well expressed by another word that Barth frequently uses in this connection: "gladness."[28]

This general characterization of the good in terms of freedom or gladness is not simply empty and formal; from the context in which they are used, they clearly imply that human flourishing involves friendship with God. But this is not all. Other distinct goods are prominent in Barth's analysis of human "freedom" in *CD* III/4. For this in-

---

26. *CD* III/4, pp. 382-83.

27. *CD* II/2, p. 556: "Of course, the command of God is also a promise. Its fulfilment produces fruit. It yields a reward. That is something which we must not, of course, overlook or deny. But we cannot and must not seek the basis of its claim in the fact that its fulfilment has this consequence, that along with blessedness, the fellowship of man with God, it brings with it the answer to the problem of human life — the only possible answer to it. The divine command, whose fulfilment has this promise, must be known and understood as grounded in itself, as having a divine basis."

28. *CD* III/2, pp. 265-85 ("being in encounter, in which we have seen the basic form of humanity, is a being which is gladly actualised by man. I think that this unpretentious word 'gladly,' while it does not penetrate the secret [of humanity] before which we stand, does at least indicate it correctly as the *conditio sine qua non* of humanity" [p. 266]).

volves not only freedom "before God" but also freedom "in fellowship" with other humans and freedom "for life,"[29] and freedom for life itself involves freedom for play and art.[30] Further, elsewhere in the *Church Dogmatics* the unification of the human self or "inward harmony" appears as one of the good effects of the divine command.[31]

Notwithstanding this, a number of putative components of the human good are missing from Barth's account altogether.[32] Knowledge of the truth and appreciation of beauty *as distinct from* friendship with God receive no consideration.[33] Skillful performance also goes unremarked. Most important of all, there is no mention in Barth's ethic of the complex good of practical reasonableness — that is, of the consistency or integrity of practical decisions.

How should we assess Barth's treatment of the human good? To start with, I judge his reluctance to make explicit reference to it to be unwarranted. His Nygrenesque assumption that self-interested desire is necessarily selfish is mistaken. Whether or not the desire for self-fulfillment or the realization of one's good is selfish, depends on how that good is conceived. It can be conceived as a state of being where the individual's natural focus of concern is outside of himself, and since the statement "It is in my interest not to be selfish and to learn to grow

29. The fourth species of freedom that Barth treats here — "freedom in limitation" — is not so easily rendered as a distinct good; however, insofar as it consists in the glad acceptance of one's status as a creature, and therefore of one's personal vocation by God to play a modest role in the redeeming of the world, it could be subsumed under the category of the good of friendship with God or "religion."

30. *CD* III/4, pp. 553-54. Barth's discussion of play and art here is brief in the extreme. But since, in his Münster-Bonn lecture on ethics of 1928-31, he discussed these topics much more extensively under the rubric of "The Command of God the Redeemer," it is possible that they would have received much fuller treatment in the equivalent section of the *Church Dogmatics* (that is, vol. V), had Barth lived to complete it.

31. *CD* II/2, pp. 726-32.

32. The components that I mention are ones identified by Germain Grisez and John Finnis. What constitutes the human good is, of course, a controversial issue. There are many and varied lists; Finnis and Grisez's is only one. Nevertheless, it makes prima facie sense to me that among the component goods are knowledge of the truth, appreciation of beauty, skillful performance, and practical reasonableness.

33. It could well be argued that knowledge of the truth about God and appreciation of his beauty are basic to the human good as Barth conceives it; but while knowledge of other kinds of truth or appreciation of other kinds of beauty may not be separable from or independent of this knowledge and appreciation, they are nevertheless distinguishable from them.

strong in care for others" is not a logical self-contradiction, such a conception of the human good is not nonsense.

The second reason adduced for Barth's coyness about the human good is also, in my opinion, inadequate. Part of his argument is that we cannot know what our own good is, and one of the reasons he gives for this is that creaturely life belongs to God and God alone has the power to decide in what its good consists. Barth here subscribes to a voluntarist understanding of divine sovereignty, according to which God, being God, has the power to do whatever he wills, and what he wills is entirely free and unconstrained. God may then decide the content of the human good from moment to moment, reinventing it at will and rendering it unpredictable. This impression is given, however, in the course of an exposition of the command of God the Creator that clearly asserts that this command has certain constant features that correspond to the "definite structure"[34] of creaturely being: it always enjoins freedom — before God, in fellowship, for life, and in limitation. Certainly, God in his sovereignty has decided that this is to be the nature of the human good, but the implication of the phrase "definite structure" is that this is a decision that God will not reverse. If that is so, and the human good has a stable, God-given nature, then in principle it is *there* to be known independently of direct reference to God.

But Barth also suggests a second reason why we cannot know our own good: not God's untrammelled power to reinvent reality at will, but human sinfulness. Whatever might be the case in principle, in fact sinfulness distorts our knowledge; this would seem to be the implication of what Barth says in the quotation above about sinners being able to live "only in the power of [God's] mercy."[35] Even so, this passage does not say that apart from God's mercy (in Christ) — apart from the Word of God — we can know nothing about the human good; it says only that our knowledge cannot be unequivocal and conclusive. So Barth is not saying that the effect of sin is such that the human good simply cannot be known, but rather that it cannot be known properly

---

34. *CD* III/4, p. 44: "Real man, man himself, is the being reflected in the grace of God addressed to man in Jesus Christ. This being is indeed a sinner, a pardoned sinner, and a child of God in hope. *But this being does not start with the sinner. It is also the creature of God, participating as such in a definite structure* [*einer bestimmten Struktur*], and knowable in this structure in the Word of God" (emphasis added).

35. *CD* III/4, p. 382.

except through the Word of God.[36] It follows that his objection should not be to every attempt to discover the nature of the human good, but only to those attempts at discovery that proceed without primary reference to God's Word.

The third reason for Barth's reluctance to make direct reference to the human good is psychological rather than epistemological, namely, that the good is realized only as a by-product of right relating to God, and that to think about it separately from God is to risk succumbing to the fantasy that it can be realized independently of him.[37] Barth adopted such a principle because he believed that, to avoid the illusion of human autarky, we must keep our attention fixed on the human creature in its spiritual relationship. Nonetheless, Barth's own tripartite differentiation of his special ethics implies that he himself recognized the possibility of considering separately the parts of an ontic whole, without forgetting their status as parts. The same is implied by the distinction Barth makes between the human freedom to be before God (and in limitation), on one hand, and the freedom to be in fellowship and to be for life on the other. The latter are not in fact independent of the former, and their dependence is made explicit; they are nevertheless considered separately. My concluding judgment on this particular point, then, is that Barth had insufficient reason not to refer to the human good directly and not to elaborate a theory of it.

As we have seen, Barth does have a particular concept of the human good — although he does not call it by that name — and he does analyze this into a number of discrete parts or dimensions. Several elements of the human good, however, are absent from Barth's account. What are we to make of this?

The absence in Barth of any reference to the good of practical reasonableness can be explained by his suspicion of the casuistical formulation and application of moral principles as an exercise in rational autarky, and so as an expression of practical atheism.[38] I have argued at

---

36. See note 34 above: the creaturely being of man is "knowable in this structure in the Word of God."

37. This is an instance of a general methodological principle of Barth's that what has no independent existence should not become an independent object of thought. For further discussion, see Biggar, *The Hastening That Waits*, pp. 158-59.

38. *CD* III/4, pp. 7-8. For detailed discussion, see Biggar, *The Hastening That Waits*, pp. 40-41.

length elsewhere that this suspicion is unfounded.[39] In brief, my argument amounts to this: that Barth was wrong to assume that methodical and systematic moral reasoning must be closed, autarkic, rationalist. On the contrary, moral reasoning is quite capable of being open to new data that requires the more or less radical reformation — sometimes even the wholesale jettisoning — of a ruling theory.

The absence in Barth's ethic of any recognition of knowledge of the truth and appreciation of beauty — insofar as truth and beauty are distinct from God — and of skill in performance as elements of the human good is symptomatic of his reluctance to consider the value of created things except in *direct* relationship with their Creator.[40] Here Barth moves within range of the criticism that Germain Grisez levels against Augustine. Grisez finds that Augustine's theology "narrows human life to its religious dimension," and in focusing so strongly on the existential goods of peace with God, within oneself, and with others, he overlooks substantive goods — including knowledge of the truth and skill in performance.[41] Although it would not be fair to say of Barth what could be said of Augustine (at least as he expressed himself in *De doctrina Christiana*) — that he regarded the enjoyment of God in heaven as the only intrinsic good to which all other, secular goods are mere means[42] — it is nevertheless true that, in Barth's thought, the spiritual (or, to use his metaphor, the "vertical") dimension of the human good so overshadows its secular (or "horizontal") components as to eclipse some of them altogether.

My overall conclusion to this discussion is that while Barth does actually have a theological theory of the human good, it is both covert and incomplete. Rather than be covert, it should be both out in the

---

39. See Biggar, *The Hastening That Waits,* chap. 1, and Nigel Biggar, "Barth's Trinitarian Ethic," in *The Cambridge Companion to Karl Barth,* ed. John Webster (Cambridge: Cambridge University Press, 2000), section V.

40. It may also be symptomatic of the limitations of an ethical method that focuses too exclusively on Christology and Scripture.

41. German Grisez, *The Way of the Lord Jesus,* vol. 1, *Christian Moral Principles* (Chicago: Franciscan Herald Press, 1983), 5.F.2, 4 (pp. 127-28).

42. Grisez, *Way of the Lord,* 34.A (pp. 807-8). Grisez is careful to note here that Augustine himself later recognized the inadequacy of the distinction — introduced in *De doctrina Christiana* — between the one good that is to be "enjoyed" (God) and all the others that should only be "used" (all temporal goods). "However," he comments, "a system which must stretch its own categories to accommodate the minimal requirements of Christian humanism leaves something to be desired" (34 n. 3 [pp. 827-28]).

open and right up front, and in order to be complete it needs to "annex" (or incorporate discriminately) data from human experience and the nontheological sciences.

The Ethical Dimension of Reconciliation: Capturing the Moral Significance of Jesus

We turn now to the second dimension of Barth's normative ethics — namely, that informed by the reconciling work of the second person of the Trinity.

The account of the moral significance of Jesus Christ, which Barth gives in the *Church Dogmatics,* is one of his most valuable gifts to Christian ethics. In his 1928-29 lectures on ethics, he had read Jesus primarily in terms of law. What Jesus signifies there is, first of all, that God's goodness reaches sinful humans through the authority of their neighbors, and their acceptance of the counsel and correction that this authority offers. By "neighbors" here Barth means social institutions or conventions such as schools and universities, law, and custom. The acknowledgment of authority requires humility, and this expresses itself in a twofold self-sacrifice: repentance, and consequently the service of other people as fellow sinners. Jesus therefore amounts, ethically speaking, to a love of neighbor that is structured by repentance and is obedient to positive social authorities.[43]

The lectures of 1959-60, which constitute what we have of *CD* IV/4, conceive Jesus' moral meaning in a strikingly different way.[44] Instead of "law" as the governing concept, we are given "invocation" — the invocation of the divine Father by his human children. This is "the primal and basic form of the whole Christian ethos."[45] As Barth puts it, Christian life is "spiritual" before it is "ethical";[46] that is to say, it is about responding to what God has done in the past and praying for him to act in the future, *before* it is about taking action ourselves in the present. Accordingly, the ethics of God the Reconciler are articulated centrally in terms of the Lord's Prayer, with a prologue in terms of baptism and an epi-

---

43. See Biggar, *The Hastening That Waits,* pp. 62-67.
44. See Biggar, *The Hastening That Waits,* pp. 67-81.
45. *CL,* p. 89.
46. *CL,* pp. 92, 157.

logue in terms of the Lord's Supper. If Christian life is spiritual first, however, it is ethical second. On the basis of their internal invocation of the divine Father — and therefore with humility, gratitude, and hope — Christians are called to act externally in a manner that corresponds to the action of God in Christ. What are the contours of such correspondent action? How does Barth characterize it? He avoids both the Roman Catholic tradition of *imitatio Christi* and the Anabaptist concept of discipleship, characterizing it neither in terms of suffering or self-sacrifice nor in terms of nonviolence. In his exposition of what he means by "correspondence," he makes almost no reference at all to the passion of Christ and cites none of the versions of "If any man would come after me, let him deny himself and take up his cross daily and follow me."[47] Even in the 1928-29 lectures, where self-sacrifice is a prominent theme, he refers to this famous saying only once.[48] Why this is so is implied in the later version of the treatise on the command of God the Reconciler, where he denies the propriety of characterizing the life of God Incarnate by any one of its moments. As he explicitly rejects monasticism as the *sole* principle, so he implicitly rejects suffering. Self-sacrifice is not *the* principle of Christian life. For the very same reason, in spite of his belief that God's action in Jesus moves the use of coercive and lethal force to the very margins of possibility as far as God's commanding is concerned, he denies that following Jesus entails principled pacifism.[49] Notwithstanding this, Barth does characterize correspondent human action in terms that, presumably, he believed to be comprehensive rather than selective. As they pray "Thy kingdom come," so Christians will act as people responsible for "the rule of human righteousness, that is, for the preservation and renewal, the deepening and extending, of the divinely ordained human safeguards of human rights, human freedom, and human peace on earth,"[50] and this will usually take the form of revolt against the "lordless powers" of political absolutism, materialism, rigid ideologies, and such chthonic (or disordered physical) powers as technology, fashion, sport, pleasure, and transportation.[51]

---

47. Matt. 16:24; Mark 8:34; Luke 9:23. I rely here on the index of Scripture references provided in Barth, *The Christian Life*.

48. Mark 8:34, in Karl Barth, *Ethics*, trans. G. W. Bromiley (New York: Seabury Press, 1981), p. 328.

49. *CD* IV/2, p. 550.

50. *CL*, p. 205.

51. *CL*, pp. 213-33. In *CD* IV/2, Barth characterizes Jesus' moral significance in

Barth's reading of the ethical import of Jesus in the *Church Dogmatics* is more thoroughly theological, more spiritual, and less Kantian than his reading in the 1928-29 lectures. Before Jesus means love for neighbor, he means faith in God and its expression in the practice of prayer. Indeed, it is because he first means faith that *when* he means love, he means love of a certain kind, namely, the love of one forgiven sinner for another, and not of the righteous for the unrighteous. Judging by the New Testament, this later reading is the better one.

The later Barth was also wise, I think, to avoid characterizing the moral meaning of Jesus in too narrow a set of terms. For one example, the tendency in some circles — not least, traditional Roman Catholic ones — to interpret Jesus as sanctioning a way of life characterized primarily by self-sacrifice or suffering is too negative. Suffering might be a means, but it surely is not the end; and should we not interpret the way of Jesus in terms of its destination rather than its (occasional) route? Moreover, the kind of suffering that Jesus actually underwent was quite specific: the forbearing endurance of slander and torture unjustly inflicted by threatened political authorities. Those who make suffering a primary characteristic of Christian life, however, invariably generalize far beyond this, tending to treat all suffering as redemptive. Thus in *The Declaration on Euthanasia of the Sacred Congregation for the Faith* (1980), Pope John Paul II wrote approvingly of those terminally ill patients who refuse painkillers "so that they can deliberately accept at least a part of their suffering and thus consciously unite themselves with the crucified Christ."[52] It is clear that the cancer patient and the crucified Christ have suffering in common, but it is not clear what is common to their respective kinds of suffering.

For another example, it seems to me that the pacifist claim to capture the moral meaning of Jesus in the narrow terms of "nonviolence" does not do full justice to the text of the New Testament. As I have argued elsewhere, the New Testament enjoins the active, generous, and enterprising desire for reconciliation, and it abjures hatred, unlov-

---

terms of self-giving, agapaic love (pp. 730f., 819f., 829f.). We may take it, therefore, that what we find in the 1959-60 draft of the ethics of reconciliation represents an explication of this love — even though it is little mentioned there.

52. In Stephen Lammers and Allen Verhey, eds., *On Moral Medicine: Theological Perspectives in Medical Ethics* (Grand Rapids: Eerdmans, 1998), p. 653. For a fuller critique of Pope John Paul II's view of "suffering" as redemptive, see Biggar, *Aiming to Kill: The Ethics of Suicide and Euthanasia* (London: Darton, Longman, and Todd, 2004), pp. 49-55.

ing anger and retaliation, ready recourse to private violence in self-defense, and violence inspired by religious nationalism. From this, however, it does not follow that the New Testament absolutely forbids the publicly authorized use of lethal violence by Christians, nor even their use of private violence *in extremis.*[53]

Nevertheless, if Barth was wise to avoid trying to capture the moral meaning of Jesus in too narrow a set of terms, the more comprehensive terms that he preferred are actually too vague and less than maximally informed by the New Testament. I think we could do better than to say that Jesus was in favor of "human rights, human freedom, and human peace" and that he was against political absolutism, materialism, rigid ideologies, and disordered physical powers such as pleasure — not to mention technology, fashion, sport, and transportation. Frankly, that is all far too slapdash, if not whimsical. What we need is a more exegetically responsible account of what we can learn from the historical Jesus about human flourishing. One plausible element of this, I suggest, is that what we learn from Jesus is how to defend and promote human flourishing under conditions of sin, namely, by responding to injustice with forbearance and compassion.

The Ethical Dimension of Sanctification: Hastening While Waiting

Of the third dimension of the ethics of the *Church Dogmatics,* I have only praise to offer. (When I say the "third dimension," I speak of that fifth volume of the *Dogmatics* that Barth did not live to complete but which is nevertheless adumbrated in what he did complete.) I regard it as one of the signal advances that the mature Barth makes over his 1928-29 lectures that here eschatology is brought right into the heart of Christian life. Moreover, I reckon his explication of its ethical import to be exemplary in the salutary tension it creates between modesty and endeavor. On the one hand the belief that God, and God alone, will bring his creation to fulfillment at the end of history should generate modesty in expectations: "It is a matter of the steps that we have to take hour by hour. . . . as people of our time in what is (even in the most extraordi-

---

53. See Nigel Biggar, "Specify and Distinguish! Interpreting the New Testament on 'Non-Violence,'" *Studies in Christian Ethics* 22, no. 2 (May 2009): 164-84; "The New Testament and Violence: Round Two," *Studies in Christian Ethics* 23, no. 1 (February 2010): 73-80.

nary case) the fairly small sphere and framework of the opportunities
we are offered and the possibilities we are given, and in the fairly narrow view of our situation and problems that we usually have, yet still,
be that as it may, as the people we now are, as God's children and not as
gods."[54] On the other hand, the hope that God *will* bring his creation
to fulfillment should also generate moral energy:

> precisely because perfect righteousness stands before them as
> God's work, precisely because they are duly forbidden to attempt
> the impossible, precisely because all experiments in this direction
> are prevented and prohibited, [Christians] are with great strictness
> required and with great kindness freed and empowered to do what
> they can do in the sphere of the relative possibilities assigned to
> them, to do it very imperfectly yet heartily, quietly, and cheerfully.
> They are absolved from wasting time and energy sighing over the
> impassable limits of their sphere of action and thus missing the
> opportunities that present themselves in this sphere. They may and
> can and should rise up and accept responsibility to the utmost of
> their power in the doing of the little righteousness.[55]

In Barth's hands eschatology bears upon the living of Christian life in
such a way as to refuse both hubris and cynicism, both ruthlessness
and callousness, and to inform it with a humane and resilient combi-
nation of humility and moral commitment. Trusting in God the
Sanctifier, we do not despise the fragments of secular achievement, and
yet we do not rest easy with them. In a nutshell: we wait upon God, but
within our waiting we hasten.

Theology as Supreme Criterion, Not Sole Source

More than once in my review I have said that I think Barth's ethics is
weakened by a failure to incorporate nontheological data. I have attributed the limitations of his understanding of the human good in part
to an excessive zeal for thinking theologically, for referring everything
directly to God and tending to ignore what does not lend itself to such
reference. I presume to call this "excessive" because the world that God

54. *CL*, p. 172.
55. *CL*, p. 265.

has created is distinct and relatively free. The Creator and his creation are always related, and the latter always depends on the former and is responsible to him. But the Creator and his creation are not the same thing; they are not identical. I say this on several grounds: first, my immediate experience of the world, where I do not find myself constantly confronted with God; second, my experience of love, which always yields freedom to the beloved; and third, my reading of the opening chapter of the book of Genesis, where God, making humankind in his own image, yields creative and discretionary freedom to him as to a vicegerent. There are some forms of human good that do not require direct reference to God — for example, knowledge of the truth about subatomic physics, or even about the moral distinction between intentional and accidental killing. One does not need to acknowledge God to recognize that friendship and the experience of beauty belong to human flourishing. The phenomena of personal intimacy and a glorious sunset take away the breath of believers and nonbelievers alike. Of course, for a believer communion with God is basic to human flourishing, but there is more to human flourishing than what is basic.

In principle, as I have argued more fully elsewhere, Barth recognizes that common sense and nontheological reflection can yield material for a Christian ethic, and that Scripture and theology are not its sole source.[56] Thus he endorses Luther's description of Hammurabi as "an exponent of the order of God."[57] He praises the Greeks for grasping in their concept of eros the fact that real, flourishing human being is "free, radically open, willing, spontaneous, joyful, cheerful and gregarious."[58] He acknowledges that Rousseau had theoretical and practical insights about politics that have an affinity with his own views of Christian political thought and action.[59] He credits Kant with expressing "the essential concern of Christian ethics" by pointing out that the concept of what is pleasing or useful cannot of itself produce the concept of what is obligatory, and he approves of Kant's definition of the ethical as that which may be expressed in terms of a universal law.[60] In

---

56. See Biggar, *The Hastening That Waits,* chap. 5, "Eavesdropping on the World."

57. *Karl Barth's Table Talk,* ed. John D. Godsey, Scottish Journal of Theology Occasional Papers no. 10 (Edinburgh: Oliver and Boyd, 1963), p. 75.

58. *CD* III/2, p. 283.

59. Karl Barth, "The Christian Community and the Civil Community," in *Community, State, and Church,* ed. Will Herberg (Gloucester, Mass.: Peter Smith, 1968), pp. 180-81.

60. *CD* II/2, pp. 650, 656.

principle, then, Barth allows theological ethics to "annex" ethical material from elsewhere — that is, to incorporate it after reforming it in the light of theological criteria. Nevertheless, in practice Barth's ethics is at best limited, and at worst weakened, by its relative neglect of philosophical resources and its relative failure to engage closely and thoroughly with empirical data. So, for example, Barth attempts a moral evaluation of suicide and voluntary euthanasia without availing himself of the valid moral philosophical distinction between what one intends, what one accepts, and what one causes; and without considering what his claim that "even the life afflicted with the severest suffering" might still be "the blessing that God intends" could possibly mean for a human being whose cerebral cortex has turned to liquid.[61]

Some excuse for these weaknesses might be found in the methodological distinction Barth makes between "theological ethics" and "Christian ethics." The role of theological ethics is to derive basic ethical principles from dogmatics; whereas the "actual handling of the problems of human life" in the light of those principles is the specific business of Christian ethics.[62] It is not entirely clear that Barth consistently thought himself to be doing only the former,[63] but even if it were, his methodological self-limitation would still be problematic for two reasons. First, the formulation of ethical principles is not separable from the moral analysis of cases. The relationship is not one-way, from the top downward. Casuistical analysis is not merely a matter of "applying" ready-made principles. On the contrary, the very meaning of principles is informed by reflection on concrete cases. The traffic is two-way, up as well as down. The second objection is this: If the theologian confines himself to only half of the ethical task, who exactly does he imagine will complete the rest? Legislators, government ministers, civil servants, managers, and pastors generally have less time for reflection than academics, and the ethical interpretation of the concrete problems of human life is often a far from simple matter. Why should professional moral theologians grant themselves the luxury of an indeterminacy that the rest of humanity can ill afford? No, a Christian ethic has to range all the way from God to mundane particulars, from the beatific to the casuistic, from the sublime to the meticulous.

61. Biggar, *Aiming to Kill,* pp. 105-7.
62. *CD* II/2, p. 542.
63. Biggar, *The Hastening That Waits,* p. 159.

Conclusion: What to Leave and What to Take

In my opening words, I said that I hope to lift my eyes again from practical cases and to refocus on the question of the moral import of believing in the God who wears the face of Jesus, and that therefore I welcomed this opportunity to consider what from Barth I would take forward to that task. Let me conclude, then, by summarizing briefly what I would leave, what I would keep, and what I would develop.

I would jettison three things: the conception of apprehending what is right (as distinct from what is one's vocation) in terms of hearing a military command of God; the proposed division of labor between theological ethics and (practical) Christian ethics; and the reluctance in practice to negotiate with nontheological sources.

I certainly would keep at the heart of ethics the spiritual relationship between God and human creatures, as embodied in acts of prayer. I would retain an economic Trinitarian structure, as I would the wise and resilient eschatological tension between modesty and hope, which amounts to a manner of life that hastens while it waits.

Finally, I would bring right to the fore and develop in the light of nontheological data a theological account of human flourishing, and I would develop an understanding of the moral significance of Jesus Christ that is at once more positive and comprehensive than "suffering" or "nonviolence" and yet more biblically specific than "revolt against the lordless powers."

3 The Spirit and the Letter: Protestant Thomism and Nigel Biggar's "Karl Barth's Ethics Revisited"

Eric Gregory

One of the more interesting developments in recent theological ethics is the emergence of what has been called "Protestant Thomism."[1] By this term, following John Bowlin, I mean the renewed influence of Aquinas's account of natural law and the virtues among Protestant moralists. This seemingly oxymoronic turn draws more explicitly from work on Aquinas as theologian than Barth as ethicist, though it benefits from recent efforts to read them together and without caricature.[2] It promotes a dynamic version of Thomism that is at once more Aristotelian and more Augustinian than scholastic Counter-Reformation moral theology that

---

1. John Bowlin, "Contemporary Protestant Thomism," in *Aquinas as Authority,* ed. Paul van Geest, Harm Goris, and Carlo Leget (Leuven: Peeters, 2002), pp. 235-51. My focus will be versions of Protestant Thomism shaped by Barthian sensibilities rather than apologists for natural law who, according to Bowlin, speak "not for the Church and the grace it confesses, but for a certain cultural and political order" (p. 251).

2. See, for example, Eugene Rogers, *Thomas Aquinas and Karl Barth: Sacred Doctrine and the Natural Knowledge of God* (Notre Dame, Ind.: University of Notre Dame Press, 1995), and Fergus Kerr, *After Aquinas: Versions of Thomism* (Oxford: Blackwell, 2002). An important common resource for these authors is Victor Preller, *Divine Science and the Science of God* (Princeton: Princeton University Press, 1967). For a recent statement by a leading Roman Catholic ethicist with long-standing interest in Barth, see William Werpehowski, "Practical Wisdom and the Integrity of Christian Life," *Journal of the Society of Christian Ethics* 27, no. 2 (2007): 55-72. Werpehowski's "Catholic Barthianism" mirrors Bowlin's "Protestant Thomism."

Preparation of this article was supported by the Center for the Study of Law and Religion at Emory University and by a grant from the John Templeton Foundation.

is sometimes held responsible for the independent rationalism of early modern moral philosophy. It is also quite different from common approaches to Aquinas in analytic philosophy of religion or moral philosophy. My response to Nigel Biggar's welcome revisiting of Karl Barth's ethics considers his remarks primarily in this contemporary context.

It is of particular interest because Biggar's earlier work on divine command and Barth's "special" ethics offered a nuanced response to the many critics of Barth's voluntarism and its supposed heteronomy.[3] By arguing that Barth's theology has resources to accommodate traditional Christian teaching on natural law in both the Catholic and Reformed traditions, Biggar in his own way was preparing the ground for "Protestant Thomism." If Biggar and others are correct, their revisionist assessment updates traditional challenges to Barth's ethics even as it promises a nuanced alternative that transcends conventional Protestant/Catholic options in moral theology. At the very least, it seems to be an option for a less anxious but still distinctively Christian ethic that may have been unavailable to Barth in his own day and has been neglected by most contemporary Barthians. I will leave it to scholars of Barth to reflect on its significance for Barth studies.

Let me begin by highlighting what I take to be the central elements of Biggar's assessment. I am helped by the clarity of his essay, especially in noting points where he thinks "Barth should have gone" rather than "where he actually went."[4] Interpretation and reconstruction are scholarly virtues that helpfully locate agreement and disagreement. Before identifying salient differences, Biggar puts forth commitments that he shares with — and learned from — Barth. They are many. They reflect the massive influence of Barth's uncompromising Christian approach to ethics. These include the priority of prayer for Christian living, the Trinitarian structure of theological ethics, the centrality of Jesus Christ and eschatology, and the evangelical significance of the

---

3. Nigel Biggar, *The Hastening That Waits: Karl Barth's Ethics* (Oxford: Clarendon, 1993, 1995). Here Biggar made a key claim that Barth did not hold "that there is no human *esse* apart from Christ, but that apart from Christ there is no human *bene esse*" (p. 162). Biggar's reading has influenced some Thomistic moral theologians. See, for example, Jean Porter, *Nature as Reason: A Thomistic Theory of Natural Law* (Grand Rapids: Eerdmans, 2005), and *Natural and Divine Law: Reclaiming the Tradition for Christian Ethics* (Grand Rapids: Eerdmans, 2000).

4. Nigel Biggar, "Karl Barth's Ethics Revisited," p. 26 above. Hereafter, page numbers for Biggar's essay are incorporated into the text.

human good for understanding God's gracious purposes in Christ. As such, Biggar shares with Barth a fundamental concern to take "the living reality of God seriously" and to assume "unequivocally that God wears the face of Jesus" (p. 26). He too is unwilling to separate Scripture and doctrine from ethics, proclamation from action, or theory from practice. Each of these commitments, however, undergoes redescription in light of Biggar's critical remarks on the limits of Barth's ethics and its account of *eudaimonia* and holiness. In this sense, we could claim that Biggar's project adheres to the spirit but not the letter of Barth's writings. The debate focuses on specification, not a wholesale choice between philosophy and theology, Christian orthodoxy and moral analysis, or some additive picture of their relation.

Biggar does advance some familiar criticisms of Barth, even as he admits tensions and implicit notions within Barth's thought that might be resolved in Biggar's hoped-for direction. He worries that Barth's formal distinction between theological ethics and Christian ethics, joined with an ambiguous notion of command cast primarily in military terms, becomes a "substitute for ethics" and leads toward a "despotic picture of God" (p. 30). Barth's misguided aversion to systematic moral reasoning and reticence about the human good, in turn, lead to moral deliberation that Biggar characterizes as "too slapdash, if not whimsical" (p. 45). In this, the great systematic theologian of the concrete is accused of delivering abstract and general moral judgments in *Church Dogmatics* and occasional writings. For example, there are too many missing steps in his provocative but unsatisfying jumps from theological pronouncement and description to specific issues like voluntary euthanasia and human rights. We might add the death penalty, war, coercion, the treatment of nonhuman animals, or the ethics of secret diplomacy to the list of Biggar's examples where more practical reasoning is demanded. Moreover, Biggar claims, Barth's suspicion of the good as the end of right action (following Nygren) betrays an unwarranted "assumption that self-interested desire is necessarily selfish" (p. 38). While theological differences are prominent, Biggar also relates these concerns to Barth's relative neglect of philosophy and nontheological empirical data. Recent Barthian-inspired discussions of the immanent Trinity or the significance of Jesus *in relation to moral and political issues* confirm these judgments.[5] It is revealing, for example, that

---

5. We might distinguish between Barth's own sustained reading of various philos-

Biggar frames his hiatus from Barth in terms of spending time "at the practical end of ethics" and "expressing a Christian intelligence in a wider public" (pp. 26-27).

Barth scholarship has sought to respond to these kinds of objections, especially in the relatively recent attention to Barth's ethical writings.[6] It is difficult to imagine the history of theological ethics in the twentieth century without Karl Barth, his defenders, and his foes. In addition to broader questions of method, discussions of voluntarism, legalism, casuistry, ecclesiology, narrative, and the event of the divine command populate a crowded landscape — especially as mediated by figures as diverse as H. Richard Niebuhr, Reinhold Niebuhr, Paul Ramsey, James Gustafson, John Howard Yoder, and their contemporary heirs.

Consider, for example, Oliver O'Donovan. Despite his sympathies with Barth's construal of ethics conforming to the shape of salvation history, he claims that Barth's attack upon natural law failed to adequately differentiate the epistemological from the ontological issues at hand. Like Biggar, O'Donovan argues that Barth's dialectics of discernment furnishes an existentialist ethic that is "far too thin to support the extensive responsibility for moral deliberation which he could claim in practice and sometimes even defend in theory."[7] O'Donovan praises Barth's *epistemological* positions given human sinfulness and the radicality of grace, but he thinks they overwhelm a properly realist (and therefore teleological) account of the "whole order of things created, restored, and transformed."[8] Despite hints of given spheres of human

---

ophers and his relative lack of attention to concepts in moral philosophy. Contemporary Barthians often draw heavily from philosophy in discussing Barth on christological and Trinitarian issues (for example, the *logos asarkos*). I think Biggar has in mind the relative neglect of ad hoc distinctions that follow the best of recent moral philosophy (i.e., directly and indirectly voluntary acts).

6. See, for example, John Webster, *Barth's Moral Theology: Human Action in Barth's Thought* (Edinburgh: T. & T. Clark, 1989); John Webster, *Barth's Ethics of Reconciliation* (Cambridge: Cambridge University Press, 1995); David L. Clough, *Ethics in Crisis: Interpreting Barth's Ethics* (Aldershot: Ashgate, 2005); and Paul T. Nimmo, *Being in Action: The Theological Shape of Barth's Ethical Vision* (Edinburgh: T. & T. Clark, 2007).

7. Oliver O'Donovan, *Resurrection and Moral Order: An Outline for Evangelical Ethics* (Grand Rapids: Eerdmans, 1986), p. 87. O'Donovan further claims that Barth ontologically subordinated creation to Christology in ways that led to "a series of frankly Apollinarian Christological conceptions" (p. 87).

8. O'Donovan, *Resurrection and Moral Order,* p. 85.

activity, the organization of Barth's ethics puts too much pressure on the doctrine of reconciliation alone and fails to provide a suitably complex account of human action and ordered loving. For O'Donovan, the reality of the resurrection of Christ (which vindicates and restores creation) provides a link between command and obedience that neither denies God's freedom nor denies human agency. This is what is meant by O'Donovan's claim that "the Spirit forms and brings to expression *the appropriate pattern of free response to objective reality.*"[9] Obedience is not an end in itself, but a means to human flourishing in delight with God's will for the good of human beings as revealed and made possible through the saving work of Jesus Christ. In other words, ethics is evangelical ("good news") only if the resurrection "does not appear like an isolated meteor from the sky but as the climax of a history of divine rule."[10]

Like O'Donovan (and myself), Biggar wants a more systematic, more eudaimonist, more exegetical, and more realist account of Christian moral reasoning that does not abandon fundamental Barthian convictions. What is interesting in Biggar's treatment, however, is the context of his own selective retrieval of Barth. Biggar's rereading of Barth is shaped by his critical engagement with the influential Finnis-Grisez school of natural law theory that rejects earlier "physicalist" readings of Aquinas.

This school, sometimes called "new natural law," claims that principles of morality cannot be derived from a metaphysical account of human nature or divinity, asserts the priority of the human good to the moral law, and places tremendous weight on concepts of personal vocation (as distinct from the right) and free choice.[11] It maintains exceptionless moral norms ("never act against a basic good"), but the goal of the theory is to offer positive guidance for human flourishing across a range of capacities and indefinite possibilities of human fulfillment. As a moral theory, it tries to combine the best of deontological and teleological ethics and avoid their weaknesses. While critical of appeals to virtue that lose purchase on moral realism and difficult cases,

---

9. O'Donovan, *Resurrection and Moral Order,* p. 25, emphasis O'Donovan's.

10. Oliver O'Donovan, *The Desire of the Nations: Rediscovering the Roots of Political Theology* (Cambridge: Cambridge University Press, 1996), p. 20.

11. For a brief summary of their account, see Germain Grisez, Joseph Boyle, and John Finnis, "Practical Principles, Moral Truth, and Ultimate Ends," *American Journal of Jurisprudence* 32 (1987): 99-151.

its advocates tend to see their primary target as the widespread appeal of consequentialist reasoning in both secular and theological ethics (especially Catholic proportionalism). According to Biggar, these features make it an attractive candidate for dialogue with a suitably reconstructed version of Barth's ethics. This reconstruction involves being set free from a theological need to ascribe to the sovereignty of God a "freedom to confound every human attempt to understand and interpret the divine will" (p. 31).[12] The bare particularity of Barth's divine command ethic, on this view, falls short of an adequate recognition of both creaturely rationality and the normative structure of created reality, which are not put in competition with God for our attention.

Elsewhere, Biggar suggestively claims that the new natural law theory is "actually formed by specifically Christian presuppositions."[13] This thought, if amplified, would find favor among critics of the Finnis-Grisez school who highlight the theological commitments of Aquinas's moral vision, especially the way in which natural law is a rational participation in the eternal law of God and human beings are always already under grace.[14] In this essay, however, Biggar seems committed to a substantive account of basic goods (i.e., knowledge of truth, appreciation of beauty, practical reasonableness, skillful performance) as noninferential reasons for action that can swing free of theological reference. Indeed, he indicates that this secular theory of value

12. O'Donovan also highlights this problematic aspect of a voluntarist legacy in modern theology: "if nothing that our minds can comprehend is in the slightest degree relevant to recognizing the authority of God's will, how is that authority to be recognized? . . . Ultimately man can do nothing but resent God's will, as he resents any other alien imposition, and shake it off if he can" (*Resurrection and Moral Order,* p. 134).

13. Nigel Biggar, "Karl Barth and Germain Grisez on the Human Good: An Ecumenical *Rapprochement,*" in *The Revival of Natural Law: Philosophical, Theological, and Ethical Responses to the Finnis-Grisez School,* ed. Nigel Biggar and Rufus Black (Aldershot: Ashgate, 2000), p. 179. For an impressive account of new natural law with particular attention to Protestant ethics, see Rufus Black, *Christian Moral Realism: Natural Law, Narrative, Virtue, and the Gospel* (Oxford: Oxford University Press, 2000). The theological commitments of the new natural law theory are most explicit in the work of Germain Grisez; see, especially, his important trilogy, *The Way of the Lord Jesus,* 3 vols. (Quincy, Ill.: Franciscan Press, 1983, 1993, and 1997); "Natural Law, God, Religion, and Human Fulfillment," *American Journal of Jurisprudence* 46 (2001): 3-36; and "The True Ultimate End of Human Beings: The Kingdom, Not God Alone," *Theological Studies* 69 (2008): 38-61.

14. See, for example, Russell Hittinger, "Natural Law and Catholic Moral Theology," in *A Preserving Grace: Protestants, Catholics, and Natural Law,* ed. Michael Cromartie (Grand Rapids: Eerdmans, 1997), pp. 1-30.

corrects Barth's (and Augustine's) *excessive* emphasis on the spiritual dimension of all goods.

For Finnis-Grisez, goods found in the first precepts of the natural law generate intermediate principles for concrete action-guidance that flesh out what Aquinas left unspecified in his treatment of natural law. They often appeal to empirical anthropology, psychology, and linguistics. The natural law, perhaps unwittingly, becomes an autonomous source of moral knowledge as right reason responds to the desirability of incommensurable yet variegated basic human goods. While I am sympathetic to most of Biggar's concerns and proposals, it is this commitment that I want to highlight as a potential cause for concern on Barthian grounds. Given the work it does for Biggar's criticism of Barth and his approach to applied ethics, it seems of foremost importance to focus on whether or not a "basic goods" or any "objective list" approach to ethics tends toward an autonomous morality unqualified by evangelical proclamation that Biggar otherwise rejects. Biggar aims to distinguish human goods on their own terms without separating them from a comprehensive theological vision. Can this moral theory consider human goods "without forgetting their status as parts" within the total sweep of divine being and action on human being and action (p. 40)? In short, can it remain *Christian* humanism?

This is not the place to pursue in detail the Finnis-Grisez school, its motivations, and its theological and nontheological critics. However, I can highlight one question. It is an old one. We can put it this way: What are the nature and purpose of the natural law? Or, more pointedly, is natural law intended to be a moral theory at all? Finnis, Grisez, and, it seems, Biggar want elements of a principle-driven theory that establishes a set of rules to guide action. It is this version of Thomism that much of the Barthian-inspired "Protestant Thomism" literature seeks to undermine. John Bowlin, for example, argues that Aquinas's account of natural law does not try to offer a "decision machine for the morally perplexed," and it is a good thing it does not.[15] The moral life is too fragile, and too contingent, for this *excessively* legal approach. This is why Aquinas devotes so much attention to the virtues

15. John Bowlin, *Contingency and Fortune in Aquinas's Ethics* (Cambridge: Cambridge University Press, 1999), p. 114. Bowlin rejects the claim that "reason's first principles can, by themselves, generate concrete moral agreement among human communities sharply divided by time and place, culture and convention" (in "Contemporary Protestant Thomism," p. 251).

in the second part of the *Summa*. Natural law does offer a minimal account of purposeful rationality, but only insofar as it delineates the shape of human reasoning as created by God and governed by his providence. Aquinas places his discussion of Christian morals in the middle of his dogmatics, between the doctrine of God and Christ. For Bowlin, natural law is not a normative theory of action as such. It is a description of those inclinations that direct us to human ends. It is agnostic as to particular ends and specific means, though Aquinas's virtue-oriented analysis of human acts places them under classifiable moral species (i.e., a violation of justice). In short, it is a description of agency and character that centrally involves the virtuous employment of practical reason through hearing the gracious command of God and the judgments of the wise (we might say, sanctified) in assessing the goodness or badness of acts.

Bowlin's reading of Aquinas, therefore, offers an approach to ethics that is "more compatible with the contingency of the human good, the indeterminacy of happiness, and the difficulty of the life of virtue."[16] It is this complex version of Thomist ethics — which I have not adequately described — that might appeal to Barthians who worry about moral theory building, overconfidence in the powers of human reason, and universal rule prescription. In fact, Bowlin argues that recent Thomistic exegesis suggests that the differences "that divide Aquinas from Barth are more apparent than real."[17] Barth and Aquinas often frustrate theorists in search of pure examples of their favored typologies. But, in short, "divine command" and "natural law," or "rationalism" and "voluntarism," may no longer be helpful categories in assessing the future shape of Christian ethics. They may serve heuristic purposes, but they also distort a more fine-grained account of contemporary debates that "range all the way from God to mundane particulars, from the beatific to the casuistic, from the sublime to the meticulous."[18] Given Biggar's reservations about some of the moral conclusions of the Finnis-Grisez school, and his partial criticism of their method, it strikes me that he should adopt some version of Bowlin's nontraditional account or, at least, identify what is missing from this account. It might allow him to maximize those features

16. Bowlin, *Contingency and Fortune,* p. 95.
17. Bowlin, "Contemporary Protestant Thomism," p. 243.
18. Biggar, "Karl Barth's Ethics Revisited," p. 48.

of Barth he wants to maintain, minimize those features of Barth he wants to reject, and make explicit those features of Barth that remain implicit.

Let me conclude this brief response. Barth's moral theology continues to exert influence in contemporary Christian ethics, even Protestant casuistry that is open and dialectical.[19] It should go without saying, however, that Barth's theological, ethical, and cultural climate was very different from our own. That "Protestant Thomism" is possible is the fruit of patient reading, restatement, and theological development since Vatican II and owes much to Barth's widespread influence in Protestant and Catholic moral theology.[20] On the whole, however, it strikes me that many Thomists have read Aquinas with Barth in mind; the task remains for Barthians to read Barth with a "revisionist" Aquinas in mind.[21] This might take the form of a conversation that relies less on what Barth opposed in his day, or placing Barth as an interlocutor, and more on what a Barthian today might constructively advance in the field of ethics, especially on moral ontology, command, grace, and human agency. The challenge of a "postsecular," "postmodern," or "post-Enlightenment" age does not mean that Barth's rebuke against the false universalism of modernity and his call for Christian particularity should be muted. To the contrary, they remain good counsel against the ideological temptations of Christian ethics and a primary resource for theological-ethical construction shaped by encounter with the Word of God. But it might mean that Barthians will need to not

---

19. For one effort to see how Barth might inform a debate in bioethics, see Eric Gregory, "A Protestant View: The Ethics of Embryo Adoption and the Catholic Tradition," in *The Ethics of Embryo Adoption and the Catholic Tradition: Moral Arguments, Economic Reality, and Social Analysis,* ed. Sarah-Vaughan Brakman and Darlene Fozard Weaver (New York: Springer, 2007), pp. 199-218.

20. As evidence, one need only look at the entries found in Stanley Hauerwas and Samuel Wells, eds., *The Blackwell Companion to Christian Ethics* (Oxford: Blackwell, 2004), and Gilbert Meilaender and William Werpehowski, eds., *The Oxford Handbook of Theological Ethics* (Oxford: Oxford University Press, 2005).

21. Notable exceptions, despite important differences, include George Hunsinger, *Disruptive Grace: Studies in the Theology of Karl Barth* (Grand Rapids: Eerdmans, 2000), and Stanley Hauerwas, *With the Grain of the Universe: The Church's Witness and Natural Theology* (Grand Rapids: Brazos, 2001). More recently, see Kevin Hector, "Apophaticism in Thomas Aquinas: A Re-Formulation and Recommendation," *Scottish Journal of Theology* 60, no. 4 (2007): 377-93, and Keith L. Johnson, *Karl Barth and the Analogia Entis* (Edinburgh: T. & T. Clark, 2010).

only revisit their imagination for Aquinas, but also attend to more recent work in the history of early modern moral philosophy, contemporary metaethics, and constructive theological ethics.[22]

Following Biggar, I have focused primarily on moral concepts in Barth's ethics rather than on his more influential reception in political theology. It is notable that Biggar and Bowlin now occupy two distinguished chairs in Christian ethics. Both took the opportunity of their inaugural lectures to reflect on theology and public life. The shared dispositions of forbearance, gratitude, and moral energy they promoted on those occasions — which challenge some more dominant voices in contemporary Christian social ethics — suggest a promising moment for the development of "Barthian Thomism" in both Anglican and Reformed circles.[23] One hope is that this approach, which joins two of the great masters of theological discourse, will help overcome the regrettable division between scholars of theology and scholars of Christian ethics. Whatever its future, that modest development within the bounds of finitude would be a fitting tribute to both Barth and Aquinas.

---

22. Recent attention to Barth in the broader context of European intellectual history also is suggestive. See Rudy Koshar, "Where Is Karl Barth in Modern European History?" *Modern Intellectual History* 5, no. 2 (2008): 333-62.

23. Nigel Biggar, "Saving the 'Secular': The Public Vocation of Moral Theology," *Journal of Religious Ethics* 37, no. 1 (March 2009): 159-78, and John Bowlin, "Some Thoughts on Doing Theology in Public," *Princeton Seminary Bulletin* 28, no. 3 (2007): 235-43.

4. Karl Barth and Just War: A Conversation with Roman Catholicism

William Werpehowski

Karl Barth's treatment of warfare in his "special ethics" of the doctrine of creation has elicited a noteworthy convergence of exasperation and complaint from a number of his most sympathetic students and commentators. For example and on one side, Oliver O'Donovan takes Barth's "descriptions of war" to be among his "least successful pages." In these starkly negative depictions "there is no gracious 'You may!' in relation to the state's use of force, so that in Barth's political theory we miss that note of redemptive divine permission which is so unforgettable elsewhere in his work."[1] The moral implications of redemptive permission for O'Donovan include the possibility that in war we may in fact seek *justice* within and as part of an established and ongoing moral order under divine governance in Jesus Christ.

The late John Howard Yoder, from another side, is no less critical, although that great spokesman for Christian nonviolent discipleship would likely not quarrel with Barth's depiction of war. A major problem for Yoder is that Barth's allowance for "just war," as it evidently *may* be commanded and therefore graciously permitted by God, appears fatally abstract on Barth's own terms. He is finally unable "to found . . . with relation to the revelation of God in Christ the advocacy of certain deviant ways of acting, such as killing when killing is other-

---

1. Oliver O'Donovan, "Karl Barth and Ramsey's 'Uses of Power,'" *Journal of Religious Ethics* 19, no. 2 (Fall 1991): 14.

I want to thank my colleagues John Bowlin, Jesse Couenhoven, Eric Gregory, David Haddorff, George Hunsinger, and Brian Williams for helping me with this essay.

wise forbidden."[2] Here, and in formal agreement with O'Donovan, Yoder takes aim at the notorious category of the *Grenzfall,* the "exceptional" or "borderline" or "frontier" case. Reliance on it for articulating the possibility that war may be commanded by God inexplicably undermines the pacifist direction of Barth's reflections. For O'Donovan, appeal to the *Grenzfall,* in connection with the claim that the use of violent force can only be an "alien work" and emergency provision of the state, involves a misunderstanding of the nature of political power, and introduces a dangerous drift toward "statism" to boot.

Criticisms akin to these have been sounded by others and across generations of Christian ethicists. Barth himself, according to Yoder, was not exactly ecstatic about what he wrote either, remarking in 1962 that "of course that was all written in 1951. . . . I cannot yet completely reject it even now. Nevertheless, I would say that it is perhaps not one of the most felicitous passages in the *Kirchliche Dogmatik.*"[3]

Recognizing the problems, contemporary theologians have sought to offer critical and internal correction. Thus Nigel Biggar specifically identifies in the *Church Dogmatics* and elsewhere just versus unjust causes, and just versus unjust intentions in responsible Christian witness to the state, while affirming that the only sort of "just war" that Barth might envision amounts to "police action."[4] David Clough, a pacifist, attempts to remove what he sees to be an inconsistency in Barth's virtual rejection of war's moral legitimacy, on the one hand, and his concession that the borderline case for war permits a state's mobilizing and preparing for it, on the other. On the contrary, Clough argues, "Christians cannot support preparations for the exceptional case in which they may be called upon to go to war; they are too busy with the emergency of peace to prepare for the distant and unlikely prospect of war, and know that war's preparations are incompatible with serious attempts to build a peaceful order."[5] On the face of it,

2. John Howard Yoder, *Karl Barth and the Problem of War* (New York: Abingdon, 1970), pp. 73-74.

3. Yoder, *Karl Barth,* p. 117 n. 7. Cf. Karl Barth, "An Outing to the Bruderholz," in *Fragments Grave and Gay,* ed. Martin Rumscheidt (London and Glasgow: Collins, 1971), p. 81.

4. Nigel Biggar, *The Hastening That Waits* (Oxford: Clarendon, 1993), pp. 38-40, 92-96, 167-75.

5. David Clough, *Ethics in Crisis: Interpreting Barth's Ethics* (Hampshire, U.K.: Ashgate, 2005), p. 98.

Biggar's and Clough's corrections appear to collide with one another. They also collide with Barth's tendency, first, to present war as beyond the pale of limits and therefore of limited police action, and second, to reject as a "worthless peace" what a nation is likely to suffer in the event that it is *not* able to protect itself in the extreme instance.

In what follows I, too, will express perplexity, present challenges, and work toward coherence and improvement, but in the context of a critical conversation between Barth and contemporary Roman Catholic approaches to war and peace. I will begin by offering an interpretation of the meaning of just war theory in theological reflection and practice. This interpretation, which draws from contemporary Catholic statements and the recent work of Oliver O'Donovan, concludes with a sketch of just war criteria or norms. Then I review Barth's treatment of ethics and war as discovered in *Church Dogmatics,* volume III, and in other sources. The exposition is in three parts, and following each I offer a commentary that engages Catholic accounts. I will propose that, for all that may be wanting in Barth's work, his "practical pacifism"[6] formally anticipates in one significant respect Catholic developments both in and around the just war theory. These developments concern the primary practical Christian commitment *to prevent war,* and include the effort to employ just war criteria for purposes of stigmatizing war *without* absolutely condemning it.[7]

Just War

The theological origin of the Christian theory of the just war is traditionally associated with the insights of Augustine and Ambrose in the fourth and fifth centuries. It offers an approach to practical reasoning about how individuals and political communities may, as O'Donovan puts it, do justice within the theater of war. It is a "discipline of deliberation" that has a certain "spirituality," the "capacity to make the re-

---

6. See *CD* IV/2, p. 550: "According to the sense of the New Testament we cannot be pacifists in principle, only in practice. But we have to consider very closely whether, if we are called to discipleship, we can avoid being practical pacifists, or fail to be so."

7. Rev. J. Bryan Hehir puts the matter this way in a March 25, 2008, address at the Joan Kroc Institute for International Peace Studies, University of Notre Dame. The lecture is entitled "Beyond the 'Challenge of Peace': Pastoral Letter for Our Day." See http://kroc.nd.edu/events/08hesburghlectures.shtml.

flecting subject conscious of his or her own responsible position before God in relation to other members of society who have their own differently responsible positions."[8] Concerned with the possible moral authority of doing justice in international relations, especially in view of an international system of sovereign nation-states, the theory depends on a morally relevant analogy with the nature and purpose of domestic political judgment, that is, the response to injustice and the attempt to rectify it, as that judgment is understood and exercised through activities such as policing and judicial functions. The idea is that, in connection with but distinct from the Christian community's divine call to seek peace through practices of self-giving love and mercy, God has also provided "a time to live, to believe and to hope under a régime" in which the world may be preserved against its own self-destruction through practices that protect the innocent and correct assaults on them through the use of force.[9] The need to use force to protect ourselves from one another would be, as Augustine had it, both a result of and a remedy for sin. Even so, the point of the use of force is to win peace and concord out of opposition, in the service of reconciliation.

So given a proposed similarity between domestic and international arrangements for securing justice, just war theory should be understood as "an extraordinary extension of ordinary acts of judgment" intended to protect the innocent against violation of their rights and well-being.[10] In an international arena that lacks a duly constituted authority for pursuing its own common good as such, states may in certain circumstances justifiably employ appropriate and limited force to oppose grave injustice for the sake of peace.

"Analogy," however, is a term that presupposes that similarities are found in the midst of deep dissimilarities. Any sensible just war theory has to register and heed the deep differences between war and domestic practices of judgment at the same time it depends on there being some moral relation between them. The vast destructiveness of war must be seen and not passed over. The relation of this destructiveness to nationalist designs bent on domination rather than justice has to be acknowledged. War's continuing and irremovable *threat* to the inno-

8. Oliver O'Donovan, *The Just War Revisited* (Cambridge: Cambridge University Press, 2003), pp. 16, ix.

9. O'Donovan, *The Just War Revisited*, p. 6.

10. O'Donovan, *The Just War Revisited*, p. 6. See also David L. Clough and Brian Stiltner, *Faith and Force* (Washington, D.C.: Georgetown University Press, 2007), pp. 51-52.

cent, especially the poor who suffer from it, must seriously figure in any practical reflection. The damage that war inflicts on warriors cannot be cruelly ignored in the name of convenient notions of "heroism" that permit us to suppose that returning soldiers can readily "get on with their lives." In short, an honest just war theory needs to face the *perils* of attaining a just and orderly peace through force of arms. We must not sanction war through myths that deny its reality, for war "dominates culture, distorts memory, corrupts language, and infects everything around it."[11] Just war theory has to resist these myths, not be co-opted by them.

On the basis of this *tension* between what would render war justifiable and what waging war so often *does* to place any easy justification of it into question, just war theory stands within but at the edges of the moral life, and gestures toward a *barely human* activity.[12]

Christological and eschatological themes heighten the complexity. The New Testament depiction of the ministry of Jesus Christ, crucified and risen, is of one who chose to confront division and conflict without recourse to armed violence. His is a ministry of reconciliation that also cautions against any self-righteous pretensions of judgment. He inaugurates a kingdom of patient love, including the love of enemies. That kingdom, although not yet and never to be perfectly realized in fallen human history, is already present to us in promise. It is understandably not unchallenging to square this route of theological witness with the carnage of war.

The eschatological reign of God, moreover, means that the kingdoms and governments of this world are all fleeting and will come to nothing. Whatever authority they have in this time between the times is divinely given and sorely limited, and eventually it will be removed and overtaken by a Lordship signaling joy and peace where God is all in all. Christians who wait for the fullness of the kingdom recognize this as they also realize that they live among others "who cannot vividly

---

11. Chris Hedges, *War Is a Force That Gives Us Meaning* (New York: Public Affairs, 2002), p. 3. For a good collection of essays that consider the similarities and dissimilarities between war and policing, see Gerald W. Schlabach, ed., *Just Policing, Not War* (Collegeville, Minn.: Liturgical Press, 2007).

12. See Paul Ramsey, *The Just War* (New York: Scribner, 1968), p. 164, and John Courtney Murray, S.J., "Remarks on the Moral Problem of War," in *War in the Twentieth Century: Sources in Theological Ethics,* ed. Richard B. Miller (Louisville: Westminster John Knox, 1992), p. 257.

imagine that democracy, freedom as we know it, America, the Constitution, are among those tragic empires . . . [that] shall have passed away."[13] The will of worldly kingdoms to wage war can bring in its train a godlike presumption that, in perverse imitation of God, must be vigilantly resisted in the light of this provision of a final reckoning.

To summarize, just war theory has to do with the manner in which practical reason seeks to do justice in war. The use of armed force may be justifiable by way of an extraordinary extension of the kinds of force and judgment we find in domestic police powers and related judicial functions. But this similarity must be recognized to exist alongside great dissimilarities that make war different, to be entered into with a unique sense of horror. The possible *duty* to resist injustice, and to resist it with firm resolve, can *also only be done with a shudder* that is sensitive to war's terrible reality.[14] Awareness of that harsh reality is *deepened* within Christian communities by faith in an already present opportunity for a discipleship, a following of Jesus, which brings to light God's reconciling mercy through nonviolent love. And the awareness is *sharpened* in the recognition that war brings the greatest temptation on the part of warring parties to defend and execute violent conflict in terms of ultimate values, "religious" values, which as such have no substance in the end.

In my reading, this double-sidedness about war informs how we are to think about the so-called just war criteria, at least as they are presented within Catholic analyses such as the 1983 American Bishops' letter, *The Challenge of Peace*. The criteria frame practical reasoning about doing justice in war, and yet have evolved as an effort to prevent war through the stringency of their requirements.[15] With regard to the right to wage war *(jus ad bellum)*, there must be present *compelling reason,* or *"just cause,"* to wage it. The serious danger and wrong that reasoning about just cause identifies cannot be merely a matter of national self-interest, or even merely a matter of self-interested "self-defense." War is waged to defend and repair a wrong that is above all damage to the in-

13. Paul Ramsey, *Speak Up for Just War or Pacifism* (University Park: Pennsylvania State University Press, 1988), p. 123.

14. Oliver O'Donovan, *In Pursuit of a Christian View of War* (Bramcote, U.K.: Grove Books, 1977), p. 5. See also William Werpehowski, *American Protestant Ethics and the Legacy of H. Richard Niebuhr* (Washington, D.C.: Georgetown University Press, 2002), pp. 100-103.

15. National Conference of Catholic Bishops, *The Challenge of Peace: God's Promise and Our Response* (Washington, D.C.: United States Catholic Conference, 1983), par. 83.

nocent, including innocent persons who are entitled to live in political communities that are self-determining and secure. "Aggression," therefore, would be a crime against the proper claims of political communities and against an international order committed to political self-determination and territorial integrity under the rule of law. Just cause also refers to a defined and limited, even if tremendously serious, political aim. It should not degenerate into a warrant for a crusade, a war waged without limits for unlimited human ends. To protect against this corruption, the bishops in *The Challenge of Peace* introduce the idea that justice in war is *comparative,* relative and not absolute, and should be pursued without any delusions that God or the right is totally on "our" side. The bishops stress this to add weight to the need to limit war, to "dampen down its destructiveness, because in a comparison of justices none escapes moral criticism."[16]

War is a public act, exercised under *legitimate authority* for the sake of the common good. The legitimacy of that authority is to be measured not only by the cause it promotes, but also by the way that cause is confirmed and confined within the *just intentions* manifest in the conduct of the war throughout its duration. What war undertakes must correspond to what its purpose is — to what just cause identifies — and what the cause identifies must correspond, therefore, to what is reasonably complained about.[17] In the course of war, what in fact is undertaken may shift from legitimate defense of political community and the international moral order to conquest, or to mainly self-interested economic gain. What is undertaken, in addition, must be *for the sake of peace,* the reconciliation between parties on terms of justice. It may appear astonishingly light-minded to insist that the contest of war must not be "essentially antagonistic," but that is the moral demand, and war *is* essentially antagonistic "if it does not intend the state of peaceful and lawful governance for the community against which war is waged."[18] "Peace" then includes "all that is comprised in a stable and settled political order, including the justice and law-governed character of relations established within it."[19]

Thus the costs and damages of war are to be continually evalu-

16. Ramsey, *Speak Up,* p. 90.
17. O'Donovan, *The Just War Revisited,* p. 52.
18. O'Donovan, *The Just War Revisited,* p. 31.
19. O'Donovan, *The Just War Revisited,* p. 59.

ated for their due *proportion* to the end of a just peace. Further, these costs and damages may be put into play as a *last reasonable resort,* and insofar as they afford a *reasonable hope of success.* One does not rush to arms, and does not refuse to count the costs, even to the point of questioning whether they might render conflict self-defeating.[20]

With regard to right conduct in war *(jus in bello),* Roman Catholic just war theory in particular poses an exceptionless moral rule that noncombatants are never to be the objects of direct attack. The defense and vindication of the innocent who suffer wrong are what may make war justifiable, and that same concern also limits the means to be employed. One must morally *discriminate* between the "guilty" and the "innocent," that is, those who are and those who are not liable to direct attack. This is typically taken to mean those who "are not fighting and are not engaged with providing those who are with the means of fighting," and others who are fighting or so engaged.[21] And when facing choices among specific military options, there is also a question of *proportionality:* "once we take into account not only the military advantages that will be achieved by using this means but also all the harms reasonably expected to follow from it, can its use still be justified?"[22] Finally, an *in bello* requirement of *just intention* applies, such that "even in the midst of conflict, the aim of political and military leaders must be peace with justice, so that acts of vengeance and indiscriminate violence, whether by individuals, military units or governments, are forbidden."[23]

The Ugliness of War

Exposition

Karl Barth's remarks on ethics and war in volume III of the *Church Dogmatics,* as part of the section "The Protection of Life," do not explicitly, or explicitly do not, take their start from just war theory. Even if he

20. O'Donovan, *The Just War Revisited,* p. 60.

21. G. E. M. Anscombe, "Mr. Truman's Degree," in *War in the Twentieth Century,* p. 242. This way of drawing the distinction has recently been challenged by Jeff McMahan, e.g., "The Ethics of Killing in War," *Ethics* 114 (July 2004): 725-29.

22. National Conference of Catholic Bishops, *The Challenge of Peace,* par. 105.

23. National Conference of Catholic Bishops, *The Harvest of Justice Is Sown in Peace* (1993), at http://www.usccb.org/sdwp/harvest.shtml.

knew much about it, and if, knowing it, his aversion to principled casuistry were not in play, any such consideration would be better placed in his doctrine of reconciliation. But Barth surely sees the practice of war to pose a question of justice or injustice. He begins "by trying to stab our consciences awake in relation to certain illusions" about warfare that may once have been but are no longer excusable. First, there can be no easy delivery of responsibility for war to the "collective body," be that the "people" or the "state."[24] Today, "everyone participates in the suffering and action which war demands," and therefore when war is waged "each individual . . . has to ask whether the war is just or unjust." Barth in fact seems to say more than this when he asserts that "each individual is himself a belligerent," and this move runs afoul of just war theory's requirement of discrimination (p. 451). Still, his major point has to do with individual political responsibility for posing the moral question, rather than with the implications of any such responsibility for liability to attack.

Second, war in general can no longer be readily vindicated in terms of high moral values that preserve and advance humanity and vital human needs. Waging war is more and more a matter of securing material and especially economic interests "as bases from which to deploy power for the acquisition of more power" (p. 452). Its reality thus also prompts us to ask what humanity is and what its needs truly are, as over against "the basically chaotic character of the so-called peaceful will, efforts and achievements of man." To put the matter bloodlessly but nonetheless precisely: the proverb "if you want peace, prepare for war" horrendously begs the question, since the peace that war and preparation for war protect is all too often an inhuman peace (p. 452).

Third, modern warfare — and here Barth refers in passing to nuclear warfare — leads us to see vividly that it is, after all, about parties seeking to kill and out-injure one another on a massive scale. Abstractions having to do with "neutralizing enemy forces" and "killing in self-defense" lose sight of the fact that "whole nations, as such, are out to destroy one another by every possible means" (p. 453).

Barth concludes: "How unequivocally ugly war now is!" (p. 453). With reference to that sphere of God's gracious activity in and for the protection of human life, he notes (in recapitulation and extension of these points) that consideration of war's justice is to be put with severe

---

24. *CD* III/4, p. 451. Page numbers placed in the text refer to *CD* III/4.

strictness because (1) all members of a nation bear a measure of responsibility for killing; (2) all antagonists implicitly pose the question of justice or injustice, and therefore of innocence or guilt, to one another;
and (3) killing in war threatens "obedience to the command of God in
all its dimensions" (p. 454). This *kind* of killing can track disobedience
and inhumanity across the board, and in any event "war is for most
people a trial for which they are no match, and from the consequences
of which they can never recover" (p. 454). An "exact calculation" of
what is at stake is called for, and that means nothing less than the admission that all affirmative answers about a war's justice "are wrong if
they do not start with the assumption that the inflexible negative of
pacifism has almost infinite arguments in its favour, and is almost
overpoweringly strong" (p. 455).

Barth intends here to contribute to correcting what he calls a "degeneration of ecclesiastical eschatology and the resultant overestima-
tion and misinterpretation of the events and laws of the present
world." He observes that in the centuries after Constantine there was
lost in Christian communities "a fairly general aversion . . . towards the
whole world of war and warring" (p. 455). He raises no objection to a
"general reckoning with war and Christian participation in it," seeing
it, *like* the recognition of the state, to be part of an honest attention to
how the church may wait for its Lord in the midst of the laws and realities of a passing aeon of sinful rebellion (pp. 455-56). He does object,
however, to Christians accommodating those realities to the point of
losing "all feeling for the . . . extraordinary nature of this possibility . . .
of mass killing for the sake of the state," for the "enormity of war."
Hence "the primary and supreme task of Christian ethics in this matter is surely to recover and manifest a distinctive horror of war and
aloofness from it" (p. 456).

Commentary

From a just war perspective and for reasons I have already noted, it is
alarming to read Barth's holding that "everyone is now a belligerent."
While my preferred reading of him is fair, there remain at this point and
elsewhere troubling indications that he either had no use for *jus in bello*
norms or thought them impossible to honor. That is, he can leave the
impression that any "just war" on his terms may also be a "total war."

William Werpehowski

While there can seem to be no positive "point of contact" between Barth and just war rules of right conduct, there is at least a sort of negative point of contact with other norms in his identifying economic motives for power as establishing no just cause, no just intention and, logically, a close relation to the "end of war," which in this case is a perverse and inhumane "peace." Here the account parallels somewhat Thomas Merton's well-known attack on American "prayers for peace" during the Cold War.

> The peace the world pretends to desire is really no peace at all.
>
> To some men peace merely means the liberty to exploit other people without fear of retaliation or interference. To others peace means the freedom to rob brothers without interruption. To still others it means the leisure to devour the goods of the earth without being compelled to interrupt their pleasures to feed those whom their greed is starving. And to practically everybody peace simply means the absence of any physical violence that might cast a shadow over lives devoted to the satisfaction of their animal appetites for comfort and pleasure.
>
> Many men like these have asked God for what they thought was "peace" and wondered why their prayer was not answered. They could not understand that it actually *was* answered. God left them with what they desired, for their idea of peace was only another form of war.[25]

Other just war themes may come through as possessing a possible complementary function. So when Barth writes of warriors on either side of conflict posing the question of justice to the other, one can introduce the idea of comparative justice — which would, of course, work to undermine any temptation to wage the total war of a crusade. The important query about the way warfare morally perverts and damages its participants may invite concern for just intention in the conduct of war, for the need, as Augustine had it, for warriors to be "peaceful in warring," and hence to "be free from the enslaving power of force." In keeping with and founding their actions, "people fighting in war have a more fundamental duty to approach war with a mind-set that keeps them from engaging in cruelty so long as the conflict lasts and helps

25. Thomas Merton, *Passion for Peace: The Social Essays,* ed. William H. Shannon (New York: Crossroad, 1995), p. 18.

70

them to look forward to living peacefully within a peaceful community when the fighting is ended."[26]

Barth's emphasis on the reality of war as a contest of killing, his resistance to abstraction, and his refusal of easy Christian accommodation after Constantine, however, covertly ask whether just war theory itself abstractly covers over that reality and is an outcome of accommodation. Nevertheless, his attention to the horror of war and to the almost overpoweringly strong "No!" of pacifism overlaps with the contemporary Roman Catholic position that just war deliberation, while *based* on a "presumption against injustice," *has its point of departure in* a "presumption against war."[27] This position has been harshly criticized for being a "functional pacifism," but I find that criticism off the mark and have argued the case elsewhere.[28] The standing concern, to repeat an earlier comment, is to stigmatize war without completely condemning it. For Barth there is a practical ecclesial need to do just that for the purpose of recovering a sense of the ugliness of war and a critical distance from the proposal that Christians killing for the state is a readily acceptable and simply inevitable state of affairs. The Catholic standpoint, in fact, is built upon a version of the eschatological character of Christian witness that Barth deems to need rehabilitation — that nonviolent resistance to injustice "best reflects the call of Jesus," but that in the present age passing away, war may yet be morally demanded.[29]

The State of Peace

Exposition

If war is what Barth has said it is, then it cannot be, in his words, a "normal, fixed and in some sense necessary part of what on the Christian view constitutes the just state, or the political order demanded by

26. James Turner Johnson, *Morality and Contemporary Warfare* (New Haven and London: Yale University Press, 1999), p. 212.

27. National Conference of Catholic Bishops, *The Challenge of Peace,* par. 89, 93.

28. William Werpehowski, "A Tale of Two Presumptions: The Development of Roman Catholic Just War Theory," in *Applied Ethics in a World Church,* ed. Linda Hogan (Maryknoll, N.Y.: Orbis, 2008), pp. 119-25.

29. National Conference of Catholic Bishops, *The Challenge of Peace,* par. 78.

God" (p. 456). The development of this claim consists of a controversial set of remarks that have appeared to some to contradict what Barth has sensibly written on other occasions. Thus when he denies that *power* does not constitute the essence of the state, he can be understood, on the one hand, to turn away from the kind of political ethic that we find in the fifth article of the Barmen Declaration, the 1938 essay "Church and State," and even the 1946 study "Christian Community and Civil Community."[30] That ethic establishes the state as entrusted with power and the threat of force to protect the innocent and punish the guilty for the sake of clearing a space for the proclamation of the gospel, as all that is also in keeping with seeking forms of "humanization" under the Lordship of Jesus Christ. On the other hand, others find Barth trying here to employ and advance a distinction between *potestas* and *potentia;* the former is "the power that follows and serves the law," while the latter "is the power that precedes the law, that masters and bends and breaks the law."[31] It is noteworthy that Barth as late as 1963 continued to wrestle with the best way to characterize the relation of "the threat and use of force" to the work of the state. He will affirm that it is the "characteristic feature of the State" but will deny that it is "an essential feature." He will allow that force "objectively and in practice . . . is inevitable," but "only as a last resource."[32]

O'Donovan, Rowan Williams, and others including myself have puzzled over the evolution of Barth's political thinking and whether it reaches to anything like settled ground. I will bypass the issue for now and instead focus on what looks like a very reasonable interpretation of one thing Barth finally means to say within the text I am explicating. He clearly means to say that a faithful Christian witness cannot "assure" the state that whatever it thinks right in the matter of war *is* right; that it "must not be given *carte blanche*"; and that Christians in

30. See, for example, O'Donovan, "Karl Barth and Ramsey's 'Uses of Power'"; Rowan Williams, "Barth, War and the State," in *Reckoning with Barth*, ed. Nigel Biggar (London: Mowbray, 1988), pp. 170-90; and William Werpehowski, "Justification and Justice in the Theology of Karl Barth," *Thomist* 50 (October 1986): 623-42.

31. Karl Barth, "The Christian Community and the Civil Community," in *Against the Stream: Shorter Post-war Writings, 1946-1952,* ed. Ronald Gregor Smith (New York: Philosophical Library, 1954), p. 40. Williams marks the distinction as "power defined in terms of the purposive capacity to serve and effect law, so as to realize harmony, as opposed to pure might, defining its own ends" (Williams, "Barth," p. 183).

32. Barth, "An Outing," pp. 73, 78.

their speaking to the state cannot merely "handle war as if it were just as natural as police action" (pp. 456, 458). There is a "true and urgent need for demythologisation" in seeking to separate *war* — organized mass slaughter that may well be mass murder — from the essence of the state (p. 458).

Otherwise, we risk holding that the political order willed and established by God may be "in itself and as such the mythological beast of the jungle, the monster with the Janus head," which by its very nature is prepared at any moment to "turn thousands into killers and thousands more into killed." The "normal" task of the state "is to fashion peace in such a way that life is served and war kept at bay" (p. 458).[33] The Christian community must do "its best for a just peace among states and nations," including the fashioning of the state for democracy and of democracy for social democracy (p. 459). Moreover, and on this last condition, the church ought to work for "peaceful measures and solutions among states to avert war," such as solid and honest alliances and agreements, international courts and conventions, mutual understanding and patience, and the education of the young to prefer peace to war (p. 460). "[R]elatively if not absolutely, in practice if not in principle, war can be avoided to a very large extent" (p. 460).

Thus the Christian community, having a keen awareness of war's terror, making a "detached and delaying movement" *away* from not only war's "normalcy" but also the state's normalcy in waging it, embarked upon securing a just peace within and among nations, and toiling to avert conflicts that are finally unnecessary, may just so also give faithful witness to the legitimacy of armed conflict "at the very last hour in the darkest of days" (p. 456). Undertaking this sequence of practices, in which the almost always "negative" of pacifism is worked out and concretely comprehended in course, renders the church capable and credible in giving this last possible witness.

Barth's unfinished ethics of reconciliation adds some depth and detail to the picture just sketched. Christian "zeal for the honor of God" is tested in acts of grateful obedience to God's command. We are summoned specifically to an entry into conflict, a revolt against the disorder of the world that follows from its faithlessness toward God. It is a disorder to which Christians have contributed and which still assails them. In solidarity with all humanity subject to this "general and

---

33. See also Williams, "Barth," pp. 184-87.

self-incurred human plight," Christians are called, without vengeance or personal anxieties, to resist the consequences of "the unrighteousness of the fall of people from God which as such ineluctably carries with it their fall from one another, the changing of their being with one another, which corresponds to their being with God, into a general being without and against one another."[34] Their struggle is *for* human right, freedom, and peace.

The unrighteousness of attempted escape from God's Lordship carries with it bondage to "lordless powers" that issue from the possibilities and powers of human beings but escape from and in turn control them. Such powers "act at their own pleasure, as absolutes, without [them], . . . according to the law by which . . . man himself thought that he should flee from God. As he did to God, so the different forms of his own capacity now do to him."[35]

Four interrelated specific implications bear on our topic. First, Christian solidarity with all humanity in sinful complicity, affliction, and reconciling promise means that revolt against disorder "is not directed *against* any people. . . . Thinking, speaking, and acting in a friend-foe relationship, that is, in favor of some people and to the detriment of others, can never be" its purpose.[36] Accordingly, Christian work for peace, and on that basis the possible witness to just war, may and must reflect that "break" with the powers of this world. Second, the lordless power that Barth names *Leviathan,* the political absolutism that subordinates right to the exercise of power and force over others for its own sake, is to be resolutely opposed. "We need to realize that no state of any kind is or has [*sic*] or will be immune to the tendency to become at least a little Leviathan. The threat of a change from the might of right to the right of might couches at the door of every polity."[37] The vigilance of a Christian "detached and delaying movement" with respect to war includes this critical stance (p. 456). Third, Christian witness also stands over against the power of *Mammon,* which we will say for now is the tyranny of money and material acquisition. This point returns us to Barth's sweeping assertions that economic interest drives recourse to war, and is in concert with "Leviathan." Fourth, propaganda, "the

34. *CL,* pp. 211-12.
35. *CL,* pp. 214-15.
36. *CL,* p. 210-11.
37. *CL,* p. 221.

particular art and masterwork" of lordless *ideologies,* would also work in concurrence with Leviathan and Mammon, as well as fuel forms of a friend-foe relationship.[38] In effect, Barth's ethics of the Christian life commend a perseverance in the struggle for human righteousness and against disorder that may discern the disordered tendencies of the state to nationalism, empire, greed, and ideological betrayal.[39]

Commentary

Two observations are in order. The first is that Barth's call for Christians to be about the "emergency of peace" as good in itself and as a condition for authentically considering the justice of war sheds some light on *The Challenge of Peace*'s seemingly odd conception that nonviolent discipleship and just war teaching "support and complement one another, each preserving the other from distortion."[40] One may understand how nonviolent witness to peace broadly considered complements and protects just war reasoning by more practically and critically identifying *what,* recalling Merton, *the peace we ought to pray for, and labor for, is and is not,* and for the sake of which justice and reconciliation are sought by means short of war. A related practice is in Christian "revolt" against rationalizations for war that keep hidden the designs of nationalism, empire, and greed. The meanings for practical deliberation of "legitimate authority," "proportionality," and "last reasonable resort" may also be better understood as we clarify the fuller contours of peace, including the sort of peace one seeks in waging war and pursuing peace in its aftermath. Most generally, nonviolent work preserves just war reasoning from distortion by affording a longer view of the meaning and conditions for peace and, with that, by the reminder of how failures in achieving a just peace may in fact have sown the seeds of war in specific instances. The possibility that just war theory may be deployed ideologically is curbed not only by a sense of war's ugliness and its likely subjection to lordless powers, but also by the fact, as John Paul II had it, that "war is the most barbarous and least effective way of resolving conflicts."[41]

---

38. *CL,* p. 227.
39. See Biggar, *The Hastening That Waits,* pp. 92-96.
40. National Conference of Catholic Bishops, *The Challenge of Peace,* par. 121.
41. John Paul II, "Message for the Celebration of the Day of Peace, 1 January 1982,"

What about the opposite direction? How does just war reasoning complete and protect nonviolent reflection and action? Consider that the terms of just war deliberation may be employed to expose how they apply, ably or badly, honestly or dishonestly, in specific historical circumstances to reach concrete practical conclusions. A politically relevant "pacifist" witness against war will and should propose against its advocates that just cause or competent authority is absent, that intentions are deceptive, that reasonable alternatives exist, that disproportion obtains, and so forth — at least for the sake of making wars *less unjust*.[42] Of course, in the view of both Barth and the Catholic Bishops, the idea that war may indeed be a genuine moral possibility for political communities additionally completes and corrects any pacifism that would categorically deny it as much.

Second, what has come to be called "Catholic peacebuilding" is in keeping with but refines and expands Barth's recommendations. In fact, this movement seeks a kind of integration that enfolds just war theory into "a more comprehensive approach to peace." "*Peacebuilding* attempts to address not only the resolution of conflict but how to build a culture that includes the prevention of conflict that leads to war, humane intervention during conflict and perhaps most important the rebuilding of a just society and a lasting peace after conflict."[43] Prevention of conflict reckons with how "at the root of war there are usually real and serious grievances: injustices suffered, legitimate aspirations frustrated, poverty and the exploitation of multitudes of desperate people who see no real possibility of improving their lot by peaceful means."[44] It links this concern with a universal vision of the common good of one human family under God, the promotion of human rights, and solidarity between affluent nations and poor, developing ones. Humane intervention during conflict addresses, with reference to the just war legacy, the varieties of warfare known today, especially those within states and involving the increas-

---

at http://www.vatican.va/holy_father/john_paul_ii/messages/peace/documents/hf_jp-ii_mes_19811208_xv-world-day-for-peace_en.html.

42. John Howard Yoder, *The Christian Witness to the State* (Newton, Kans.: Faith and Life Press, 1964), p. 49.

43. Robert Schreiter, "The Future of Catholic Peacebuilding," *Origins* 38, no. 3 (May 29, 2008): 34.

44. John Paul II, *Centesimus Annus,* par. 52, at http://www.vatican.va/holy_father/john_paul_ii/encyclicals/documents/hf_jp-ii_enc_01051991_centesimus-annus_en.html.

ing vulnerability of noncombatant populations. The rebuilding of just and peaceful societies introduces the demands of what is now regularly referred to as *jus post bellum,* the kind of practical judgment and action that attends to transitional justice, reparations, the rebuilding of civil society, and the further possibilities of reconciliation between parties at odds.[45]

Waging and Preparing for War

Exposition

Barth anticipates his discussion of just cause for war with a short statement of the kinds of causes that fail to measure up. These include national expansion, achieving political unity, vindicating injured honor, correcting threatening shifts in the international power balance, concern about the internal affairs of another nation, and advancing one's own nation's "historical mission." He further denies that the continued independent life of a people or state will always constitute a valid cause when that life comes no longer to have any "meaning [or] basis" (p. 461). Just cause for war is present only on the condition that "in and with the independence of a nation there is entrusted to its people something which, without any claim or pretension, they are commissioned to attest to others, and which they may not therefore surrender" (p. 462). What is this divine commission that a people is summoned to defend? It is "the preservation of the political conditions under which justice is attested" as constitutive of God's provision for an order of legitimate political authority.[46] These conditions include the ordering of power under law to preserve a common life from chaos and destruction, and intentional promotion of fellow humanity, a mutuality of human right, freedom, and peace that moves ideally (but not necessarily) in the direction of democracy and social democracy.

When a nation's political sovereignty as bound up with such a divine commission is directly threatened or attacked, the people of that

45. Schreiter, "Future of Catholic Peacebuilding," p. 34. See *Pursuing Just Peace: An Overview and Case Studies for Faith Based Peacebuilders,* ed. Mark M. Rogers, Tom Bamat, and Julie Ideh (Baltimore: Catholic Relief Services, 2008).

46. Biggar, *The Hastening That Waits,* p. 93.

nation not only may but must resist. An unthreatened third party may also find itself obliged, by treaty or otherwise, to fight in aid of its similarly vulnerable "weaker neighbor." Peacetime preparation for this and only this kind of defensive war is morally demanded, and yet Barth insists that in this "rare case" of a just war the demand to wage it is "unconditional," that is, "independent of the success or failure of the enterprise, and therefore of the strength of one's own forces in comparison with those of the enemy" (p. 463).

The discussion ends as it began, with attention to individual responsibility for moral judgment. The Christian in his or her capacity as citizen cannot avoid or defer a "supremely personal interrogation" about facing the terrible reality of war or not, about seeking peace or not, about working to avoid war or not, about naming false reasons for war or not, and finally, against this background, about hearing the command in the emergency case to accept war, military training, and the prospect of killing (p. 466). In a remarkable excursus on conscientious objection, Barth argues that the practice of military conscription supports the most serious because personal attention to the problem of war, and that what *perpetuates* war is any Christian "Pharisaic attitude" that would leave war and its "moral odium" to "others" (p. 466). The crucial point for our purposes is the commendation of a Christian's legitimate refusal of military service in wartime when the cause for war is unjust. It would be, Barth thinks, "a great gain for peace" if governments had to account for the press of personal judgment in this way; moreover, the assistance of the Christian community insofar as it speaks to the validity of this judgment of free conscience — which is to say the validity of the case that a particular war is unjust — would concretely embody how the church can be what it should be, a "retarding factor in regard to war, a genuinely unreliable element upon whose cooperation it is impossible to count unconditionally" (p. 469).

Commentary

I said earlier that just war theory depends on a morally relevant analogy between the moral nature and purpose of warfare and domestic policing and judicial functions. We find no clear or direct or explicit appeal to such an analogy in Barth's 1951 statement on war, and that is in keeping with his reluctance in that text to "normalise the extraordinary."[47] He surely has the issue of analogy in mind when he asserts *dissimilarity*; Christians must not "handle war as if it were just as natural as police action" (p. 458). In his "table talk," Barth does comment that "a soldier or a policeman is not a murderer," and he makes similar allusions elsewhere.[48] In 1941, for example, he refers to the war against Germany as "a large scale police measure which has become absolutely necessary to repulse an active anarchism."[49] This remark follows an account of Romans 13:1-7 that implies that there is a common basis for domestic judgment and the police action of war. There may also be resources in Barth's consideration of self-defense and capital punishment for affirming the analogy. God has not abandoned the common life to confusion and chaos, he says, and can will that an individual "may rise up quite simply in honour and defence of the law and order which protects the community and oppose the one who is deliberately on the point of breaking it," even by killing "on the extreme edge" (pp. 435, 436). And punishment generally is based "on the necessity of defending the state and therefore all its members against arbitrary crime and disorder," though Barth in the end proposes a comparison *the other way,* from war, if you will, to legitimate capital punishment for high treason during its course, and hence when the very existence of the state is at stake (p. 443).

But whatever he said and whenever he said it, Barth definitely requires something like the idea, one that I think is also necessary to make sense of Roman Catholic teaching, that moral resort to war is "an extraordinary extension of ordinary acts of judgment."[50] His limited case for strictly defensive war cannot be theologically coherent without it. After all, what needs defending is the independent life of community as it is bound up with a political order intending justice and therefore included within the redemptive purposes of God in Jesus Christ. Any such order, we should suppose, finds itself objectively within the reach of these purposes. To protect and preserve the right through defensive war in the concrete case is to witness to God's patient and gracious gift of time and space for the proclamation of the gospel and the amend-

47. O'Donovan, *The Just War Revisited,* p. 19.

48. *Karl Barth's Table Talk,* recorded and edited by John D. Godsey (Edinburgh: Oliver and Boyd, 1963), p. 80.

49. Karl Barth, *This Christian Cause* (New York: Macmillan, 1941), no pagination. Also see Barth, "An Outing," pp. 77-79.

50. O'Donovan, *The Just War Revisited,* p. 6.

William Werpehowski

ment of life, and just so "by resisting disorder, restraining, by compulsion where necessary, the mutual destructiveness of sinful human beings, creating equity and harmony."[51] The vocation of the state is carried over to establish the warrant for war within an international frame.

If we accept this proposal, then a few other standing issues in Barth's account fall somewhat into line. The circumstances within which one may hear a divine command to wage war include that there be a strong presumption against it, because of what the reality of war threatens and because, for the sake of justice and peace, ongoing work on behalf of fellow humanity and the avoidance of conflict may promise to hit nearer the mark. War may be waged only as a last resort and with all unjust warrants and intentions exposed and renounced. Preparation for war is imaginable insofar as it intends sufficient defense, and inasmuch as it does not succumb to what Barth saw in 1951 to be an "armaments industry . . . which is always forging ahead on its own account, which is closely linked with many other branches of industry, technical science and commerce, and which imperiously demands that war should break out from time to time to use up existing stocks and create the demand for new ones" (p. 452). In fact such military-industrial complexes ought to be resisted. Even Barth's claim that questions of success or failure must be put to one side in the exceptional case of a just war can make at least some sense, because a firm witness to just order under God when it is utterly threatened honors that order perhaps adequately for the sake of a genuine peace. At the least, there is the necessity of introducing the norms of just conduct that Barth appears never positively to consider; for both the defense of just order and the "break" with the terms of a friend-foe relationship cannot countenance practices that would directly assault the innocent and the conditions for humane social existence.[52]

51. Williams, "Barth," p. 187.

52. But also see Barth, "An Outing," p. 83, where Barth concedes that he erred in his 1951 *Church Dogmatics* statement: "In connection with the idea of the just war, I should have said that, in considering the question of whether a war is just or not, not only its cause and meaning must be taken into account, but also the manner of its waging. Had I done that, I should have been bound to conclude that no nuclear war can be a just war." We remain a bit disappointed in the end, however, because the specific reason Barth gives here for his opposition is not directly in terms of the *jus in bello* considerations of discrimination and proportionality. Instead, it is that nuclear war, "which from the outset means the end of all

80

But this attempt to bring Barth closer to Roman Catholic just war theory is not fair to the power of his vision unless we undertake a reverse move that entertains bringing the latter closer to him; for he reminds us implicitly that "just war theory" may, like self-defense and "high ideals," become an abstraction that distracts us from war as mass killing and from a necessary witness to peace. So we now have to look, albeit too briefly and incompletely by way of conclusion, at two implications for Catholic communities aligned with just war reflection of Barth's radical call "to recover and manifest a distinctive horror of war and aloofness from it" (p. 456).

If pacifism is almost entirely right, if nonviolent resolution of conflict best reflects the call of Jesus, and if, therefore, as Barth and Roman Catholic teaching agree, there is a strong presumption against war, then the practices of Catholic communities ought to reflect these truths more closely. First, for example, within families and parishes the discernment of vocations before God ought to emphasize and enable the virtues of peacemaking, nonviolent service for the common good, and critical attention to the corruptions of nationalism, greed, false ideologies of martial heroism, and the perpetuation of "us" versus "them" forms of self-glorification and demonization.[53] For over forty years, Roman Catholic teaching has supported, as did Barth, "selective conscientious objection" by "those who cannot . . . serve in specific conflicts they consider unjust."[54] However, the Second Vatican Council

---

things," "makes waging war senseless." That is, there can be no possible political purpose for a war that means the end of all human purposes. Compare the sharp statement in par. 80 of Vatican II's *Pastoral Constitution on the Church in the Modern World* that "every act of war directed to the indiscriminate destruction of whole cities or vast areas with their inhabitants is a crime against God and man, which merits firm and unequivocal condemnation." http://www.vatican.va/archive/hist_councils/ii_vatican_council/documents/vat-ii_cons_ 19651207_gaudium-et-spes_en.html.

53. On these themes in Catholic reflection, see *The Harvest of Justice Is Sown in Peace* (see n. 23 above), including the U.S. Bishops' caution that "moral reflection on the use of force calls for a spirit of moderation rare in contemporary political culture. The increasing violence of our society, its growing insensitivity to the sacredness of life and the glorification of the technology of destruction in popular culture could inevitably impair our society's ability to apply just war criteria honestly and effectively in time of crisis."

54. National Conference of Catholic Bishops, *The Harvest of Justice Is Sown in Peace*. An important difference is that Catholic support of "SCO" (selective conscientious objection) status extends to the endorsement of *legal protection*. Barth does not think that the state can realistically provide this, and, indeed, supposes that a test of Christian au-

also seems to say that legitimate objection to military service may extend beyond such individuals. The Catholic tradition's exemption of clergy from fighting in war rightly prompts an inquiry into whether Christians or others in other social roles — "doctors or teachers or others whose work seems especially opposed to bloodshed," or "others who have adopted a particularly pacific or prophetic lifestyle" — may be exempted from the duty to fight in what may even be deemed a just war. Such an inquiry surpasses what Barth requires in the emergency situation, but that is only to say that he may overreach in claiming that a duty to fight in this case is indefeasible, and that there are features of Catholic moral traditions that may disclose why this is so.[55]

Second, Roman Catholic educational instruments and institutions must more clearly and critically teach how it is that just war theory may be, while admitting the justifiability of war as a last resort, a form of practical reasoning that aims also and especially to prevent war. To take a case that strikes close to home at my own university, Reserve Officer Training Corps (ROTC) programs "should organize their curricula to train officers thoroughly in the just war criteria. Training should be so thorough, in fact, that resisting unjust orders and selective conscientious objection to unjust wars becomes normative."[56] A related requirement is that in their public witness to parishes and to governments, Roman Catholic bishops should provide genuine guidance through careful moral argument, but may also be expected in these arguments "to oppose the war unless arguments in favor of its justice are overwhelming."[57]

---

thenticity would be to recognize and accept the moral necessity of punishment for conscientious objection. To pursue "alternative service" or legal protection appears to him to amount to dishonest evasion.

55. *Gaudium et Spes,* par. 79, at http://www.vatican.va/archive/hist_councils/ii_vatican_council/documents/vat-ii_cons_19651207_gaudium-et-spes_en.html. See Joseph Boyle, "Just War Thinking in Catholic Natural Law," in *Christian Political Ethics,* ed. John A. Coleman, S.J. (Princeton and Oxford: Princeton University Press, 2008), p. 226. The theme of testing for vocation is central in Gerald W. Schlabach's analysis in "Practicing for Just Policing," in *Just Policing, Not War,* pp. 97-105.

56. Schlabach, *Just Policing, Not War,* p. 104. Cf. Boyle's response to Vitoria's argument that questions of individual doubt regarding military service in war should resolve themselves in deference to the state, pp. 225-30. On the contrary, "obedience is justified only when honest moral reflection reveals no reason to think that there is a crime, and obedience is not morally justified as long as one has a reason for thinking the war is criminal, or as long as one negligently fails to determine whether such a reason exists" (p. 230).

57. Schlabach, *Just Policing, Not War,* p. 102.

5. Barth and Werpehowski on War, Presumption, and Exception

John R. Bowlin

Barth's remarks on war, justice, and exception in the special ethics of his *Church Dogmatics* III/4 come burdened with all kinds of trouble and woe, all sorts of antinomies and contradictions. About this, nearly all commentators agree. Some, like Oliver O'Donovan and John Yoder, wonder whether those remarks hang together well with the rest of Barth's theological enterprise.[1] Others, like David Clough and myself, worry about the internal consistency of those remarks and wonder whether this local inconsistency, once noted, can be avoided, given Barth's other remarks about moral judgment and moral rule under the command of God.[2] Bill Werpehowski stands in this company of complaint and worry. He takes note of these troubles with Barth's remarks, and yet the great virtue of his paper is that he doesn't dwell on them. Or more precisely, he doesn't dwell on them in order to dismiss and condemn but rather to redeem and improve. In this instance the medium of redemption is conversation with the Roman Catholic just war tradition, and the fallout is a somewhat saved Barth. Somewhat saved, I

---

1. John Howard Yoder, *Karl Barth and the Problem of War and Other Essays,* ed. M. T. Nation (Eugene, Oreg.: Cascade Books, 2003), and Oliver O'Donovan, *The Just War Revisited* (Cambridge: Cambridge University Press, 2003).

2. David Clough, "Fighting at the Command of God: Reassessing the Borderline Case in Karl Barth's Account of War in the *Church Dogmatics,*" in *Conversing with Barth,* ed. J. C. McDowell and M. Higton (Aldershot: Ashgate, 2004), pp. 214-26.

I want to thank Matthew Puffer for editorial advice on the penultimate draft of this essay.

say, because on Werpehowski's able and graceful rendering, Barth is simultaneously rehabilitated and yet ever lost.

By Werpehowski's lights, Barth's rehabilitation comes as we note a number of traditional just war distinctions and norms imbedded in his remarks about politics and war and as we see how Barth anticipates recent developments in Catholic just war theory, developments that accent the irreducible horror of war, the peacemaking functions of the state, and the primacy of our practical commitment to prevent war. And yet at the same time, Werpehowski quite rightly insists that Barth's remarks on war remain incomplete. They stand without deliberate reflection on the analogy between the purposes of policing and those of war, without noting the connections between ordinary and extraordinary political judgment, and, perhaps most troubling, they conclude without serious reflection on the justice of means, on discrimination, double effect, and proportionality.

In what follows, I want to continue the conversation that Werpehowski has started between Barth and the Catholic just war tradition, in part to pose questions to Bill, in part to voice my own puzzlement about Barth's efforts, in part to propose alternative modes of rehabilitation.

Barth discusses warfare under the heading "The Protection of Life," which he describes as his attempt "to elucidate the literal wording and meaning of the biblical commandment: 'Thou shall not kill'" and to consider "the difficult problem of [the] exceptional case." It is this problem, Barth tells us, that is the "main theme" of this subsection.[3]

Now when philosophers and theologians speak of commandments and prohibitions, of presumptions against this or that, and of exceptions to each, we should expect them to be as precise as possible. If precision is lacking, then we should press our questions. What exactly is being prohibited, what presumed against, and what does the exception regard, the presumption or the prohibition? My own hunch is that, when it comes to war and murder, Barth is not as precise or consistent as he should be given the seriousness of the matter. So too, I think this lack of precision and consistency makes it difficult to determine what exactly Barth's remarks about war ultimately amount to even as I suspect that these local deficits have everything to do with Barth's struggle to remain faithful to his other theological commitments. So, as I indi-

---

3. *CD* III/4, pp. 397-98.

cated, Werpehowski thinks that Barth anticipates the presumption against war that we now find in Catholic social thought, a presumption expressed most prominently in *The Challenge of Peace,* the 1983 pastoral letter on war and peace from the U.S. Conference of Catholic Bishops. But I am not convinced that Barth's views are spelled out with enough clarity to make this claim, to draw this comparison.

Werpehowski's argument goes something like this. Barth refuses to let us love war. He paints its hard reality in stark and bloody colors. He drains it of all glory, valor, and heroism. He unmasks its false glamour and displays its raw ugliness. He debunks the distinction between friend and foe, between complicity and innocence. And he confronts us with war's tremendous costs in modern times, costs that include not only life and limb but also virtue and soul. War corrupts judgment, it enflames desire, it encourages suspicion and fear and thus perpetuates itself. Because this is what war is and does, and because Christians are obliged to work tirelessly for peace and to resolve disputes nonviolently whenever possible, and because "war is the most barbarous and least effective way of resolving conflicts," we must conclude that for Barth "the circumstances within which one may hear a divine command to wage war include that there be a strong presumption against it."[4]

So goes the argument. But what does it mean for there to be a presumption against this or that course of action? And what does a negative presumption involve in the context of war? Well, I suppose it means something like this. There is a presumption against some action, let's call it x, when, everywhere and always, resort to x stands in need of justification. Everywhere and always reasons need to be offered in defense of this resort, and the burden of proof is always on the person who makes it, not on the person who asks for a reason that might justify the resort.

If this is right, then to say that Barth shares with the U.S. Catholic Bishops a presumption against war is to say that he thinks it always makes sense to ask for reasons in defense of this resort, presumably reasons that refer to the gracious commands of God. It means that, for Barth, it always makes sense to ask, "Why opt for *that* method of confronting injustice and securing peace and not some other?" And it means that the burden of proof is *always* on those who make this resort. When confronted with *this* "why" question, this doubt about mo-

---

4. William Werpehowsi, "Karl Barth and Just War," pp. 75 and 80 above.

John R. Bowlin

tive and action, they are obliged to respond and can be faulted if reasons fail them.

It is worth noting that most human actions do not proceed under this cloud of doubt. Most have no presumption against them. Most do not provoke "why" questions of this kind everywhere and always. Rather, most provoke questions of this kind in relation to some agents, actions, and circumstances but not all. Suppose it is 6 A.M. and my wife is sitting at the breakfast table eating a bowl of cereal. Does this act provoke enough puzzlement to justify the question "Why are you doing that?!" Probably not. Indeed, were I to pose this question to her, she would no doubt be within her epistemic rights to ignore this request for reasons and, with a grunt and a scowl, return to her meal. If, by contrast, I find her in the kitchen baking a cake in the middle of night, say at 2 A.M., then it makes perfect sense (I think) to ask for reasons that might make this act both intelligible and justified at this late hour. As before, she may scowl and grunt, but I am owed an answer, and she's likely to provide one.

So then, given this (admittedly rough) distinction between actions that have a presumption against them and those that do not, the question is this: Does Barth believe that the burden of proof is always on the person who resorts to war in order to confront injustice and secure peace? Does he think that everywhere and always war making proceeds under this cloud of legitimate doubt? Werpehowski, as I said, thinks he does, and I don't deny the strength of the case Bill has made, but at the same time I am not convinced that the textual evidence is as straightforward as Bill assumes. Consider what Barth says about war as a response to unjust aggression. Can we regard that response as just?

> The obvious answer is that there may well be bound up with the independent life of a nation responsibility for the whole physical, intellectual and spiritual life of the people comprising it, and therefore their relationship to God. It may well be that in and with the independence of a nation there is entrusted to its people something which, without any claim or pretension, they are commissioned to attest to others, and which they may not therefore surrender. It may well be that with the independence of the state, and perhaps in the form of the legally constituted society guaranteed by it, they would also have to yield something which must not be betrayed, which is necessarily more important to them than the pres-

86

ervation of life itself, and which is thus more important than the preservation of the lives of those who unfortunately are trying to take it from them. It may well be that they are thus forbidden by God to renounce the independent status of their nation, and that they must therefore defend it without considering either their own lives or the lives of those who threaten it. Christian ethics cannot possibly deny that this case may sometimes occur. The divine command itself posits and presents it as a case of extreme urgency.[5]

In cases like these, a people confronted with aggression *must* respond with war. They may not surrender. They must not yield lest they defy God's command.

Notice how emphatic are these remarks, how pressing the necessity, and notice how they shift the burden of proof from the one who asks for reasons that might justify resort to war to the person who would doubt that this resort makes sense in this instance. Once this shift has been made, it is the person who considers war a presumptuous response to unjust aggression who must now address doubts and answer "why" questions. It is as if Barth thinks the question, "Why respond to unjust aggression with violent means?" is equivalent to asking my wife, "Why are you eating a bowl of cereal at 6 A.M.?" Both questions deserve a grunt and a scowl and nothing said in reply. Or better yet, it is as if Barth shares something like Michael Walzer's presumption in *favor* of war when, as Barth says, there is an "attack on the independence, neutrality, and territorial integrity" of a people, an attack on their life together, their collective freedom, and the common goods that accrue in that shared life.

Barth makes these remarks as he imagines aggression against tiny Switzerland, which in turn makes his position all the more Walzeresque.[6] Walzer's defense of war as the presumptive response to unjust aggression emerges in reflection on the Finns' response to Soviet belligerence at the start of WWII. The Soviets wanted a small bit of Finnish territory, a strip of empty bog-land on the western flank of Leningrad. The Finns refused the requests, and the Soviets invaded to get what they wanted. Outnumbered and outclassed, the Finns had no rea-

5. *CD* III/4, p. 462.
6. He writes: "I may remark in passing that I myself should see it as such a case if there were any attack on the independence, neutrality and territorial integrity of the Swiss Confederation, and I should speak and act accordingly" (*CD* III/4, p. 462).

sonable hope of winning this fight and every reason to believe that the harms incurred would be disproportionate. And yet for reasons largely identical to those provided by Barth, Walzer insists that the Finns were right to fight. For the sake of their life together and for the just affairs they have sustained in that life, they ought to meet force with force. They must take up arms. Unjust aggression against their rightful sovereignty must be opposed. They may not surrender.

What follows? It is not at all clear. Werpehowski is right to insist that the bulk of Barth's remarks tilt toward a presumption against the resort to war, and yet his remarks about aggression and sovereignty deny that presumption. We are left with an inconsistency, and it is not the only one of this kind that confounds Barth's discussion. At other key moments, inconsistency with regard to command, presumption, and exception reappears, and, as I said, makes it difficult for us to say what his account of war actually entails.

Consider another such example. Barth would have us interpret the biblical command not to kill as an implicit command not to murder. As such, God's command

> is not a plain and simple prohibition of every kind of extinction of human life by human decision and action. Such an understanding of Ex. 20:13f. and par. is excluded by the fact that the killing of men by men is not only reported in Old Testament stories, and often without any objection to such action, but in many passages it is even directly enjoined. . . . Again, the New Testament interpretation of this commandment in Mt. 5:21f. does not attack killing as such but radicalises the concept of murder (cf. I Jn. 3:15). He who is angry with his brother and calls him Raca or fool incurs the judgment of the commandment in the same way as he who in the simple sense of the term wilfully takes the life of another. It is tacitly assumed that there is a form of killing which as such is not murder.[7]

This interpretation of the command places Barth in a lineage of Christian reflection on killing that runs from Augustine to Aquinas to Calvin, a lineage that regards killing as indifferent, at least at the start of moral analysis, and murder as unjust killing. By these lights, it is murder that is prohibited by God, not killing in general. What is commanded is that we do no injustice with respect to human life, created

7. CD III/4, pp. 398-99.

by God and given as gift. What is assumed is that we find no blanket condemnation of killing in Scripture but rather killings of various kinds, some of them just, others not.[8]

At the same time, we find Barth admitting that the New Testament witness against killing of any kind is so strong that we should take caution as we deploy this distinction between the just and the unjust. The rebuke Jesus offers to James and John in Luke 9:56 ("the Son of Man has not come to destroy men's lives but to save them") and his reply to sword-wielding Peter in Matthew 26:52 ("Put your sword back into its place; for all who take the sword will perish by the sword"), while not finally decisive in their condemnation of deadly violence, nevertheless come pretty close. These stories indicate that Christ would have us regard most talk of just killing as fraudulent. The disciples think they are making just resort to deadly violence, but Christ unmasks that resort as a hoodwink and a lie that need to be "rejected . . . as a will to murder."[9]

Notice the puzzle, then, as it regards the character of the exceptional case. We have a prohibition commanded, "Thou shalt not murder," and we have the New Testament presumption against the thought that there could be just killings of any kind. When sinful creatures say

---

8. See Augustine, *Contra Faustum Manichaeum* 22.73; Aquinas, *Summa Theologiae* I-II.1.3.3; 18.8-9 (hereafter *ST*); and John Calvin, *Institutes of the Christian Religion* 4.20.10-12. Richard Miller argues that Aquinas ought not to be counted in this company, but there are good reasons to doubt this conclusion ("Aquinas and the Presumption against Killing and War," *Journal of Religion* 82 [2002]: 173-204). Thomas regards the distinction between killing and murder as so thoroughly unobjectionable that he uses it to help his reader distinguish an action that is indifferent in its moral species from one that is not (*ST* I-II.1.3.3). Actions indifferent in their moral species, actions like walking, eating, and yes, killing, are good or evil, not in themselves, but only in relation to their ends and circumstances (I-II.18.9). Any particular instance of these actions will of course be good or evil (I-II.18.8), but we will not be able to offer a proper moral description of it until we take note of the end it was chosen to achieve and the circumstances within which it resides. An action initially indifferent in its moral species will, for us, remain so, until we know these things, and presumably it can be judged good in relation to some intentions and circumstances, evil in relation to others. This is what it means for an action to be initially indifferent, and presumably an initially indifferent killing will be murderous or not for precisely these reasons, and it will be described as such once these reasons are known. If this is right, if Aquinas does indeed regard killing as initially indifferent, then he would regard a presumption against it as equivalent to a presumption against walking or eating, which of course he doesn't do.

9. *CD* III/4, p. 400.

they have killed justly, we should suspect a lie and a swindle. Given these two — the prohibition and the presumption — the exception could, in principle, regard either. And notice further, how morally distinct these two possibilities are. If the exception is to the prohibition, then, at least on a literal reading of the matter, the God who commands the exception enjoins injustice. God prohibits murder, and, in the exceptional case, God commands murder. If, by contrast, what is commanded is an exception to the New Testament presumption against killing, a presumption justified by sin's eagerness to consider every expedient murder a just killing, then it is a just killing that is commanded, not murder. No exception is made to the prohibition against injustice in general or to murder in particular, for what God commands in the exceptional case is just killing. So which is it?

Apparently it is both. In his discussion of suicide, Barth works with a clear and precise distinction between just killing and murderous injustice. He writes: "We must start with the unequivocal fact that when self-destruction is the exercise of a supposed and usurped sovereignty of man over himself it is a frivolous, arbitrary and criminal violation of the commandment, and therefore self-murder. To deprive a man of his life is a matter for the One who gave it and not for the man himself. He who takes what does not belong to him, in this case only to throw it away, does not merely kill; he murders. There is no ground on which to justify or authorise this."[10] At the same time, Barth admits that it is certainly possible "for the gracious God Himself to help a man in affliction by telling him to take this way out[.] In some cases perhaps a man can and must choose and do this in the freedom given him by God and not therefore in false sovereignty, in despair at the futility of his existence, or in final, supreme and masterful self-assertion, but in obedience."[11] And Barth insists that this "permission and command to destroy . . . cannot be regarded as a suicide in the bad sense."[12] It is not murder that is imagined in this exceptional case, but a just killing at the command of God.

Fair enough. But now consider what Barth says about killing in war, alluded to earlier by Werpehowski. His realism is cold and unflinching, and it comes packaged with three assumptions. First, "It is

10. *CD* III/4, p. 404.
11. *CD* III/4, p. 410.
12. *CD* III/4, p. 411.

an illusion to think that there can be an uncommitted spectator" in a nation at war. All are now military personnel, "each individual is himself a belligerent."[13] Second, there are no longer wars of aristocratic honor or national pride. Today, all wars are fought to acquire wealth, land, and power. War is a kind of shopping for the power classes, whose material and economic interests drive peace from our homes and gladness from our hearts. And finally, there are no restraints in modern war. "[W]ar does in fact mean no more and no less than killing, with neither glory, dignity nor chivalry, with neither restraint nor consideration in any respect."[14]

Notice what emerges from these points as regards the exceptional case. Barth assumes that war in the modern age is total, that discrimination is impossible, and that noncombatant immunity is a quaint relic from the moral past. This is what war now is. This is what warring nations now do. They disregard the innocent; they take up arms and they commit murder. If *this* is the substance of war, if this is what God commands and authorizes in a limit case, then the exception imagined is not to the New Testament presumption against killing but to the biblical prohibition against murder. On this reading, Barth is recommending that, in certain extreme circumstances, and on the command of God, we may do evil that good may come, that we may kill shopkeepers and children in order to secure the political freedom of our homeland. This is quite a claim. I can't quite imagine assigning to it Barth, particularly after considering his remarks about suicide, and yet I do think it emerges quite seamlessly from what he says about killing in war.

What follows this time? I am inclined to think that little does other than the need to admit that Barth's discussion of killing and murder, war and exception, stands in need of precisely the kind of rehabilitation that Werpehowski's efforts have begun. At the same time, it is not clear to me that these inconsistencies can be resolved. Suppose Werpehowski is right. A presumption against war and killing does indeed dominate Barth's discussion. If that presumption falters in his treatment of aggression and national sovereignty, then perhaps he should have abandoned that treatment in order to retain that presumption. This approach would not only bring internal consistency to Barth's treatment of war, but it would bring that treatment into line with his well-known suspicion of

13. *CD* III/4, p. 451.
14. *CD* III/4, p. 453.

theology's service to the nation-state. And, as Werpehowski points out, this accent on the presumption against war and killing would create significant points of agreement between Barth's efforts and recent developments in Catholic social thought.

These benefits cannot be denied, but neither can the moral costs of this accent. The problem is not, as some commentators have argued, that this talk of a presumption against war and killing allows pacifism into the just war tradition through the back door.[15] No, the problem is that it tempts us to invite injustice in. Begin with a presumption against war and killing and you will most likely assume that this presumption can be put aside only in the gravest circumstances and for the most pressing reasons. Reduce moral reflection to consequentialist calculations of this kind and you may find yourself compelled by grave circumstances to do injustice for the sake of the good. Package those reasons in talk of God's command and the outcome is much the same.

No doubt, great evils accompany war and great sorrow the loss of life, and yet if we begin our reflections here, with these evils and losses and with a presumption against their causes, then we are likely to conclude that arms can be taken up only as we locate some good or collection of goods that in our minds or by God's command justifies that resort. In the absence of that good or that collection, we will have no reason to fight. When present, we will have no reason to retreat. In each instance, the relevant goods and evils at stake determine our conduct, not our concern for justice, not our commitment to the right.

Again, if we begin with the undeniable evil of death and with the presumption against killing, and if we kill only as some good justifies that evil and overcomes that presumption, then we will give little (if any) attention to the moral content of the means we employ as we kill. Our aim will be to avoid evil, which in this instance entails nothing more than keeping deaths to a minimum. Keeping the body count low will govern our choice of means. And of course, if that count can be kept low by resort to indiscriminate or disproportionate means, then what reason have we to forgo them? We might say that our commitment to the just and the right provides such a reason, and no doubt it would, but we have already decentered that commitment in a presumption against killing that gives priority to lives lost and saved, not to the just or unjust manner in which lives might be taken or protected.

15. George Weigel, "Moral Clarity in a Time of War," *First Things* (January 2003).

Suppose we take seriously these worries about the presumption against killing and war and reassert the centrality of justice in our reflections about these matters. And suppose we follow Werpehowski's lead and seek to rehabilitate Barth's efforts. In that event, we would most likely recast his account of killing in war along the lines of his account of killing and suicide. That latter account makes no presumption against killing in general, but rather distinguishes just and unjust killing and then prohibits injustice absolutely while leaving open the possibility of just self-slaughter at the command of God. By these lights, there would be no presumption against killing in war. Rather, there would be an absolute prohibition against unjust killing and a faithful recognition that a God who loves justice might nevertheless command us to oppose tyrants and thugs with deadly violence. As in the case of just suicide, these killings would be not murderous but just and due.

This sounds right, this analogy between suicide and war and this accent on justice, but consider the obstacles Barth would have to overcome to adopt this scheme, obstacles that he himself puts in place. The best way to see this trouble is to note the *disanalogies* between these cases. If and when the command to kill comes to the potential suicide, it comes in the privacy of her own relationship with God. The image Barth provides is of a solitary individual in the wee hours of the soul's dark night, who hears God's command and then acts. No justification is offered other than the theologian's counterfactuals: "Who can say that it is absolutely impossible for the gracious God Himself to help a man in affliction by telling him to take this way out? . . . Who can really know whether God might not occasionally ask back from man in this form the life which belongs to Him? . . . Can we, therefore make a simple equation of self-destruction with self-murder?"[16]

Perhaps not. But now consider the difference that war makes. War is a public act. Suicide is too, of course, but we are tempted to think that it is not, and Barth's portrait encourages us to succumb. But war poses no such temptation. If waged in response to the real command of God, and if the killing that results is considered just, not murderous, then those who recommend its violence must be prepared to respond to requests for justification, presumably with reasons that refer both to the God who commands and to the justice of the acts commanded. They will have to say how the just character of these acts, these killings, com-

---

16. *CD* III/4, p. 410.

pares to the just character of other acts. Moral reasoning is done by analogy, and analogies will have to be made. I imagine Christians will find themselves saying something like the following: "This war must be fought because God has commanded it. These means may be employed because God has authorized them. The justice of the actions we propose can be seen, as in all just acts, in their object, intention, circumstances, and consequences." And of course, it is precisely this reply, this resort to analogy, that would give Barth pause. As any reader of Anscombe or Ramsey knows, talk of object and intention, circumstances and consequences, is just-war talk.[17] It refers to the criteria that the just war tradition has made explicit over the centuries, and it is precisely criteria of this kind that Barth resists. By his lights, these criteria threaten God's authority to distinguish the just and unjust by divine command. They exhibit our desire to stand free of that authority, to determine (or more modestly, to discover) the just and the unjust on our own, without first discerning God's command or conceding the sources of our agency in God's gracious will. As Barth sees it, these criteria are evidence, not of our moral seriousness or faithful obedience, but of our sin.

The dilemma, Barth's and ours, should now be obvious. More often than not, the public character of war making compels those who would commend its violence to offer reasons that might justify what they say and do, reasons that distinguish just from unjust objects, intentions, circumstances, and consequences. Reason giving of this kind tends to generate reflection on norms and cases, and it is reflection of precisely this kind that Barth hopes to avoid. If we hope to resolve the various inconsistencies that confound Barth's reflections on war, then it would seem that we have reached a point where his commitments forestall our efforts. He can't accept what we recommend without forsaking those commitments, and we can't accept those commitments without noting the inconsistencies they generate.

I close with an uncontroversial diagnosis and a recommendation for a different mode of rehabilitation. The inconsistencies that we find in Barth's account of killing and war follow in large measure from his resistance to absolute prohibitions and his contempt for flat-footed ca-

---

17. Elizabeth Anscombe, "War and Murder," in *Ethics, Religion, and Politics,* Collected Philosophical Papers, vol. III (Minneapolis: University of Minnesota Press, 1981), pp. 51-61; Paul Ramsey, *The Just War: Force and Political Responsibility* (New York: Scribner, 1968).

suistry, and each of these follows in large measure from his account of moral norms. Norms, he assumes, are templates of human action that govern and prescribe with independent authority. They are prior to history and agency, and we appeal to their prescriptions in order to shape and control each. In this mode, moral reasoning is largely a matter of applying a template, of determining the course of action prescribed in this or that circumstance by this or that norm. As the template, not the Word of God, is the authority that matters, and as poor sinners must determine its proper application, Barth can't help but conclude that when a moralist speaks of norms we should hear a sinner's desire for self-sovereignty. If this is what moral reasoning involves and if this is how we regard moral norms, then Barth is surely right to complain. And if Barth is right to complain, then the inconsistencies in his account of killing and war that accompany this complaint are unavoidable. We will simply have to tolerate them.

But what if this account of moral norms is misleading? What if it fails to depict the way we actually reason about moral matters? What if norms are less like transcendent templates and more like principles already embedded in practices? In that event, moral reflection will begin with those practices, and the norms that reflection yields will abridge what we already do. They will describe the judgments implicit in those doings and suggest ways that similar practices might be revised. If we begin with the assumption that God commands and that by grace the just obey, then moral reflection would be designed to make explicit those norms already embedded in obedient practice, already found in the lives of those who hear the Word of God and who bear witness to the justice it commands. If we were to proceed in this way, we would put aside Barth's Kantian-driven fears and follow his Hegelian-inspired instincts. We would take note of his treatment of just cause, where he plainly begins with examples and cases — of unjust aggression and legitimate political sovereignty — and then works to express the principles embodied in an obedient response to injustice. Following his lead, we would extend this practice and reflect on the means employed in war. We would consider examples of obedient witness to the God who at times commands war and yet always prohibits murder. We would distill the norms implicit in that witness and thus provide the *jus in bello* constraints that Barth does not. We would, in other words, continue in a slightly different vein the rehabilitation of Barth's reflections on war that Bill Werpehowski has already begun.

6. Barth and Democracy: Political Witness without Ideology

David Haddorff

Although Barth never finished *Church Dogmatics* IV/4, including, most likely, a long excursus on the state and politics, we know more about his political thought than any other area of his practical ethics. Not only did he write and speak more about political matters, but he also participated, intensely at times, in the political process. Whether as the student leader in the Swiss Zofinger Union, the activist "Red pastor" of Safenwil, a leader in the Confessing Church, an outspoken supporter of the war against Hitler's Germany and critic of Swiss neutrality, an advocate for peacemaking between East and West during the emerging Cold War, or a supporter for nuclear disarmament in the late 1950s, Barth remained politically active throughout his life. Even if one dislikes his theology, one cannot but appreciate his courage, defiance, and conviction in his political decisions and actions. As a Swiss Reformed Social Democrat, he was an apologist for neither capitalism nor communism, political liberalism nor communitarianism, nor for a purely "Christian" or purely secular state. Still, for all his dialectical maneuvering, he does boldly say in 1946 "that the Christian line" following from the gospel moves in the direction of the "democratic state."[1] Indeed, a decade later he says: "Democracy is not in the middle between anarchy and tyranny, but is *above* both, above this dichotomy."[2] Both

---

1. Karl Barth, "The Christian Community and the Civil Community," in *Community, State, and Church: Three Essays*, with a new introduction by David Haddorff (Eugene, Oreg.: Wipf and Stock, 2004), p. 181.

2. *Karl Barth's Table Talk*, ed. and trans. John Godsey (Richmond: John Knox, 1963), p. 81.

anarchy and tyranny are shaped by the power of *potentia,* or "naked power" that "masters and bends and breaks the law," whereas democracy, as a just state, attempts to rise above this struggle for power through *potestas,* or the "power that serves the law."[3] Barth prefers democracy because it limits power, protects individuals and communities, and encourages responsible participation by standing under a constitutional rule of law.[4]

This essay examines Barth's political thought with the intention of both describing its development and relating it to current trends in Christian political ethics. In brief, it uses two methodological tasks in order to make two basic arguments. First, in the *descriptive* mode, this essay constructs a framework for how Barth might have addressed the topic of democracy in his unfinished ethics of reconciliation. From his diverse political and theological writings, we get several narratives from which he could have drawn in finishing *CD* IV/4. Second, in the *comparative* and *evaluative* modes, it relates Barth's thought to contemporary trends within political ethics. My argument is simply that Barth's thought still matters, especially in today's often polarizing context. Barth teaches us to think theologically about politics and democracy in a way that challenges everything we think we *know* about politics. In short, he teaches us that Christian political ethics, as a form of Christian *witness,* seeks to be free of ideology.[5]

Barth's thought stands as an alternative to what Daniel Bell, Jr., calls the two main streams of Christian political thought today, namely, the "dominant" and "emergent" traditions.[6] The dominant

---

3. Barth, "The Christian Community," p. 177.

4. As I am using the word, "democracy" refers to both the governmental *process* and procedures, such as universal suffrage, which offer individual citizens and social groups the opportunity to participate in the governance of the civil community, and the *form* of government, enforced by the rule of law, that gives individuals and communities their rights, while providing safeguards against the abuse of these rights through emerging arbitrary power and authority of individuals or factions within the civil community. For a helpful discussion of democracy and Christianity, see John W. DeGruchy, *Christianity and Democracy: A Theology for a Just World Order* (Cambridge: Cambridge University Press, 1995).

5. Similarly, Frank Jehle writes: "Barth aims for politics that is free of ideology." Frank Jehle, *Ever Against the Stream: The Politics of Karl Barth, 1906-1968,* trans. Richard and Martha Burnett (Grand Rapids: Eerdmans, 2002), p. 42.

6. Daniel Bell, Jr., "State and Civil Society," in *The Blackwell Companion to Political Theology,* ed. Peter Scott and William T. Cavanaugh (Oxford: Blackwell, 2004), pp. 423-38.

tradition includes various types of political theology, liberation and feminist theology, and public theology. This diverse group shares the basic conviction that the state and civil society are the "principal agents of social and political change," while the church's political role is limited to the "guardian of abstract values."[7] Furthermore, civil society fosters a kind of redemptive space of "democratic freedom," limiting the state's power while imparting a positive vision for the future. In contrast stands the emergent tradition of John Howard Yoder, Stanley Hauerwas, Oliver O'Donovan, and John Milbank. This group, says Bell, rejects the "modern nation-state's claim to the right to organize human community in its own image," and instead "finds the political correlate of the Christian *mythos*, not in the secular state and civil society, but in the church."[8] Radically different, this group sees civil society as a kind of hegemonic, disciplinary space where individuals are shaped by social, cultural, or technological ends of society. Bell's categories are too neat to include someone as dialectical as Barth. Like the dominant view, Barth supports Christian responsibility for statecraft and civil society, but like the emergent view, he affirms a political church, so when the church ceases being political, it ceases being a witness.

Another framework to consider is Barth's own typology, first developed in his 1928-29 *Ethics* lectures, and later in *CD* II/2. Here he distinguishes his theological ethics from three other approaches: (1) one extreme is the "synthesis" or "apologetic" type, which assimilates Christian ethics into a generalist or common language like philosophy; (2) the other extreme is the "diastasis" or "isolationist" approach, which *contrasts* Christian ethics to generalist ethics, thus limiting Christian normative claims to the confines of the church; and (3) a third approach is the mediating theory of Thomistic moral theology, which allows the particularity of the theological to build upon the generality of natural law.[9] Although Barth appears to prefer the last, mediating theory over the other two extremes, they all err by beginning with ethical method *itself* — that is, they begin by placing together in conversation theology and philosophy, or particular and general truth claims. Instead, Barth begins with God's triune agency and then seeks to develop

---

7. Bell, "State and Civil Society," p. 429.
8. Bell, "State and Civil Society," p. 435.
9. For these discussions, see Karl Barth, *Ethics*, trans. Geoffrey W. Bromiley (New York: Seabury Press, 1981), pp. 19-33, and *CD* II/2, pp. 519-35.

a command ethics that is resilient of methodology and dialectical in movement.[10] His approach stresses neither identification (synthesis), difference (diastasis), nor mediation (natural law), but rather a dialectical movement toward distinctiveness *within* relatedness and participation *without* assimilation.

The framework for this essay surfaces from a conversation, in the mid-1950s, between Barth and an unnamed English-speaking student, as described in *Karl Barth's Table Talk*. In no doubt a rather humorous moment, a student posed the question to Barth: "If Thomas Jefferson had read the *Church Dogmatics* and *Church and State* before he wrote the Declaration of Independence, how do you think he would have opened this text?" Barth responds to the question, first admitting its difficulty, but then proceeds to revise Jefferson's famous preamble. Barth says: *"We hold these truths to be evident, . . . that all men are created . . . in togetherness and mutual responsibility . . . and that they are endowed by their Creator with freedom of life within the bounds of a rightfully established common order."*[11] In this concise and thoughtful statement, Barth concentrates on the three important factors that belong to any theological discussion of democracy, namely, considerations about truth, ontology, and responsibility. Taking these into consideration, the three parts of the essay are entitled (1) "Truth and Democracy," (2) "Being and Democracy," and (3) "Ethics and Democracy." Within this threefold structure I generally follow a chronological movement within Barth's thought. So, the first part concentrates on his political writings of the 1930s-1940s, with some reference to *CD* II/2; the second part is on the doctrine of creation in *CD* III; and the third part is on the doctrine of reconciliation in *CD* IV.

Truth and Democracy

In replacing Jefferson's term "self-evident" with "evident," Barth comments that moral truths are "evident" only from the "will of God" and not "natural theology."[12] Barth's defiant "No" against natural theology

10. Nevertheless, we see some interesting parallels with Bell's groupings. The method of the dominant group often relies on "synthetic" or natural law theories, which draw heavily from the social sciences and philosophy. The second contrastive method used by the emergent group tends toward the "diastasis" or isolationist model.

11. *Karl Barth's Table Talk*, p. 77.

12. *Karl Barth's Table Talk*, p. 77.

David Haddorff

has caused many critics to say he denies moral realism *itself,* that is, a common understanding of moral truth learned through the shared experience of human reflection and discourse. One recent example of this criticism is Peter McEnhill, who says Barth's "narrow" "Christomonism" forces him "to separate his whole theology from the reality of human experience" and the possibility of creation-based political ethic.[13] McEnhill uses Barth to criticize John Milbank, but then turns around and argues that Barth is not really useful for Reformed political thought. What Barth's critics often overlook is that in rejecting natural theology, Barth never rejects a general ethics, but only seeks to *distinguish* this from theological ethics. Moral realism is not denied; it finds its ground in the theological realism of God's divine agency and revelation. In other words, moral truths, including democratic ones, begin with God's Word and not with our own reflection as self-determinative autonomous moral agents.

Barth's early writings are largely deconstructive of the synthesis of theology and politics championed by liberal theology. In 1916, he writes that political ethics remains "only *parabolic*" of its "heavenly analogue" because it cannot be *strictly identified with God's action in history.*[14] Yet this negative diastasis, however strong, is usually answered by the "Yes" of responsible service and witness toward God and our neighbor. Thus, in 1925, he contends that Christians are obligated to act responsibly in the "tasks of industry, science, art, politics and even religion."[15] Seeking to move beyond this No/Yes dialectical pattern, Barth's first significant discussion of the state is found in his *Ethics* lectures, where he places it within his ethics of reconciliation. This move is significant in itself, as it departs from the more creation-based "two kingdoms," "orders of creation," and natural law approaches. God's reconciliation in Christ makes it possible for mutual service and fellowship to exist in "the double order of church and state."[16] In *Ethics,* Barth describes the just state as constitutional and democratic, as the "power of the state

13. Peter McEnhill, "'The State We're In': A Reformed Response to Some Aspects of John Milbank's Theory of Church and State," in *Reformed Theology: Identity and Ecumenicity,* ed. Wallace M. Alston, Jr., and Michael Welker (Grand Rapids: Eerdmans, 2003), p. 135.

14. Cf. Karl Barth, *The Word of God and the Word of Man,* trans. Douglas Horton (New York: Harper and Row, 1957), p. 320.

15. Barth, *The Word of God,* p. 173.

16. Barth, *Ethics,* p. 441.

comes from the people," and its public task, "the upbuilding of society," takes place under the constitutional rule of law.[17] Although these lectures are more constructive than his earlier writings, what is missing in them is a definitive analysis of how church and state are actually *related* under reconciliation, and how the church's witness impacts the state's identity, structure, and concrete tasks.

This would change in the 1930s, when Barth is forced to become a leading theological voice of the Confessing Church and its struggle against the German Christians and Nazism. As the principal author of the 1934 Barmen Declaration, Barth calls the church to listen only to the Word of God, which claims authority over all ecclesial and political life. Moving beyond *Ethics,* Barth claims that the church *reminds* the state that it is a responsible agent of peace and justice in the world. The state, in turn, gives the church its *freedom* to witness to God's kingdom. Thus, the agencies of church and state are distinguished and *related,* so that both are seen as *witnesses* to Christ's Lordship. This allows the church to evaluate the state, not just through civil law, but in light of the gospel. Barmen's critics saw latent "anarchist" themes that undermined the authority of social institutions, grounded in God's ordered creation. Nevertheless, Barth is not an anarchist but a democratic constitutionalist who realized that the traditional law-gospel pattern of Protestant theology could not challenge the tyrannical ideology of the German Christians who identified the divine law with the human *laws* of German society.[18]

Hence a year later, in his essay "Gospel and Law," Barth further challenges the two kingdoms theology of the German Christians by insisting that the gospel comes *before* the law, and that the law is the "form" of the gospel whose "content" is grace. He states succinctly: "From what God does *for* us, we infer what he wants *with* us and *from* us."[19] In reversing the law-gospel relation, both church and state fall

---

17. Barth, *Ethics,* pp. 448-49.

18. For a longer discussion of the Barmen Declaration and how it relates to Barth's political thought as a whole, see my monograph, David Haddorff, "Karl Barth's Theological Politics," in Barth, *Community, State, and Church,* pp. 1-69.

19. Karl Barth, "Gospel and Law," in *Community, State, and Church,* p. 78. In his most developed discussion in *CD* II/2, Barth succinctly states: "The one Word of God is both Gospel *and* Law" (*CD* II/2, pp. 511ff.). He further writes: "As the doctrine of God's command, ethics interprets the Law as the form of the Gospel, i.e., as the sanctification which comes to man through the electing God" (*CD* II/2, p. 509).

under the gospel, which provides a stronger argument against the ideologies of nation, race, and people. Barth demonstrates that when the law is *separated* from its gracious content, both its form and content are invariably shaped, not by the gospel, but by some ideology.

The theology behind the law/gospel distinction has wide-ranging implications for political ethics. The gospel as judgment unmasks our "self-evident" moral truths as false ideologies or illusions. In the 1941 public letter to British church leaders, Barth chastises them for relying too heavily upon natural law in their political moral judgments. "All arguments based on Natural Law are Janus-headed. They do not lead to the light of clear decisions, but to the misty twilight in which all cats become grey. They lead to — Munich."[20] Barth often cites the failure of the "Munich Agreement" as evidence of the pernicious effect of natural law reasoning in political decisions. By failing to "honour democracy" and defend the norms "of justice, of freedom, and of responsibility," Western democracies provided an opening for the triumph of the Nazi regime to emerge and flourish.[21] According to Barth, natural law reasoning by itself cannot distinguish "between a legitimate state and robber state, between democracy and absolute dictatorship."[22] The lurid example of the German Christians *reminds* the church that its political reflection and action begin with the gospel, not natural law.

What bearing, then, does the gospel have on democracy? In his 1938 essay "Church and State," Barth claims that the doctrine of justification provides a more coherent relation between church *and* state. Here the church's primary role is one of *intercessor* and witness; that is, in being the church, it "expects the best" from the state, demonstrating that it belongs "originally and ultimately to Jesus Christ."[23] On this christological basis, the "democratic conception of the State," says Barth, is a "justifiable expansion of the thought of the New Testament."[24] So, the argument for democracy emerges from the "evident" truths of the gospel of reconciliation, and not natural law or creation.

20. Karl Barth, *A Letter to Great Britain from Switzerland* (London: Sheldon Press, 1941), p. 17.
21. Karl Barth, *The Church and the Political Problem of Our Day* (New York: Scribner, 1939), p. 70.
22. Karl Barth, "The Churches of Europe in the Face of War," in *The Church and the War* (New York: Macmillan, 1944), p. 5.
23. Karl Barth, "Church and State," in *Community, State, and Church*, pp. 140, 118.
24. Barth, "Church and State," p. 145.

It is divine justification that establishes a "true order" that as a "concrete law of freedom" enables the state to embody a "true order of human affairs — the justice, wisdom and peace, equity and care for human welfare."[25] Barth would explore these themes further in his most important political essay, the 1946 document "The Christian Community and the Civil Community." Here he presents the thesis that the "real church" is the model and prototype of the "real state."[26] Indeed, this is why "the existence of the State [is] an allegory, an analogue to the Kingdom of God which the church preaches and believes in."[27] The inner circle of the Christian community, in witness and reminder, reveals to the outer circle of the civil community that it too is centered in Jesus Christ, granting to the civil community its identity, structure, and vision of its place within God's kingdom.

Furthermore, this essay culminates with a list of twelve analogies between the church and the civil community.[28] Drawing from a list of Christian doctrines, beliefs, and practices, Barth uses these analogies to both defend and reject certain aspects of political society. For example, the church supports the civil community when it serves its citizens, with particular emphasis on assisting the poor, but criticizes it when it serves various ideological causes. Likewise the church supports constitutional democracies of impartial justice, including the separation of governmental powers, but rejects totalitarian and authoritarian governments. Again, the church supports the equality and freedom of all citizens but rejects the extremes of individualism and collectivism. Again, it supports cultural plurality and religious diversity, freedom of speech and the press, but rejects political deception, secrecy, and coercion. Taken together, these analogies justify the promotion of civil laws protecting social and economic justice, basic human rights, self-determination, political equality, equal protection, and the freedom to engage in the public life of civil society. Drawing parabolic analogies between the two communities gives the civil community a path to follow in being an indirect *witness* to God's kingdom. It seeks not only to preserve order and security, but to rid the community of disorder, violence, and injustice through balancing the power of individual rights

25. Barth, "Church and State," pp. 147-48.
26. Barth, "The Christian Community," p. 186.
27. Barth, "The Christian Community," p. 169.
28. Barth, "The Christian Community," pp. 171-79.

with communal responsibilities. Still, we recall, it is the church's witness, both visibly and conceptually, that provides secular polity with another way of conceiving power, authority, responsibility, participation, and plurality.

Barth's theology of the political church places him in close proximity to the ecclesial politics of the emergent group. Still, the general movement of ecclesial politics is toward the *separation* of the two communities, whereas for Barth the movement is toward the *relation* of the two communities under Christ's rule. Ecclesial politics, for example, says that God uses the state to preserve order, but only so the church can carry out its mission; the state has no direct access to the kingdom of God except through the church. As John Howard Yoder puts it, "The meaning of history — and therefore the significance of the state — lies in the creation and work of the church."[29] The *esse* of the state as "fallen power" is contrasted to the *esse* of the church, as redeemed polis.

By contrast, Barth argues that God's agency prioritizes Jesus Christ over both church and state in salvation history. The civil community, even in its secularity, does not fall outside the parameters of God's reconciliation. It is true that the civil community is ignorant of its true calling, but even in its flawed judgment and apparent disregard for the gospel, it can still give *indirect* witness to God's kingdom in its role as a just state. Despite Barth's reluctance to affirm a "Christian" form of politics, he writes, the "essence of Christian politics" is a "constant direction, a continuous line of discoveries on both sides of the boundary which separates the political from the spiritual spheres, a correlation between explications and applications."[30] Where the "boundary" is, there is overlap and mutual sharing. The church can learn from the world how to be the church because the freedom of the Word of God can speak to the church through secular parables of the kingdom. These parables, says Barth, can "illumine, accentuate or explain the biblical witness in a particular time and situation."[31]

It is this general openness to outsiders, coupled with an intense commitment for social and political responsibility, that leads Jeffrey Stout in his book *Democracy and Tradition* to see Barth, and his inter-

29. John Howard Yoder, *The Christian Witness to the State* (Newton, Kans.: Faith and Life Press, 1964), p. 13.

30. Barth, "The Christian Community," p. 180.

31. *CD* IV/3.1, p. 115.

preter George Hunsinger, as an alternative to the "new traditionalists" Milbank and Hauerwas.[32] In this book, Stout develops a pragmatist public philosophy that seeks to be inclusive of all the voices of democracy, including the intensely theological. Stout believes that Barth's ethics provides a theologically orthodox, politically engaging, and open-ended model for Christian political thought and action. Stout's point here is generally correct, as Barth says the "truth itself demands complete openness. From the standpoint of the truth itself thoroughgoing conservatives are as useless as thoroughgoing modernists."[33] Yet it must be added that this "complete openness" does not imply indecision, ambiguity, or relativism. Instead of looking for normative principles to guide our actions, Barth suggests we seek what is "intrinsically valuable." Barth writes: "And what is intrinsically valuable truth is the command of God which always surpasses what we consider worthy either to be retained or to come, which always transcends our hypotheses and convictions of yesterday, to-day and to-morrow."[34] Hearing and responding to God's moral command is a journey of discovery in which we learn what is "intrinsically valuable." This remains an ongoing task of judgment, discernment, and action. What matters for democracy is more than a common ethical language, or a common set of moral practices; it is a common commitment to be mutually responsible in freedom under the rule of law. This law is "evident" or made visible by the gospel, which establishes the freedom, responsibility, and openness necessary to be witnesses to God's kingdom.

Being and Democracy

Radical Orthodoxy has rightly shifted the conversation about moral epistemology into the underlying issue of ontology. The ethical strategy of much contemporary social science and philosophy is to overcome the anomie of the isolated postmodern self by seeking to find ways of relatedness within difference through ethical action. Yet, as John Milbank and others have reminded us, ethical action, however

---

32. Jeffrey Stout, *Democracy and Tradition* (Princeton: Princeton University Press, 2004).

33. *CD* II/2, p. 648.

34. *CD* II/2, p. 648.

conceived, cannot address the more fundamental problem of modern ontology, and with it, the inevitability of postmodern nihilism. Unlike a Trinitarian participatory ontology that affirms that we are created for communion, the secular self is flattened, materialistic, monistic, and self-absorbed. Secular thought hopes for a revived democratic socialism, but it can never achieve this, because it cannot overcome the metanarrative of ontological separateness that leads to personal isolation, exclusion, and violence. Rather, only with theology, with its ontology of participation, is a true account of politics possible.[35]

In Barth's revision of Jefferson's preamble, we also see a challenge to modern secular accounts of the human self. We recall that Barth replaces the word "equality" with the words "togetherness" and "mutual responsibility." He writes: *"We hold these truths to be evident . . . that all men are created . . . in togetherness and mutual responsibility."*[36] Barth omits the word "equal" because, he says, it remains too abstract and "formal," thus too detached from the actual structure of human relationships. Being "created equal" is possible only because we are created in "mutual togetherness and responsibility," which presupposes covenant relations. This is why, in his 1946 essay, he uses the analogy of Christian equality, established in baptism, as the basis for the political doctrine of "equality, freedom and responsibility of all adult citizens."[37] True equality presupposes God's prior action of grace, which further leads to the practice of ecclesial inclusiveness, and this by analogy relates to supporting the ethnic, racial, sexual, or religious differences within civil society. Moreover, since the church's inclusiveness is "catholic," the civil community must be willing to resist all "abstract, local, regional and national interests" that infringe upon the unity within difference of the wider world. Both communities must resist the parochialism of the "immediate city boundaries," and instead seek to practice "understanding and cooperation within the wider circle."[38] Still, Barth is not a strict internationalist, nor a localist or nationalist for that matter. He believes that the unity within the church, as local and universal, can model a particular kind of wide-ranging cooperation from the lo-

---

35. See John Milbank, "Materialism and Transcendence," in *Theology and the Political: The New Debate,* ed. Creston Davis, John Milbank, and Slovoj Žižek (Durham, N.C.: Duke University Press, 2005), pp. 394-426.

36. *Karl Barth's Table Talk,* p. 77.

37. Barth, "The Christian Community," p. 175.

38. Barth, "The Christian Community," p. 178.

cal to the international levels in civil society, which challenges all of these territorial authorities to reject hegemonic rule.

Most Christian ethicists in the dominant tradition would not dramatically disagree with Barth's practical ethics but only with the *methodological* basis in which these analogies are grounded. As stated earlier, these critics often fault Barth for not having a general ethics based on naturalistic sources or a creation-based ethics. William Schweiker, for example, applauds Barth's ethics of responsibility but criticizes him for not providing a realistic account of the goodness of finite existence or what Schweiker calls the "integrity of life."[39] In pluralistic societies Christians must be able to talk about the good of creation *by itself* without appeal to christological or ecclesiological premises. Schweiker understands theological ethics, then, as a "kind of hermeneutical phenomenology," a "way of analyzing and articulating the lived structure of reality in order to provide orientation and guidance for life."[40] By concentrating so heavily on the particularity of God's command, Barth neglects the very *human* process and power of hermeneutical moral reasoning, personal moral agency, and moral action. In Schweiker's synthetic approach, the "integrity of life" provides an account of community and moral and political responsibility, which is essential for the future of democratic society.

Like Schweiker, Barth prioritizes human dignity in his political thought, but would add that such a belief cannot be sustained by simply affirming the "integrity of life." Barth, too, strongly affirms the integrity of life in his ethics of creation, but adds that such a claim cannot be separated from, or ignore, God's action as reconciler and redeemer. Life itself, says Barth, can never be our "ethical lord, teacher and master."[41] Indeed, he further warns: "In theological ethics the concept of life cannot be given this tyrannical, totalitarian function."[42] Rather, in various places, but especially in *CD* III/2, Barth redefines human nature as dynamically interrelated with God and others in being and act.

> Man generally, the man with the fellow-man, has indeed a part in the divine likeness of the man Jesus, the man for the fellow-man. As

39. William Schweiker, *Theological Ethics and Global Dynamics: In the Time of Many Worlds* (Oxford: Blackwell, 2004), p. xix.

40. Schweiker, *Theological Ethics,* p. xxi.

41. *CD* III/4, p. 326.

42. *CD* III/4, p. 326.

man generally is modelled on the man Jesus and His being for others, and as the man Jesus is modelled on God, it has to be said of man generally that he is created in the image of God. . . . It is inevitable that we should recall the triune being of God at this point. God exists in relationship and fellowship. As the Father of the Son and the Son of the Father He is Himself I and Thou, confronting Himself and yet always one and the same in the Holy Ghost. God created man in His own image, in correspondence with His own being and essence. He created Him in the image which emerges even in His work as the Creator and Lord of the covenant.[43]

Barth's *actualism* and *relationalism* (or personalism) say that being and action cannot be understood apart from the history of Jesus Christ. He reveals the personal being and gracious action of God as Trinity, and humanity as covenant-partner with God. Human dignity is visibly manifested in the real man, or "true human," discovered in the incarnation where God chooses to be "with" us and "for" us in Jesus Christ. Just as God is essentially a relational being or being-in-relation, so too is humanity seen as being-in-relation with others. Between the human and divine, therefore, is what Barth calls an *analogia relationis,* or analogy of relations. Just as God is relational, so too is humanity relational; there is not just being, but being-in-encounter. Yet, this analogy is possible only because God has bound himself to our humanity in Christ, making every person a fellow-person of Jesus Christ, and full-fledged covenant-partner with God. Barth writes: "The ontological determination of humanity is grounded in the fact that one man among all others is the man Jesus. So long as we select any other starting point for our study, we shall reach only the phenomena of the human."[44] Only in our being in Christ, as our representative head, is it possible to be in relation with other persons. Without Christ, we are only left with the isolated monads of God and humanity, a deistic God, and a Nietzschean humanity, or as said earlier, ontological separateness. In Christ, humanity can "realize the togetherness of man grounded in human freedom" in which persons are neither slaves nor tyrants but friends and companions.[45]

This "being-in-encounter," this "I-Thou" relation, has important implications for political participation. In *CD* III/2 Barth writes: "If I

43. *CD* III/2, pp. 323-24.
44. *CD* III/2, p. 132.
45. *CD* III/2, p. 271.

and Thou really see each other and speak with one another and listen to one another, inevitably they mutually summon each other to action."[46] First, being able to truly see the other face-to-face implies being open to the needs, desires, and hopes of the other, or participating in the life of the other. Truly being in fellowship and "mutual openness" rejects the impersonal relations so often found in bureaucratic structures and relations that serve causes and ideologies rather than human dignity.[47] Second, this "mutual openness," this I-thou relation, allows us to truly hear and speak with others, further participating in their good. Conversation that is not mutually beneficial serves other personal or ideological interests that prohibit the civil community from living out its mission for freedom, justice, and peace. Third, our mutual seeing and conversing also lead to mutual assistance that makes full participation in justice possible. Where there is no mutual assistance, there is movement away from social justice and toward ideologies based on interests of the self, group, or nation. Regarding this, in the 1946 essay he says the church "will always choose the movement from which it can expect the greatest measure of social justice."[48] In participation we learn more fully what it means to be human and to act in mutual togetherness and responsibility.

Now that we've looked at togetherness and participation, we must consider further Barth's view of responsibility. In *The Christian Life,* Barth discusses how Christian moral responsibility exists in three spheres or "circles" of Christian existence, namely, the personal, the ecclesial, and the worldly (social). First, responsibility occurs in *relation* to the other. Ethical action, says Barth, implies "being in the openness of the one to the other with a view to and on behalf of the other."[49] An ethic *for* others means loving and serving others, but also giving others freedom to be responsible to their own conscience.[50] Second, responsi-

---

46. *CD* III/2, pp. 260-61.

47. Barth writes: "Bureaucracy is the form in which man participates with his fellows when this first step into mutual openness is not taken," namely, because of the intention of serving a cause, structure, or program rather than the true needs of the other (*CD* III/2, p. 252).

48. Barth, "The Christian Community," p. 173.

49. *CD* III/2, p. 250.

50. In *Ethics,* Barth writes: "Violation of freedom of conscience, no matter how well intended, always means that the others upon whom I force myself with the claim of my conscience no longer hear their own" (p. 494).

bility occurs in *relation* to the Christian community. A Christian ethic that does not include responsibility to the church cannot be *Christian,* or as Barth puts it, the Christian "stands or falls with the cause of the church."[51] We've seen how this ecclesiological dimension serves as a visible dividing line between dominant and emergent traditions. Much Christian social ethics concentrates on the individual's relation to society (or the world), while avoiding the church altogether. This is a problem, as neglecting the church means neglecting the gospel witness and thus opening the door to some other false or illusionary gospel of ideological power. The third and last sphere of the Christian life is the "world." The Christian does not *choose* to be in solidarity with the world, says Barth, but "is in solidarity with it from the very first."[52] "It is here in this outermost circle," Barth adds, that the Christian life "has its practical scope or has none at all."[53]

This threefold notion of responsibility places Barth in tension with both the dominant and emergent groups. As we've seen, the dominant view undervalues Christology and ecclesiology, and with it, cuts itself off from the doctrine of justification and the church's witness. Although the emergent group is closer to Barth on these points, it also undervalues the secular world by overvaluing the church. Barth's acceptance of the truths of secular parables is generally a problem for ecclesial politics, especially in Radical Orthodoxy. Milbank criticizes Barth for having a "secular theology" that accepts the secularity and heretical nature of other disciplines without offering a real alternative.[54] In other words, Barth's theology is too narrowly defined by the method of dogmatics and exegesis. Instead, Milbank insists that theology should "claim to be a metadiscourse" and position itself as "the queen of the sciences for the inhabitants of the *altera civitas*."[55] Milbank, for example, deconstructs the ontology of secular post-Marxist thought with the hope that it will embrace a theological construct of participatory ontology of peace. That is, he develops a kind of negative apologetic that seeks to reveal the emptiness of the secular in

51. *CL,* p. 190.
52. *CL,* p. 194.
53. *CL,* p. 195.
54. See John Milbank, Catherine Pickstock, and Graham Ward, eds., *Radical Orthodoxy: A New Theology* (London and New York: Routledge, 1999), p. 33.
55. John Milbank, *Theology and Social Theory: Beyond Secular Reason* (Oxford: Basil Blackwell, 1990), p. 380.

order to then fill it with the theological, fulfilling the created aspirations lying behind the mask of secularism.

The political ethics of Radical Orthodoxy is right to point us in the direction of participatory ontology and ecclesial politics, but it does not provide a helpful language for being responsible "with" and "for" others in the secular world. In refusing to give the secular its freedom to be *other* than the church, it has no way of explaining how it is *related* to the church. Milbank's theology demands a Christian victory over the secular. In contrast, Barth would say the threat to the church is not the secular per se, but the ideology of secular*ism* — the reduction of all speech *to* the secular — particularly as it replaces or is placed "side by side" with the Word of God.[56] Yet, it is not so much the secularism "out there" as the secularism "in here" that is dangerous to the church and the world. The church must be free from ideology to give witness to the gospel. In doing so, it also gives freedom to the secular, or secularity of the *other,* and in so doing acknowledges the Spirit's freedom to speak through secular parables. Radical Orthodoxy has difficulty valuing the secularity of the world because it begins not with the freedom of the Word of God but with the "social reality" of the church as polis. For Barth, Christian responsibility cannot be limited to the sphere of the church; it is dialectically linked with spheres of personal and worldly existence that stand under the authority of the Word.

Ethics and Democracy

Christian political ethics includes not only concepts of truth and being, but also freedom and order. Again, recalling Jefferson's preamble, Barth replaces the phrase "inalienable rights of life, liberty, and the pursuit of happiness" with the phrase *"freedom of life within the bounds of a rightfully established common order."*[57] He then says: "I do not like the notion of individual rights. . . . The State must protect the *freedom* (not 'liberty' . . .) of man, which means also responsibility. Freedom and re-

56. This distinction is evident in Barth's comparison between two types of "secularism." The "absolute" form emphatically rejects God's Word, and the "relative" form proclaims belief in God while indirectly rejecting the freedom of God's Word. Regardless, both forms are not hegemonic, and in either case, Christ is able to raise up witnesses from both secular spheres (*CD* IV/3.1, p. 118).

57. *Karl Barth's Table Talk,* p. 77.

sponsibility are not opposed, but go together. Freedom of life cannot be described in terms of individual existence, but of *community*. . . . The State has to protect men who are constituted by togetherness and responsibility within these bonds."[58] All democratic societies struggle with the tension between individual rights and communal responsibilities. Yet the emphasis on social responsibility, Barth says, "was never made particularly clear in the classic proclamations of so-called 'human rights' in America and France."[59] Barth is not against individual rights per se, but seeks to place them within the covenant framework. Similar to his view of "equality," he seeks to place them within the "context of the realization that true human existence means existence together with one's fellow men."[60] So, the denial of togetherness and responsibility leads to a rejection of human freedom, amplified in the extremes of radical individualism and collectivism. First, the error of individualism denies the reality of the *social* self, and with it, the self's freedom to be *in relation* with the other. Second, the error of collectivism denies the individual self, and with it, the freedom to be *oneself* in relation to the other. This judgment is christologically grounded: the first error denies the common humanity in Jesus Christ as the one representative of all humanity, and the second error denies the one person of Jesus Christ. What is needed is balance, as neither individuals nor the group interests should have the last word. Rather, the civil community and the church stand for mutual responsibility of free persons within a "rightfully established common order."

Barth's constant return to the christological center continuously places him at odds with the "dominant" versions of political theology, which often begin with the structure of critical theory or social analysis. In discussing topics such as freedom or political order, much political theology begins with a structural analysis of the worldly powers or hegemonic structures, like militarism, tribalism, or globalization, and then seeks to find ways to limit their power through the matching power of *political* agency — through democratic politics. This means that if Christians are to make any difference in the world, they can do so only as political agents, seeking to "transform" the power of state-

58. *Karl Barth's Table Talk,* p. 77.
59. Barth, "The Christian Community," p. 174.
60. Karl Barth, *God Here and Now,* trans. Paul M. Van Buren (London and New York: Routledge, 2003), p. 8.

craft, by fostering subversive and resistant political agency in radical democratic politics. In short, human freedom becomes possible through political agency, which makes democratic politics possible and saves humanity from the hegemonic powers. Now this entire scheme can be developed without any discussion of God's agency or the relationship between human and divine agency, and without any conversation about Christian *witness* to God's action.[61] Human freedom cannot be liberated through democratic political agency by itself, as this would be an ideology of *democratism,* not democracy.

To reiterate, no person can be a "genuine free person" without being joined to Christ — the "real man" and source of human freedom. Reconciliation is an objective reality accomplished by God once through the covenant of grace, and we become aware of this knowledge through faith. What Christians do with this faith knowledge is important, as they learn not only what they are liberated *from* but also what they are liberated to *do.* Christian freedom becomes possible in discipleship and vocation, which liberates the person from solitude and isolation and brings the person into fellowship and community. It is eschatologically realist, in that it is *confident* yet *cautious* of its task in the world. Disciples are confident because Christ, not the democratic power of statecraft, has defeated the potentially hegemonic powers, and they are *cautious* about making absolute judgments or determining absolute courses of action as yes or no, risking further ideological reductionism. Hence, unlike political theologies that strategize how humanity will gain victory and freedom over the powers, Barth says all powers have only a "relative and limited" power because they have been defeated by Jesus Christ.[62] The powers are not intrinsically hegemonic, but act *as if* they are because humanity infuses them with hegemonic power. So, it is not the powers themselves but the *ignorance* of the powers that serves as the greatest potential threat to humanity's freedom.

What are these powers? In *The Christian Life,* Barth mentions sev-

---

61. Regarding globalization, for example, many writers draw from the social sciences for their discussion of hegemony and moral agency. So, as Cynthia Moe-Lobeda says, globalization "disables moral agency by disabling democracy," and Rebecca Todd Peters adds that a "democratized understanding of power ought to serve as the context for exercising moral agency." Cynthia Moe-Lobeda, *Healing a Broken World: Globalization and God* (Minneapolis: Augsburg/Fortress, 2002), p. 4; Rebecca Todd Peters, *In Search of the Good Life: The Ethics of Globalization* (New York: Continuum, 2004), p. 23.

62. *CL,* p. 216.

eral, but for our discussion two are particularly relevant, namely, ideology and Leviathan. First, "wherever we find 'ism' there lurks an ideology," says Barth, and with it, "man is more or less on the point of losing his freedom or has already lost it."[63] Whether ideologies are "macro" or "micro," whether they are grand metanarratives like liberalism or communism or the micro-ideologies of slogans and propaganda, they all promise freedom and solidarity through absolute loyalty in thought and practice. This is why the Christian political voice is free, he says, to "speak very conservatively today and very progressively or even revolutionarily tomorrow — or vice versa."[64] Christian political ethics stands as an *alternative* to all ideological positions. The second power is Leviathan, which raises the question of the "demonic" in politics. It consists in the idea of "empire," which in turn can be found in any "monarchical, aristocratic, democratic, nationalistic, or socialistic idea."[65] Leviathan's power, then, is not principally located in an evil tyrant or group of tyrants but in a totalitarian *system* or program in which the power of dissenting or alternative voices is eliminated, or where human freedom is suppressed. Even Western democracies, says Barth, are not "immune to the tendency to become at least a little Leviathan."[66] One important task of political ethics, therefore, is to give witness to their defeat in Christ by unmasking and resisting their power.

Political ethics, furthermore, as a form of witness, must seek to establish a *"rightfully established common order,"* which gives *indirect* witness to God's kingdom.[67] Returning to the 1946 essay, Barth maintains that just as "disciples of Christ, the members of his Church do not rule, they serve," so too, the civil community should reject any form of political ruling that does not serve the civil community's good.[68] In a just state, he says, power "serves the law," but in an unjust state power "masters and bends and breaks the law."[69] What is this just state? It is worth noting that the English term "just state" is a translation of either the

---

63. *CL*, p. 226.
64. Karl Barth, *Against the Stream: Shorter Post-war Writings, 1946-52*, ed. Ronald Gregor Smith, trans. E. M. Delacour and Stanley Godman (New York: Philosophical Library, 1954), p. 91.
65. *CL*, pp. 219-20.
66. *CL*, p. 221.
67. *Karl Barth's Table Talk*, p. 77.
68. Barth, "The Christian Community," p. 177.
69. Barth, "The Christian Community," p. 177.

German *rechten Staat* or *Rechtsstaat*. The first term, *rechten Staat,* is usually translated as "just state" or "righteous state" or "proper state." This is the term Barth commonly uses in his political writings when discussing the identity, structure, and purpose of the state. The second, more loaded word, *Rechtsstaat,* is used less often but interestingly is found frequently in the 1938 essay "Church and State" in relation to the gospel of divine justification. *Rechtsstaat* does not translate well into English. It can mean "rule of law" or "constitutional state," or more expansively, "constitutional state under the rule of law." It implies that the state's authority is grounded in law, not the power or will of the ruler, or even the will of the people. The law of the *Rechtsstaat* embodies justice and a commitment to the common good.[70] In theory, *Rechtsstaat* could apply to any state with a firm constitutional understanding of law, such as a constitutional monarchy or republic. Regardless of its particular form, Barth writes in the 1946 essay: "The church always stands for the constitutional State [*Rechtsstaat*], for the maximum validity and application of that twofold rule (no exemption from and full protection by the law), and therefore it will always be against any degeneration of the constitutional State [*Rechtsstaat*] into tyranny or anarchy."[71] Indeed, *Rechtsstaat* also serves as a vision or hope of what the civil community ought to be, a truly just state. According to Barth, "there never has been a perfect constitutional State [*Rechtsstaat*], and there never will be this side of Judgment Day."[72]

Political ethics, then, evaluates the direction in which *Rechtsstaat* points as it carries out its twofold obligation of "no exemption from

70. Yet, what makes a state a *Rechtsstaat?* German historians, with few exceptions, have described the regimes of the Second Reich (1871-1918), the Third Reich (1933-1945), and the German Democratic Republic (DDR, 1949-1990) as *Unrechtsstaat,* meaning that these states have violated basic human rights and freedoms of individuals, and have not based their laws on constitutionality, but have declared them by historical and circumstantial fiat. Barth, too, uses this word, *Unrechtsstaat,* when referring to the Nazi regime, but he also uses it to discuss any state that collapses into anarchy or tyranny, including the possibility of Western democracies. In the 1946 essay, he writes: "Conversely, no democracy as such is protected from failing in many or all of the points we have enumerated and degenerating not only into anarchy but also into tyranny and thereby becoming a bad State [*Unrechtsstaat*]" ("The Christian Community," p. 181). For a discussion about the historical legacy of *Rechtsstaat,* see Girish N. Bhat, "Recovering the Historical *Rechtsstaat,*" *Review of Central and East European Law* 32 (2007): 65-97.

71. Barth, "The Christian Community," p. 172.

72. Barth, *Against the Stream,* p. 96.

and full protection by the law."[73] The event of gospel proclamation in the church, for Barth, serves as an analogy for how the civil community *protects* the basic principles of free speech, free assembly, and freedom from search and seizure. Thus, gospel proclamation negatively critiques the state that seeks to *exempt* itself from this "rule of law," and challenges any restrictions on free speech, practice of government-sponsored clandestine operations, including covert actions, secret police, and secret diplomacy. Moreover, in a *Rechtsstaat,* power must be balanced. So in another analogy, Barth uses the example of the diversity of spiritual gifts within the church to argue for a separation of powers within government.[74] No one branch of government, or one group within society, can embody all powers of government. This is why the *Rechtsstaat,* or "constitutional state," has legislative, executive, and judicial powers, which make, judge, and enforce the rule of law.[75]

In reading Barth's 1946 essay, John Howard Yoder criticizes Barth for mixing "civic virtues" and "human rights" with actual church practices, which "weakened the case he could have made, and thereby dispensed some readers at the time from any effort to take it seriously in detail."[76] According to Yoder, Barth was aware of this problem and corrected himself in *CD* IV/2 by expanding on the "public" nature of church law.[77] Is there a discrepancy between these two accounts as Yoder claims? In Barth's discussion of the paradigmatic significance of church law in *CD* IV/2, we see some parallels with the 1946 essay.[78]

73. Barth, "The Christian Community," p. 172.

74. Barth, "The Christian Community," pp. 175-76.

75. Barth's affirmation of the separation of government powers is first developed in his *Ethics* lectures. Because these lectures were given in three cycles from 1928 to 1933, it is interesting to see how Barth made changes in his revisions. Indeed, the changing political situation in Germany from 1929 to 1933 forces him to change his understanding of how democracy is structured. For example, in 1929 he says leadership emerges as an "event which is the mutual venture of the leaders and the led," and that both leaders and citizens are "called by God's grace to do the work of the state," but in 1933 he adds the negative statement that the "leader may also be a usurper with great power of suggestion" and the forceful statement that the "state comes from the people." See Barth, *Ethics,* pp. 448-49.

76. John Howard Yoder, *Karl Barth and the Problem of War and Other Essays on Barth,* edited with a foreword by Mark Thiessen Nation (Eugene, Oreg.: Cascade Books, 2003), p. 184.

77. Yoder repeatedly makes this point in various essays. For these, see Yoder, *Karl Barth,* pp. 76-77, 115-18, 141-43, 172-73, and 183-84.

78. *CD* IV/2, pp. 723-24.

First, church law in its pure form simply *serves* the other as its end, which simplifies and transcends the complex, self-interested strategies of much secular law. Second, church law, in its witness to Christ, points beyond society to a divine law that rules and *judges* the world and all human law. Third, church law demonstrates how law can be based on mutual *trust,* not coercion. Fourth, church law demonstrates to the world that law should place *value* on the community's welfare, or as he puts it, the "total self-giving of each to all."[79] Fifth, the church demonstrates how mutual *fellowship* and human *equality* can be practiced within a community of free persons, while rejecting society's emphasis on achievement, materialism, and power. And sixth, the church demonstrates to society that the law is a free gift of God that remains *open-ended* and *dynamic.* It is not a "frozen or static pond, but must be a living stream continuously flowing from the worse to the better."[80]

Yoder is right to claim that Barth is more cautious here in drawing direct parallels with secular polity, but this does not prove that Barth has altered his earlier position. Indeed, later in this same section Barth immediately turns the argument around and places the church in a learning role. In its relationship to the world, he writes, it is possible that the "children of the world prove to be wiser than the children of light, so that in the question concerning its law the Church has reason to learn from the world . . . receiving from it the witness which it ought to give."[81] The point is not that Barth loosely attaches "civic virtues" with ecclesial doctrines or practices, as Yoder claims, but rather *how* the civil community and the church ought to be governed under law as the "form" of the gospel. Again, Barth does not assume that analogies always univocally go in the direction of the church to the world, but go back and forth, between the two communities, whose common center is Jesus Christ.

Here, again, Barth challenges the emergent group's preoccupation with ecclesial practices as the basis to shape character and behavior in the Christian polis. There is a diverse rendering of these practices in the emergent group, from Yoder's five practices in *Body Politics* to a more ecclesiastically formal sacramental and hierarchical ranking of

79. *CD* IV/2, p. 724.
80. *CD* IV/2, p. 724.
81. *CD* IV/2, p. 725.

the practices, as found in Radical Orthodoxy.[82] Most ecclesial politics follow this latter route and ground an alternative politics in a high-church doxological or liturgical expression, made concrete and consummated in the Eucharist.[83] This general trend dominates in *The Blackwell Companion to Christian Ethics,* edited by Stanley Hauerwas and Samuel Wells, which uses the church's liturgy as the way to "discern and embody Christ's life in the world."[84] The editors' basic argument here is: "Christianity is not principally something people think or feel or say — it is something people *do.*"[85] In short, worship practices become paradigmatic of all other moral acts.

It is Hauerwas's concentration on practice that leads him, in his Gifford Lectures, to criticize Barth's theology for not moving from the "truth" to the "practice" of Christian witness.[86] As I understand Hauerwas's criticism, Barth lacks a sufficient doctrine of the sanctified visible church as the body of Christ, which unites Christians with their Lord in their faithful witness through the sacraments and practices of the church. Yet, is this true? Like Hauerwas, Barth repeatedly claims that the purpose of the church in the world is to *be* the church, that is, to bear witness to the reality of Jesus Christ. Still, for Barth the church's witness consists primarily of *God's* action, to which persons correspond in responsible action, whereas for Hauerwas divine agency principally emerges through the *human* action of the Christian community. For Hauerwas, the truth of Christianity is made visible in Christian witness, which becomes embodied in specific actions that bear witness to the truth of the gospel and the Spirit's presence in the world. For his part, Barth draws a firmer distinction between Christianity's intelligibility, which rests in the objective revelation in God's

82. Yoder's five practices include: baptism, Eucharist, "binding and loosing," "freedom at the meeting," and the "universality of gifts." See John Howard Yoder, *Body Politics: Five Practices of the Christian Community before the Watching World* (Nashville: Discipleship Resources, 1992).

83. For Milbank and Catherine Pickstock, for example, the Eucharist conjoins the material with the "infinite depth" so completely that "God as the participated truth is fully present, without lack, in the material bread and wine which participate." John Milbank and Catherine Pickstock, *Truth in Aquinas* (London: Routledge, 2001), p. 81.

84. Stanley Hauerwas and Samuel Wells, eds., *The Blackwell Companion to Christian Ethics* (Oxford: Blackwell, 2004), p. 26.

85. Hauerwas and Wells, *Blackwell Companion to Christian Ethics,* p. 37.

86. Stanley Hauerwas, *With the Grain of the Universe* (Grand Rapids: Brazos, 2001), pp. 144ff.

Word, and the task of Christian witness, which remains the "declaration, exposition and address, or the proclamation, explication and application of the Gospel" as revealed in that Word.[87] For Barth divine agency cannot be strictly identified with ecclesial practices or human acts of Christian witness, which risks making God's action contingent upon human action. Otherwise, we might ask, once the church has the proper practices to perform, is it really necessary to continue to discuss God's action in the world? Such a view seems to limit divine agency and freedom, while also placing a heavy burden on the church in getting its practices right. The church is burdened to carry God's action of divine justification to the world.

Conclusion

Barth did not leave us a comprehensive theology of democracy, but he did leave a comprehensive theology from which to reflect about theological politics. We have seen how the political themes of togetherness, responsibility, freedom, and order all emerge from a theology governed by the Word of God and directed to the welfare of the individual and the civil community. More than just a political ethics telling us what we must do, Barth offers an open-ended political vision of Christian witness. In our political witness, we are driven upward and outward, that is, upward in our attentiveness to God's commanding presence and outward into the presence of others in the world. In so doing, we discover two possible errors of judgment. These are: (1) by stressing the *homogeneity* of world and church, persons inevitably endorse a kind of "Christian secularism," or "secular Christianity"; and (2) by stressing the church's *otherness* from the world, persons create a false separation between themselves and the world, leading to an exclusion from and resentment of the world.

So, on the one hand, the dominant tradition (or what Barth calls "apologetics") moves toward the error of *homogeneity,* while the emergent tradition (or what Barth calls "isolationist") approach of ecclesial politics is continually tempted by the error of *otherness.* The first view remains tempted by utopian, and sometimes ideological, visions of humanity, society, and the world. The second view shifts the primary

87. CD IV/3.2, p. 843.

agent in the world from civil society to the church. It is the church that saves us from the ravages of secularism and liberalism, by providing its inhabitants, through its ecclesial practices, a new mythos and polis. In both cases, what seems to be missing is priority of divine agency in Jesus Christ, which breaks down the tension between the two polarizing perspectives, namely, the freedom established in the political agency of statecraft and the freedom established in ecclesial practice. Again, for Barth there is only one polis, one kingdom of God, of which the church and civil community both bear witness.

In the last section of the *CD* IV/4 fragments, Barth says that Christian witness neither identifies its own human strategies with the kingdom of God nor over "against" it but "alongside" it, and in so doing, human "righteous action" will be "kingdom-like."[88] He further says: "They are absolved from wasting time and energy sighing over the impassable limits of their sphere of action and thus missing the opportunities that present themselves in this sphere. They may and can and should rise up and accept responsibility to the utmost of their power for the doing of the little righteousness."[89] Barth's modest claim for humanity to do a "little righteousness" — to do only what is "possible" — seems out of step with the often *heroic* claims of some political theology that envisions a transformed human moral agency, democratic politics, ecological restoration, or a more equitable economy. Yet Barth is not telling us to remain dormant, but to act decisively and responsibly here and now, but in so doing, we must first pray: "Thy kingdom come, Thy will be done, on earth as it is in heaven." In our praying, we must also be cautious of the temptation to be a *heroic* church. The church is no more "graced" than the state in its relation to the kingdom of God, as both are in a condition of sin and grace. Both stand under the promise of redemption. Ecclesial politics tells us that only by remaining a contrast or dissident community, a *counterpolis* within the larger world, can the church demonstrate to the world the truth of the gospel. Barth would generally concur: the Christian must continually "swim against the stream." He would, however, add that we are swimming in "mutual togetherness and responsibility" with the civil community for the "freedom of all persons," within a "common order under law." In this way, the church can remind the civil community what

88. *CL,* pp. 265, 266.
89. *CL,* pp. 265.

it means to be a true democracy, and the civil community in its democratic form can remind both church and world, by its indirect witness, what it means to be a community of free persons within God's covenant of grace.[90]

90. For a more comprehensive account of Barth's ethics of witness, see my *Christian Ethics as Witness: Barth's Ethics for a World at Risk* (Eugene, Oreg.: Cascade Press, 2010).

7. Karl Barth and the Varieties of Democracy: A Response to David Haddorff's "Barth and Democracy: Political Witness without Ideology"

Todd V. Cioffi

I

I want to thank David Haddorff for a fine essay on Barth's political ethics and treatment of democracy. The topic is not an easy one by any means, and Haddorff has done an admirable job. My comments therefore are mostly intended to enrich and clarify, and only at times to challenge, this construal of Barth's political theology and affinity for democracy.

As Haddorff notes well, Barth, in his 1938 essay "Church and State,"[1] claims that the basis of the state's identity and activity is the person and work of Jesus Christ — and especially God's reconciliation of the world, including the state, *in* Jesus Christ. Haddorff explains that for Barth the church enlightens the state as to its belonging "originally and ultimately to Jesus Christ," which more specifically means that the state is freed, under Christ's reconciliation, to be a community of peace and justice.[2] It is on this "basis" that democracy is the favored choice for state government, and thus is an expansion of New Testament thinking. And yet, it is not entirely clear, at least in Barth's 1938 essay, how Christ's reconciliation of the world and the state leads us to suppose that democracy is to be prized over other forms of govern-

---

1. See Karl Barth, "Church and State," in *Community, State, and Church: Three Essays,* with a new introduction by David Haddorff (Eugene, Oreg.: Wipf and Stock, 2004).

2. Haddorff, "Barth and Democracy: Political Witness without Ideology," p. 102 above. Hereafter, page numbers for Haddorff's essay are incorporated into the text.

ment. While Haddorff moves quickly from "Church and State" to the 1946 essay "The Christian Community and the Civil Community," I want to pursue this problem in the 1938 essay, and suggest that a key development in *CD* II/1-2 helps in setting up the latter essay, which is often seen as Barth's "mature" political theology, including his support of democracy. By turning to *CD* II/1-2 before examining "The Christian Community and the Civil Community," I think we will be led to a slightly different conclusion, or perhaps a slightly different emphasis, than Haddorff provides as to the character of Barth's support of democracy and the *particular kind* of democracy that is under consideration.

The thesis of the essay "Church and State" is, in Barth's words, to establish "a connection between justification of the sinner . . . and the problem of justice, the problem of human law."[3] However, while Barth provides an innovative claim that the fact of divine justification necessitates a connection to and a particular view of human justice, especially as practiced by the state, he does not adequately uncover the "material" connections and implications of divine justification for human justice. That is, Barth never makes fully explicit how the doctrine of justification supplies the content for human justice. Consequently, it is not sufficiently clear what the basis is for any form of government, let alone democracy. Rather than democracy having a substantial material connection to divine justification, it seems that democracy is to be preferred based on more practical reasons — democracy seems to provide the best social space for the church's preaching of divine justification.

Throughout "Church and State" Barth develops an appeal for democracy based on the *church's* relationship to the state (and not necessarily Christ's), and specifically the church's *need* of the state. Barth writes, "The behaviour towards the State which [the New Testament epistles] demand from all Christians is always connected with their behaviour towards *all* men."[4] Barth continues, "since it is our duty to pray for all men, so we should pray in particular for kings and for all authority, *because it is only on the condition that such men exist* that we can 'lead a quiet and peaceable life in all godliness and honesty.'"[5] The

---

3. Barth, "Church and State," p. 101.
4. Barth, "Church and State," p. 128, emphasis Barth's.
5. Barth, "Church and State," p. 128, emphasis added.

church needs the state because the church "needs freedom in the realm of all men in order to exercise its function towards all men."[6] In this sense, the state, says Barth, "will have to be the servant of divine justification."[7] Apparently, democracy best allows the Christian to participate in the shape and direction of political life — the state's authority, laws, care and maintenance of these laws, and peaceable negotiation of political struggle — and through such participation can help ensure that the state maintains the right sort of political and civil freedoms in order that the church can be the church. The church's interest in democracy, then, is more nearly practical than material in terms of the relationship between divine justification and human justice. Indeed, Barth writes at the end of the 1938 essay, "the guarantee of the State by the Church is finally accomplished when . . . all that can be said from the standpoint of divine justification on the question . . . of human law is summed up in this one statement: the Church *must have freedom to proclaim divine justification*."[8] With this in mind, I want to turn to CD II/1-2 and take note of a shift in Barth's thinking, one that begins to provide the material connections between divine justification and human justice, or for our purposes, God's mercy and democratic life.

II

Positioned in the middle of a discussion of the doctrine of God, Barth claims, "The mercy of God lies in His readiness to share in sympathy the distress of another, a readiness which springs from His inmost nature and stamps all His being and doing."[9] God's willingness to share in human suffering is a "sympathetic communion" with humanity, and is a giving of God's very self to the plight of humanity.[10] Moreover, this "sympathetic communion" takes the form of God's "self-revelation, reconciliation and sanctification, the form of His covenant with Israel, the form of Jesus Christ."[11] In terms of the moral life, Barth

6. Barth, "Church and State," p. 129.
7. Barth, "Church and State," p. 131.
8. Barth, "Church and State," p. 147, emphasis Barth's.
9. CD II/1, p. 369.
10. CD II/1, p. 371.
11. CD II/1, p. 371.

holds that "to be a person means really and fundamentally to be what God is, to be, that is, the One who loves in God's way."[12] All this, we discover, is "grounded [in] the justification of the sinner in Christ and the forgiveness of sins."[13]

With this, we find a key development in Barth's thinking on the relationship between divine justification and human justice. In just two pages of fine print, in *CD* II/1, §30, Barth draws the connections between God's mercy and righteousness, or divine justification and human justice and by implication the church's political stance in the world. The logic of these relations goes something like this: *as* persons are reconciled to God, *so now* they must fulfill the ministry of reconciliation. There is a "straight line," as Barth puts it, from God's mercy and righteousness to a "very definite political problem and task."[14] Turning to II/2, we find a short section on the political ramifications of God's mercy, as a form of God's election of sinful humanity. For an illustration, Barth draws upon Paul's letter to the church in Rome, chapter 13.[15] Although Paul intended his political exhortations for the Christian, the apostle's call to political responsibility, which is based on God's mercy, is, according to Barth, a call for all persons, for God's mercy has been extended to all women and men in Jesus Christ. "[The Christians'] nobility," writes Barth, "obliges them, not to something which is not binding upon all men, but to a life which, because it is binding upon all men, must at all costs be lived out among all men as a token of its universal obligatoriness."[16]

Given that Paul's letter to the church in Rome is primarily about God's reconciliation of the sinner in Jesus Christ, Barth contends that political responsibility, for both the Christian *and* the non-Christian, entails the "ministry of reconciliation."[17] Political life, then, is fundamentally about *fellowship by way of reconciliation*. We get a glimpse of what a political ministry of reconciliation may look like by returning to *CD* II/1. At the conclusion of the fine print section noted above, Barth suggests that the political attitude that must follow from God's righteousness and mercy results in two concrete aims. He writes, "[One]

12. *CD* II/1, p. 284.
13. *CD* II/2, p. 167.
14. *CD* II/1, p. 386.
15. *CD* II/2, pp. 713ff.
16. *CD* II/2, p. 715.
17. *CD* II/2, p. 720.

cannot avoid the question of human rights. [One] can only will and affirm a state which is based on justice."[18] To Barth's mind, then, a just state — or a state that recognizes and preserves human rights — allows not simply space for the church to preach justification, but space for the state to participate analogically in God's reconciling activity in history and for the world. "By any other political attitude," Barth continues, "[one] rejects the divine justification."[19] What we must note further is that for Barth to speak of a just state in terms of acknowledging and upholding human rights, and so forth, is also to begin to affirm the democratic state. For, as we shall see, Barth argues that human rights, and the like, are best recognized and secured within a democratic form of political life.

III

At this juncture we have found a key link between Barth's 1938 essay "Church and State" and his 1946 essay "The Christian Community and the Civil Community." The possibility and necessity for the church's and the state's witness to the rule of Christ are the reality of divine justification. Moreover, it is the *character* of divine justification that must inform the Christian and non-Christian in pursuing justice, the rule of law, and most importantly democracy. Given this, we are better able to see in the 1946 essay Barth's unfolding of the significance of divine justification not simply for the political realm but particularly for an affirmation of democracy, and most importantly, the *various types* of democracy in which Barth seems to be interested.

In "The Christian Community and the Civil Community" Barth holds that the church and the state can inform one another of an "external, relative, and provisional order of law" that reflects "the original and final pattern of . . . the eternal Kingdom of God and the eternal righteousness of His grace."[20] This reciprocity between the church and the state is possible, Barth claims, because both church and state share "a common origin and a common centre," namely, Jesus Christ.[21] Barth

18. CD II/1, p. 387.
19. CD II/1, p. 387.
20. Karl Barth, "The Christian Community and the Civil Community," in *Community, State, and Church*, p. 154.
21. Barth, "The Christian Community," p. 156.

illustrates this by way of concentric circles with a common center. Christ is the center of the circles, which represent the Christian and civil communities. With Christ as the center, the church is the inner circle, and the civil community is the outer circle. Because both communities find their center in Christ, both communities can witness to and serve Christ and his kingdom. While both church and state pursue distinct goals — the church its confession of Jesus Christ and the state its care for political and civil life — they remain unified by and in Christ in their purpose, means, and ends, which is to reflect the kingdom of God in their own unique way. Consequently, for Barth, no stark division and no undifferentiated unity should be encouraged or allowed to develop between church and state. In other words, both church and state possess unique callings, and yet they complement one another in their service to Christ. However, there is a key aspect of Barth's 1946 essay that needs to be brought out more fully, namely, Barth's appeal to divine justification and how this informs his interest in democracy and various kinds of democracy. To see this, I want to provide a brief analysis of the 1946 essay by starting in the middle of the essay with the fifteenth of thirty-five sections.

In section 15 Barth writes, "The Church is based on the knowledge of the one eternal God, who as such became man and thereby proved Himself a neighbor to man, by treating him with *compassion* (Luke 10:36f.)."[22] For Barth to suggest that God treats humanity with "compassion" is no small matter. Indeed, as we noticed in *CD* II/1, Barth holds that God is in "sympathetic communion" with humanity, giving himself for and to humanity's plight, which takes the primary form of reconciling humankind to himself.[23] Here Barth makes a connection between God's compassion and God's reconciliation of humanity, or God's justification of humanity in Jesus Christ. What sets the church apart from the state, then, and indeed the rest of the world, is not that God's compassion has been directed only to the church, but that the church *knows* that God's compassion and reconciliation are effective for all humankind. The knowledge of God's reconciliation of humanity is what guides the church in its mission in the world, especially in the political realm. The church knows that no human being stands outside the compassion of God, but in fact stands reconciled to God by way of

22. Barth, "The Christian Community," p. 171.
23. *CD* II/1, p. 371.

divine justification in and through Jesus Christ. Barth's reference, therefore, to God's compassion in the middle of his 1946 essay is an *indirect* reference to God's justification of the ungodly.

The upshot of identifying the relationship of the Christian community and civil community to divine justification in this essay is that both the Christian and the civil communities should work in concert for, as Barth puts it, the "provisional humanising of man's life."[24] The emphasis on humanizing persons' lives is carried over in Barth's more explicit reference to divine justification and the political realm in section 16 of the essay, giving us a direct link between divine justification and the state. "The Church is the witness of the divine justification, that is, of the act in which God in Jesus Christ established and confirmed His *original claim* to man and hence man's claim against sin and death."[25] The phrase "original claim" stems from Barth's treatment of God's eternal decree to be humanity's covenant partner in *CD* II/2. The divine claim on humankind refers to the "right" God has on humanity, establishing and confirming the "basis and justice," as Barth contends, of "man's situation."[26] The result is that, by way of divine justification, humanity stands in the "right" before God and one another, which for Barth translates into a sense of dignity before God and human beings. Such dignity has significant civil and political implications, for human dignity as granted by way of divine justification, says Barth, results in "human rights" and specific political polity. For example, in reference to God's compassion, in section 15 of the essay Barth argues that political agendas must serve human beings, otherwise "man, human dignity, [and] human life" will be "trampled underfoot."[27] In section 16 Barth suggests that God's claim on humanity corresponds politically to "equal protection for all," which is to be preserved by way of a "commonly acknowledged law" within a "constitutional State."[28] At this point we are able to discern an important aspect of the movement from divine justification to political life, namely, from God's claim on humanity in Jesus Christ to the state's obligation to provide for a humane environment in which human flourishing can occur. To the degree that the state *indirectly* reflects God's merciful claim on humanity, the

24. Barth, "The Christian Community," p. 155.
25. Barth, "The Christian Community," p. 172, emphasis added.
26. *CD* II/2, p. 561.
27. Barth, "The Christian Community," p. 171.
28. Barth, "The Christian Community," p. 172.

state is analogously reflecting the logic of the inner connection between justification and justice.

Barth begins to make more explicit what the movement from divine justification to political life should look like in section 17 of the 1946 essay. "The Church is witness of the fact that the Son of man came to seek and to save the lost. And this implies that — casting all false impartiality aside — the Church must concentrate first on the lower and lowest levels of human society. The poor, the socially and economically weak and threatened, will always be the object of its primary and particular concern, and it will always insist on the State's special responsibility for these weaker members of society."[29] Such language reflects the language found in *CD* II/1. God shares in "sympathetic communion" with human suffering, giving the church and indeed the state a ministry of reconciliation that attempts to ease the suffering of persons within a society. Barth puts it this way, "the connexion between justification and law in all its relevance for that between Church and state" is reflected in the church's and the state's just treatment of the "weak" in society. In no uncertain terms, Barth asserts, "By any other political attitude [one] rejects the divine justification."[30] The logic between justification and justice displayed in II/1 is repeated in the 1946 essay. That is, *as* God reconciles humanity by way of divine justification, *so too* the church and the state are "called" to engage in a ministry of reconciliation (justice) to the oppressed. To the degree, then, that the state, particularly at the encouragement of the church, shows mercy to the disadvantaged, and indeed all persons, it is indirectly participating in the ministry of reconciliation to which God calls the church and all persons.

Beginning with section 17 of the 1946 essay, Barth draws out more explicitly the implications of how both the church and the state can and should reflect analogically the kingdom of God and divine justification. For instance, Barth concludes that as women and men are called to be children of God, by way of God's grace and love, so, too, the state must guarantee the basic right of its citizens to carry out their decisions in the political sphere unencumbered by the state. Or, because the church knows that God's "anger and judgment . . . lasts but for a moment, whereas His mercy is for eternity," the political community is to enact

29. Barth, "The Christian Community," p. 173.
30. *CD* II/1, pp. 386-87.

violence as a political solution only as an *"ultima ratio regis"* and only for a limited time. Indeed, given God's mercy, the state "must . . . do all it can to see that no price is considered too high for the preservation or restoration of peace at home and abroad except the ultimate price which would mean the abolition of the lawful State and the practical denial of the divine ordinance."[31] Barth concludes these examples of how the state can reflect the kingdom of God by making clear that they only illustrate "analogies and corollaries of that kingdom of God in which the Church believes and which it preaches, in the sphere of the external, relative, and provisional problems of the civil community."[32]

Barth's examples are not meant to establish a closed political "system," but simply to show how the Christian community and indeed the civil community can move in "a constant direction, a continuous line of discoveries on both sides of the boundary which separates the political from the spiritual spheres, a correlation between explication and application."[33] By providing such examples, the Christian community is drawing the line connecting the gospel's explication to its application in the political sphere. As such, the line drawn by the church is not a direct witness to its gospel, but an indirect one, as a "reflection" in its "political decisions." The success of the church's decisions and application of the gospel in the political sphere, therefore, is contingent not on the success of making known to the state its "Christian premises" but on the fact that the church's political decisions are simply *better* decisions in the political and public arena. The church's political decisions and actions, like the state's, are to be a "witness only to Christian truths" and particularly divine justification.[34]

Consequently, as Haddorff notes in his paper but only in passing, Barth suggests in this essay that the Christian community should prefer democracy as the form of government that best reflects divine justification and God's kingdom. In the light of divine justification, it is easier to see why this is the case for Barth. For instance, as God justifies humanity against sin and its destructiveness, so should the state provide equal protection under the law for all persons, protecting its citizens against the destructiveness of anarchy and tyranny and thus moving in

---

31. Barth, "The Christian Community," pp. 178-79.
32. Barth, "The Christian Community," p. 179.
33. Barth, "The Christian Community," p. 180.
34. See Barth, "The Christian Community," p. 183.

the direction of a constitutional state.[35] Or, as God has set persons free and called persons to free association in the church, so should the state guarantee the freedom of its citizens to make lawful decisions in regard to certain spheres of life, such as family, education, and the like.[36] Further, as the Christian community seeks to identify the gifts of the Spirit among the faithful, thereby providing a social space where individual Christians make distinctive contributions to the life and direction of the church, so should the state seek to separate the different political functions of the state, such as the legislative, executive, and judicial tasks.[37] Finally, as God speaks his word freely to humanity, and particularly the church, so should the state allow for free speech within the political realm.[38] Here, then, Barth concludes that these analogies — informed as I have suggested by his understanding of the gospel of divine justification and the connection it has to political life — point the church and no less the state in the direction of democracy.[39]

While such analogies lead Barth to support a "constitutional state," or a form of democracy based on and guided by the rule of law, as noted above, he also suggests that democratic life should prize social justice seemingly above all else. For instance, at the beginning of the analogical connections between the New Testament and the political realm in the 1946 essay, Barth writes, "And in choosing between the various socialistic possibilities (*social-liberalism? co-operativism? syndicalism? free trade? moderate or radical Marxism?*) it will always choose the movement from which it can expect the greatest measure of social justice (leaving all other considerations on one side)."[40] For Barth, "socialistic possibilities" are to be prized, even within the context of constitutional democracy (or within some form of *political liberalism*), because socialism places great stress on the equal and just arrangements of its citizens and, in Barth's mind, tends more than other forms of government to protect the most vulnerable citizens of a society.[41] As we

---

35. Barth, "The Christian Community," p. 172.

36. Barth, "The Christian Community," p. 174.

37. Barth, "The Christian Community," p. 175.

38. Barth, "The Christian Community," pp. 176-77.

39. See Barth, "The Christian Community," p. 182.

40. Barth, "The Christian Community," p. 173, emphasis added.

41. As is well known, Barth's connection to socialism was strong throughout his life, even if varied. On Barth's connection to socialism, see George Hunsinger, ed. and trans., *Karl Barth and Radical Politics* (Philadelphia: Westminster, 1976).

shall see, one of the more interesting choices for Barth, it appears, will be democratic socialism, or what he calls in the list above "social-liberalism." It is understandable why Barth emphasizes the "socialistic" concern even while affirming democracy, for in his mind the movement from divine justification to the political realm requires it.

With the foregoing in place, I want to return to a more direct engagement with Haddorff's essay, suggesting that he has not provided the needed emphasis on Barth's relating of divine justification and the political realm. In particular, it is important to emphasize that Barth's support of democracy includes his concern that the democratic state be a "social democracy."

IV

Barth's interest in democracy is a result of his conviction that from God's justification of the sinner a "straight line" is drawn to a "very definite political task." And it is this "straight line" that I think needs to be made more up front and center in Haddorff's account of Barth's political ethics, especially in Haddorff's treatment of Barth's understanding of the I-Thou relationship and its potential to inform Barth's political theology.

For example, turning to *CD* III/2 and III/4, Haddorff wants to uncover Barth's "creation ethics," in terms of human relationships, as *a* basis for Barth's democracy. Here, Haddorff rightly notes that for Barth human life *as such* can never be our "ethical lord, teacher and master."[42] Instead, it is human life *as related* to God and others that forms the basis for the moral life and perhaps political life. However, we must not lose sight of *how* exactly human life relates to God.

For Barth, the God-human relationship at root is fundamentally marked by God's mercy and compassion — or God's sympathetic communion with humanity in and through Jesus Christ. While Haddorff helpfully points us to, as he calls it, Barth's rich account of human "being-in-relation," I think we need to say more about the distinct character of such relatedness (p. 108). Haddorff is just right, to my mind, when he begins to move us in the direction of seeing human relatedness as human equality by claiming that for Barth "true equality

42. *CD* III/4, p. 326.

presupposes God's prior action of grace" (p. 106). In other words, while there is no doubt that Barth mounts up an impressive notion of divine-human and human-human "togetherness" in *CD* III/2 and III/4, it is "togetherness" that has as its beginning and end God's covenant of reconciliation of the world in Jesus Christ. We must not forget that for Barth creation is the external basis of the gracious and reconciling covenant God has with humanity in Jesus Christ. In this sense, I think Haddorff's account of Barth's creation ethics and its use in contributing to Barth's political ethics needs to be more tightly connected to Barth's ethics of reconciliation.[43]

Why is this important to keep in mind? When divine reconciliation is kept at the forefront, as I am suggesting that Barth wants to do, we discover *not only* that the preferred form of government is democracy, but what *kind* of democracy is needed. For instance, Haddorff often notes that Barth's democracy is constitutional democracy. The reason this is so, Haddorff suggests, is that democratic constitutionalism "limits power, protects individuals and communities, and encourages responsible participation by standing under a constitutional rule of law" (p. 97). In what appears to be a summary statement, Haddorff writes, for Barth, "What matters for democracy is more than a common ethical language, or a common set of moral practices; it is a common commitment to be mutually responsible in freedom under the rule of law" (p. 105). As far as it goes, Haddorff's exposition represents Barth well. Indeed, Haddorff is often restating what in fact Barth says. Yet, I think more needs to be said about the kind of democracy Barth is seeking.

We must keep in mind that for Barth God's mercy depicted in *CD* II/1, or as Barth further describes it in the 1946 essay, God's concern for the plight of the weakest among us, moves us to a definite political problem and task. According to that essay, "The Church is witness of the fact that the Son of man came to seek and to save the lost. And this implies that — casting all false impartiality aside — the Church must concentrate first on the lower and lowest levels of human society. The poor, the socially and economically weak and threatened, will always be the object of its primary and particular concern, and it will always in-

---

43. On the connection between Barth's ethics of reconciliation and creation ethics, see John Webster, *Barth's Ethics of Reconciliation* (Cambridge: Cambridge University Press, 1995).

sist on the State's special responsibility for these weaker members of society."[44]

The direction in which we must move for Barth, it seems, is not just along the lines of constitutional democracy but of some form of democratic government that seeks economic and class equity or "social liberalism," which we could identify as democratic socialism. For Barth, democracy must include *economic* democracy, or an equitable distribution of market resources, otherwise, as George Hunsinger notes, "democracy" in Barth's view "is hobbled."[45] The concentration of economic power in the hands of a few will necessarily skew participatory democracy in the direction of the powerful. As Kathryn Tanner points out in her essay in this volume, Barth thought capitalism was an acid of society, ultimately destroying social relations and exploiting, and indeed creating, the socially and economically weak.[46] Indeed, in an essay from *Against the Stream,* Barth acknowledges that democracy without socialism is nothing more than "dust thrown in the eyes of the people," for it lacks a redistribution of economic and social power.[47]

Democratic socialism, then, appears to more nearly reflect the realities of divine justification and its connection to human justice, the "straight line" from God's mercy and compassion in Jesus Christ for humanity's plight to concrete aims that seek justice for all citizens but particularly for the weak and threatened. Unfortunately, this piece is missing in Haddorff's paper. And when Haddorff does quote Barth to the effect of the church pursuing "the greatest measure of social justice," which comes from the 1946 essay and explicitly links the church's concern for social justice to "the Church's witness that the Son of man came to seek and save the lost," he places the quote at the tail end of his discussion on human relatedness in *CD* III/2 and not in connection to divine justification, as Barth seems to want to do (p. 109). Thus, an important element of Barth's understanding of democracy may be lost in Haddorff's construal of it.

In the end, while democracy is the direction in which Barth pre-

44. Barth, "The Christian Community," p. 173.

45. See George Hunsinger, "Karl Barth (1886-1968)," in *The Teachings of Modern Christianity on Law, Politics, and Human Nature* (New York: Columbia University Press, 2006), p. 365.

46. For Barth's critical comments on capitalism, see *CD* III/4, p. 544.

47. Karl Barth, "The Church between East and West," in *Against the Stream: Shorter Post-war Writings, 1946-1952* (New York: Philosophical Library, 1954), p. 134.

fers to move, it is clear, by Barth's own admission, that no one form of government is *the* Christian choice, not even one particular kind *or kinds* of democracy. For Barth, the theologian ought not to be constrained by any one "system," whether theological or political. As he reminds us in his *Table Talk,* where he claims, "I must confess I do not like the term 'democracy'; there should be a better term."[48] Indeed, Barth's concern is not a political system per se, but the mercy and compassion of God reflected in our political arrangements — God's justification of the sinner and the new life that springs from this divine act. And so it is, near the end of "The Christian Community and the Civil Community," that Barth writes, "What we have said here needs to be extended, deepened, and particularised."[49]

48. *Karl Barth's Table Talk,* ed. John D. Godsey (Richmond: John Knox, 1962), p. 81.
49. Barth, "The Christian Community," p. 180.

8. Crime, Punishment, and Atonement: Karl Barth on the Death of Christ

Timothy Gorringe

Karl Barth preached regularly at, and visited prisoners in, Basel jail from 1954 onward. In 1960, the day after his seventy-fourth birthday, he traveled to Fulda to address German prison chaplains. Barth was in fine form, reminding his hearers of the excellent German law that prescribed a siesta after lunch and engaging sharply with a whole range of questions about crime and punishment. The record of the event is a splendid testimony to Barth's profound humanism, what we might call "the humanism of election."[1] Barth approaches offenders in the light of his understanding of election, according to which all human beings are elect in Christ and only Christ is "elected to destruction" for our sakes. Three themes stand out in particular: the solidarity of the rest of the community with criminals; an insistence on punishment as a form of care *(Fürsorge)*; and an insistence that punishment cannot be understood as expiation. What this grounds is, as we would hope, a deeply humane approach to offenders. Unfortunately this humanity has not characterized Western approaches to offending in general, and it may be that understandings of the death of Christ play some role in that. Tracing intellectual causality is always problematic, as the forty-year debate about Lyn White's claims regarding Christian responsibility for the ecological crisis shows. I have attempted to argue elsewhere that the Anselmian under-

---

1. The talk and engagement with questions can be found in Karl Barth, *Gespräche 1959-1962*, ed. Eberhard Busch (Zürich: Theologischer Verlag, 1995), pp. 53-90. I am grateful to Karlfried Froehlich of Princeton Theological Seminary for drawing my attention to this material.

standing of the atonement did influence Western structures of affect in a retributivist direction.[2] At the heart of the argument are two points: Anselm's insistence that God could not just forgive sin (as his interlocutor, Boso, suggests) but that Christ's death was required for that forgiveness, and that punishment alienates rather than heals. In his account of the atonement Barth gives Anselm a fairly wide berth, but I am going to suggest that he nevertheless follows an unreconstructed understanding of punishment, one not in line with his understanding in his meeting with prison chaplains. Followed through consistently, this could have led to a different approach to offenders than the one we actually find, or alternatively he could have modified his account of the death of Christ. I begin with a preamble about sin, crime, and punishment.

Sin and Crime

Every Christmas when English-speaking Christians sing the carol *In Dulci Jubilo,* they come across the line "Deeply were we stained *per nostra crimina.*" The Latin word *crimen* means charge, accusation, reproach, fault, guilt, scandal. It is, of course, the word from which we derive our word "crime." In the carol it obviously means "sin." How are they related? "If a man commits adultery with the wife of his neighbor, both the adulterer and the adulteress shall be put to death" (Lev. 20:10). This is an example of something that, in postexilic Israel, seems to have been both a sin and a crime, but in present-day Western society remains a sin but is no longer a crime. In some Muslim societies, as we know, it remains both. In common parlance, people commonly conflate sin and crime, even at a sophisticated level. Thus the former master of the rolls in Britain, Lord Denning, wrote: "In order that an act should be punishable it must be morally blameworthy." A certain kind of immorality should be a necessary, though not sufficient, condition of criminality. "It must be a sin."[3] Turning that around, the theologian Hastings Rashdall wrote: "A crime is simply a sin it is expedient to repress by penal enactment."[4] This seems to be saying that some sins so affect the

---

2. Timothy Gorringe, *God's Just Vengeance* (Cambridge: Cambridge University Press, 1996).

3. Alfred Thompson Denning, *The Changing Law* (London: Stevens, 1953), p. 112.

4. Hastings Rashdall, *The Theory of Good and Evil: A Treatise on Moral Philosophy* (Oxford: Oxford University Press, 1907), 1:296.

wider community that they have to be proscribed by law, and thereby become crimes, while other sins may be the target of disapprobation but are not penalized. But of course, unjust states may criminalize moral forms of behavior (as eighteenth-century England criminalized ancient traditions of using the commons, or apartheid South Africa criminalized mixed-race marriages), while society may sanction and even reward forms of behavior that many might consider sinful and might perhaps want criminalized (such as some forms of financial trading, arms trading, and gambling). The gap between sin and crime that these distinctions indicate can also be seen by the fact that while, according to Scripture, all humans are sinful, only a tiny percentage come through the criminal justice system. The relation between sin and crime, therefore, is not one of identity, but common issues are involved in both. Both "sin" and "crime" describe patterns of behavior that damage human society, and therefore the possibility of being human, to varying extents and which therefore constitute boundaries that need marking.

In early modern Europe the criminal was the paradigm sinner and, because all humans were sinners, the paradigm human being. Looking at the criminal, people said, "There, but for the grace of God, go I." Charles Wesley could draw on prison imagery in his redemption hymns:

> Long my imprisoned spirit lay
> Fast bound in sin and nature's night;
> Thine eye diffused a quickening ray,
> I woke, the dungeon flamed with light;
> My chains fell off, my heart was free,
> I rose, went forth and followed Thee.

To look at the criminal was to acknowledge the sin we both shared. In his talk with chaplains Barth insisted on this over and over again, alluding to a wonderful story about Niemöller. When Niemöller was locked up for opposing the German Christian movement, the prison chaplain met him and asked in surprise, "My brother, why are you in prison?" To which Niemöller replied, "My brother, why are you *not* in prison?"[5] Barth uses the story, tongue in cheek, to suggest that we are

---

5. Barth, *Gespräche*, p. 82, author's translation.

all offenders. We are all unclean. Hence the fundamental presupposition of prison chaplaincy is "an unreserved solidarity" with inmates.[6]

This understanding of the criminal or sinner was linked to an understanding of redemption: the prisons built for such people were penitentiaries, or reformatories. There was no illusion about the darkness of the human heart, but at the same time there was a belief that God wished to save all, and the offer of salvation applied to the prisoner as much as to anyone else. This is fundamental to Barth's approach to offenders. Chaplaincy is quite simply a matter of letting prisoners know that in Christ God has reconciled, justified, and sanctified them.

This paradigm changed in two ways, neither of which can be quite identified with the influence of the Enlightenment. First, beginning in the 1890s we have the emergence of the penal welfare era, which, it has been said, assumed the perfectibility of man, saw crime as a sign of an underachieving socialization process, and looked to the state to assist those who had been deprived of the economic, social, and psychological provision necessary for proper social adjustment and law-abiding conduct.[7] In ways made familiar to us by Robert Bellah and others, therapy replaced the idea of redemption.

Today we are in a different situation in which crime is regarded as rational maximizing behavior, explicable by reference to standard motivational patterns, and where the key issue is to control crime. Control theories, says David Garland,

> begin from a much darker vision of the human condition. They assume that individuals will be strongly attracted to self-serving, anti-social, and criminal conduct unless inhibited from doing so by robust and effective controls, and they look to the authority of the family, the community, and the state to uphold restrictions and inculcate restraint. . . . this way of thinking has tended to reinforce retributive and deterrent policies insofar as it affirms that offenders are rational actors who are responsive to disincentives and fully responsible for their criminal acts.[8]

6. Barth, *Gespräche*, p. 63, author's translation.
7. David Garland, *The Culture of Control: Crime and Social Order in Contemporary Society* (Oxford: Oxford University Press, 2001), p. 15.
8. Garland, *The Culture of Control*, pp. 15-16.

This darker vision might seem to resonate with an Augustinian understanding of the human, but in fact it is quite different in two ways. First, for the Christian tradition sin is a pathology. Sin may be universal, but it is not normal. Behind this understanding is the view of Adam Smith and David Ricardo, and ultimately of Mandeville, that of course we seek our own best interest, and on the whole this works to the good of all. Secondly, it has no vision of redemption.

Ways of Dealing with Sin and Crime

There are three broad ways of dealing with sin and crime. The first is to seek to protect society at large, often by sequestration. Punishment is not the issue; protection is. This is the view most commonly associated with utilitarianism. It has a theological response in understandings of scapegoating, but I shall not pursue it here.

The second way is to deal with sin or crime by punishment. On this view wrongdoing requires retribution. Our own societies are profoundly retributive, and thus this response might seem self-evident, and belief in the necessity of punishment lies deep in the biblical and theological imagination. Barth himself treads warily around the issue. The extensive debate on the theory of punishment, however, amply demonstrates that the need for punishment cannot be taken for granted. A whole variety of reasons for punishment is adduced: because society cannot turn a blind eye to the assumption that "crime pays"; because offenders deserve it; because we have to stop people committing further crimes; because crime should be denounced; because we have to reassure the victim that society cares about what has happened; because we have to protect society from dangerous or dishonest people; because we have to allow offenders to make amends for the harm they have caused; because we have to ensure that the laws are obeyed; because criminals have to repay their debt to society; because sin or crime upsets a balance that must be restored; because sin or crime requires expiation, atonement, or annulment in order to wipe the slate clean, to start afresh.

One of the most cogent accounts of the need for punishment is given by Simone Weil in *The Need for Roots*.[9] Beginning with commu-

---

9. Simone Weil, *The Need for Roots* (London: Routledge, 1987).

nity, she argued that crime places us outside the chain of obligations that bind every human being to every other one. Punishment, in her view, is what welds the offender back into the community. To punish people is to respect them, by showing that we still consider them part of the community. Punishment, in her view, ought to be an honor. It both wipes out the stigma of crime and must be regarded as a supplementary form of education, compelling a higher devotion to the public good.

Punishment, then, takes the wrongdoer seriously as a moral agent, and a sane offender has a right to be punished rather than manipulated or ignored. Punishment seeks to prevent continuation in hardness of heart, and to promote a return to goodness. It is a "transforming agent." In a similar vein others have spoken of punishment as a symbol, an outward and visible sign of an inward and spiritual disgrace, which seeks both to forestall the consummation of wrongdoing and to promote its annulment.

Weil herself went on to set out the objections to this kind of argument, citing the discredit attaching to the police, the irresponsible conduct of the judiciary, the prison system, the permanent social stigma cast upon ex-convicts, the scale of penalties that provides a much harsher punishment for ten acts of petty larceny than for one rape or certain types of murder, and even provides punishments for ordinary misfortune. All this, she argued, made punishment of this ideal type impossible. In an unjust society the relative degree of immunity should increase, not as you go up, but as you go down the social scale, because otherwise the hardships inflicted will be felt to be in the nature of constraints, or even abuses of power, and will no longer constitute punishments. For there to be punishment there has to be justice. What she was calling for, therefore, was a complete reordering of society.

In addition to the objections Weil raises, it is also the case that punishment, far from bringing people to repentance, often hardens them. "Generally speaking," said Nietzsche, "punishment makes men hard and cold; it concentrates; it sharpens the feeling of alienation; it strengthens the power of resistance. . . . punishment *tames* men, but it does not make them 'better.'"[10] George Bernard Shaw agreed, arguing that to punish retributively was to injure persons, "and men are not im-

---

10. Friedrich Nietzsche, *The Genealogy of Morals,* in *Basic Writings of Nietzsche,* trans. and ed. Walter Kaufmann (New York: Modern Library, 1968), pp. 517-19 (II:14, 15).

proved by injuries."[11] Retributivism is a way of saying that two blacks make a white. "We get the present grotesque spectacle," he wrote, "of a judge committing thousands of horrible crimes in order that thousands of criminals may feel that they have balanced their moral accounts."[12] Weil thinks of punishment as purifying, but it can embitter and break as well. The Norwegian criminologist Nils Christie speaks of Western law as "pain law" because it is an elaborate mechanism for administering "just" doses of pain. Why do we do that? Because we have been educated to believe that humiliation and suffering are what justice is about and that evil must be held in check by harshness rather than by love and understanding. This, says Christie, stands up to the scrutiny neither of experience nor of moral sense. If offenders need to learn that they are persons who matter, who have both the capacity and the responsibility to make good choices, who ought to respect others and cope peacefully with frustration and conflict, they are unlikely to do that if they are dealt with by violence. Violence breeds nothing but violence. The North American psychiatrist James Gilligan, who has spent a lifetime working with violent offenders, considers that punishment routinely leads to worse violence. Punishment eases the feeling of guilt, but it does nothing whatsoever to bring about a more reconciled society.[13] Of course, Christie and Gilligan are assuming that criminals are redeemable.

This is the focus of the third way of dealing with crime, rehabilitation, which aims to restore the criminal to society. Rehabilitation was the norm in both Europe and North America for the first six decades of the twentieth century, and then gave place to a new round of retributivism, but at the same time in many places around the world an alternative to retributivism began to be urged that has, as some of its advocates note, ancient roots, including roots in the Hebrew Bible and in the New Testament. This has come to be known, over the past forty years or so, as "restorative justice."

---

11. George Bernard Shaw, in Sidney Webb and Beatrice Webb, *English Prisons under Local Government* (London: Longmans, Green and Co., 1922), p. xiv.

12. Shaw, in Webb and Webb, *English Prisons,* p. liv.

13. James Gilligan, *Preventing Violence* (London: Thames and Hudson, 2001).

Shalom and Restorative Justice

The United Nations defines restorative justice as a "process in which the victim, the offender and/or any other individuals or community members affected by a crime actively participate together in the resolution of matters arising from the crime."[14] Justice here is the concern of the whole community, and not of legal professionals and a judge who is paid by the state. The process is a palaver, in which everyone can have his or her say in defense of, or in accusation of, the accused. The victim is not sidelined but is, to the contrary, a prominent player in the whole process. The object is that the victim should have justice done to him or her, rather than justice being meted out to the offender. At the end of the day, however, the desired aim is not to punish whoever the guilty party might be, but to bring healing, reconciliation, *shalom,* to the community. It is an implication of this process that crime is viewed primarily as a breakdown in relationships rather than as a breach of the law. Justice, in turn, is the restoration of relationship, something that cannot be decreed by statute but only decided by debate and negotiation. The process allows a much more complex understanding of human agency, guilt, and responsibility than the conventional justice system, which is organized around victim and offender, guilt, and innocence.[15]

14. Daniel Van Ness, Allison Morris, and Gabrielle Maxwell, "Introducing Restorative Justice," in *Restorative Justice for Juveniles: Conferencing, Mediation, and Circles* (Oxford: Hart Publishing, 2001), p. 13.

15. A recent handbook of restorative justice identifies key elements:

- There will be some relatively informal process that aims to involve victims, offenders, and others closely connected to them or to the crime in discussion of matters such as what happened, what harm has resulted, and what should be done to repair the harm and prevent further wrongdoing.
- There will be emphasis on empowering ordinary people whose lives are affected by a crime or wrongful act.
- Some effort will be made by decision-making processes to promote a response geared less toward stigmatizing and more toward ensuring that wrongdoers recognize and meet a responsibility to make amends for the harm they have caused in a manner that directly benefits those harmed, as a first step toward their reintegration into the community of law-abiding citizens.
- Decision makers or those facilitating decision making will be concerned to ensure that the decision-making process and its outcome will be guided by certain principles or values that, in contemporary society, are widely regarded as desirable in any interaction between people, such as respect being shown for others;

As the Mennonite scholar Howard Zehr notes, the focus of restorative justice on restoring the whole has parallels, and not just analogies, with the idea of *shalom* in the Hebrew Bible.[16] There, he argues, doing justice is not primarily about punishing the offender but about putting right the damaged whole, which has made the crime possible. In a way that is crucial for our understanding of both criminal justice and atonement, *shalom* is reestablished after judgment, but by forgiveness. Israel's sins are forgiven (Isa. 40:2), and God then reestablishes the covenant of peace (Isa. 54:10). Restorative justice, we could say, is about reconciliation.

It seems probable that Jesus' preferred phrase for God's project, "the kingdom of God," embraces what was meant by *"shalom."* This is why Jesus says that the nonviolent will inherit the earth (Matt. 5:5) and why he insists on not resisting enemies and loving the enemy. Jesus concludes many of his encounters with the words "Go in peace." His healing ministry both fulfills the messianic promises and, as a result, establishes *shalom* between people and between humankind and God. Barth takes this up in his account of the "direction" of the Son in *CD* IV/2. What follows from the resurrection, he argues, is "the power to spread peace." Salvation is a form of healing: "a healing of the rent, a

---

violence and coercion are to be avoided if possible, and inclusion is to be preferred above exclusion.

- Decision makers or those facilitating decision making will devote significant attention to the injury done to the victims and to the needs that result from that and to tangible ways in which those needs can be addressed.
- There will be some emphasis on strengthening or repairing relationships between people and using the power of healthy relationships to resolve difficult situations. Cf. Gerry Johnstone and Daniel W. van Ness, *Handbook of Restorative Justice* (Cullompton, U.K.: Willan, 2007), p. 7.

Another pair of scholars writing on criminal justice, Sullivan and Tifft, contrasts needs-based justice with the economies and paradigms of rights-based and deserts-based conceptions of justice. They argue that rights-based conceptions distribute power according to social position or location; deserts-based according to efforts, talents, achievements, and failures. Both of these are violent conceptions of power. Rather, we should meet the needs of all parties as those define their own needs. The goal is equality of well-being. Success as a healing community will depend on how needs oriented our primary social institutions are. Dennis Sullivan and Larry Tifft, *Restorative Justice: Healing the Foundations of Our Everyday Lives* (Monsey, N.Y.: Willow Tree, 2001), p. xi.

16. Howard J. Zehr, *Changing Lenses: A New Focus for Crime and Justice* (Scottdale, Pa.: Herald, 1990).

closing of the mortal wound, from which humanity (and openly or secretly every man) suffers. It consists in the removal of antitheses; the antithesis between God and man; then the antithesis between man and man; and finally the antithesis between man and himself. In this sense salvation means peace."[17] As applied to punishment, Barth argues that the state has a divinely instituted duty of care for all its citizens and that punishment is to be understood as an exercise of this duty of care with regard to offenders. It involves education that seeks to help the offender understand why she or he should obey the law. "Und das ist eine heilsame Sache."[18]

This has a close analogy with the argument of the criminologist Antony Duff, who argues that punishment is a communicative exercise that seeks to persuade the offender, by rational moral argument, of the wrongness of his or her conduct. It seeks to arouse the repentant recognition of guilt, which is a form of pain. "Such pain must be mediated and aroused by his own understanding of and judgment on his conduct. . . . Blame thus seeks the participation of the person blamed: for its aim is not a kind of suffering which I can impose on him, but one which he must impose on himself."[19] It seems to me that this is precisely what Barth is aiming at.

Karl Barth on Atonement

I turn now to Barth's account of the atonement. With much of the Western Christian tradition, he opts for forensic imagery in exploring the significance of the death of Christ. It is on this exploration that I am going to focus, the seventy-two pages entitled "The Judge Judged in Our Place,"[20] but it is essential to note that Barth regarded the whole of *CD* IV/1, IV/2, and IV/3 as his exposition of the doctrine of reconciliation. Reacting to nineteenth-century British debates about atonement, R. C. Moberly had insisted that there was no Calvary without Pentecost.[21] Barth agrees, giving us a massive pneumatology and a corresponding

17. *CD* IV/2, p. 314.
18. Barth, *Gespräche*, p. 66.
19. R. A. Duff, *Trials and Punishments* (Cambridge: Cambridge University Press, 1986), p. 59.
20. *CD* IV/1, pp. 211-83.
21. R. C. Moberly, *Atonement and Personality* (London: Murray, 1909).

doctrine of the church in these volumes that sketch the "subjective realisation of the atonement."[22] This is not a narrowly religious affair. The
church is "in its deepest and most proper tendency . . . worldly." "It is holy
in its openness to the street and even the alley, in its turning to the pro-
fanity of all human life — the holiness which, according to Rom. 12:5,
does not scorn to rejoice with them that do rejoice and to weep with
them that weep."[23] There is the basis here for a profound understanding
of restorative justice. In focusing on the forensic imagery we must also
not forget that the doctrine of reconciliation for Barth is the account of
the humiliation of God and the exaltation of human beings. In Christ's
death the regeneration and conversion of human beings take place.
"They took place in Jesus Christ as the Crucified because it is finally and
supremely in His cross that He acted as the Lord and King of all men,
that He maintained and exercised His sovereignty, that He proved his
likeness to the God who is so unassuming in the world but so revolutionary in relation to it, that He inaugurated His kingdom as a historical actuality."[24] The emphasis on the humility of God is, arguably, the dominant note of *CD* IV/1 and IV/2 and the key to Barth's thought about
reconciliation. Again, although he expressly tells us at the beginning of
CD IV/3 that the theme of the true witness is simply the making plain of
what has been established in the previous two volumes, nevertheless the
account of Jesus as Victor anticipates the fragmentary material under
"The Lordless Powers,"[25] where an account of criminal justice might well
have found a place. Barth's treatment of *nomos* in his *Romans,* although
understood there as religion, opens the way for a critique of criminal justice. It is essential to bear this in mind. "The Judge Judged in Our Place"
is seventy-two pages amongst nearly three thousand that deal with reconciliation. It is not that in these pages we find "the doctrine of atonement" and elsewhere something different. Rather, Barth recasts the traditional thinking of atonement in this massive exposition of
incarnation, death, and resurrection, the meaning of sin, justification,
and sanctification, as well as of pneumatology and ecclesiology. With
those caveats I turn to Barth's exploration of the forensic metaphor.

Barth notes the importance of what he calls the "military" meta-

---

22. *CD* IV/1, pp. 643, 644, 645.
23. *CD* IV/1, p. 725.
24. *CD* IV/2, p. 291.
25. *CL,* pp. 213-33.

phor, better known as *Christus Victor,* and the cultic one, the theology of sacrifice. Drawing on Blumhardt, he explores the former in *CD* IV/3 but in his first volume on reconciliation opts for the forensic. He begins from the claim of the New Testament that in Christ we encounter "the Judge of the world and of every man."[26] This is glossed with the sense "Judge" has in the Hebrew Bible: "He is the One whose concern is for order and peace, who must uphold the right and prevent the wrong." The judges of the Hebrew Bible were "helpers and saviours in the recurrent sufferings of the people at the hand of neighbouring tribes." An understanding of judgment in this sense will lead in the direction of restorative justice, but curiously, given his theological method, Barth qualifies his acknowledgment of the biblical sense of judging, on which he could have built, by noting, "this involves judging in the more obvious sense of the word, and therefore pardoning and sentencing."[27] "Obvious" here means in the retributive sense familiar from Western criminal justice. He goes on to quote from the *Dies Irae,* a majestic but ultimately pagan hymn about Zeus rather than the God and Father of Jesus Christ. Unlike that poem, he wants to expound Christ's coming as Judge as good news, not a threat. In his exposition of 1 Corinthians 13 Barth quotes Blumhardt: "The Saviour is not a destroyer."[28] The good news is that Christ died "for us," and Barth attempts to expound this under four headings. He argues that Christ took our place as judge. He took our place as the judged. He was judged in our place. And he acted justly in our place. "If the nail of this fourfold 'for us' does not hold," Barth writes, "everything else will be left hanging in the void as an anthropological or psychological or sociological myth, and sooner or later it will break and fall to the ground."[29] How does he understand this, and how does it help us understand the criminal justice process?

Jesus as Judge

The first of these four headings, that Jesus took our place as judge, is the most innovative. Barth has argued that "all sin has its being and or-

26. *CD* IV/1, p. 217.
27. *CD* IV/1, p. 217.
28. *CD* IV/2, p. 837.
29. *CD* IV/1, p. 273.

igin in the fact that man wants to be his own judge. . . . The whole world finds its supreme unity and determination against God in looking for justification from itself and not from God. . . . Not all men commit all sins, but all men commit this sin which is the essence and root of all other sins."[30] Guilt, says Paul Ricoeur, is "a way of putting oneself before a sort of invisible tribunal which measures the offence, pronounces the condemnation, and inflicts the punishment; at the extreme point of interiorization, moral consciousness is a look which watches, judges, and condemns; the sentiment of guilt is therefore the consciousness of being inculpated and incriminated by this interior tribunal; it is mingled with the anticipation of the punishment."[31] But Barth assumes that we also externalize this interior tribunal, judging others as well. To be human means to want to be the judge of both myself and my neighbor. But the fact that Jesus is my Judge means not only that the dream of divine likeness is ended (in this case, in acting as a Judge) but also that I am freed from judging: "The loss which we always bewail and which we seem to suffer means in reality that a heavy and indeed oppressive burden is lifted from us when Jesus Christ becomes our Judge. It is a nuisance, and at bottom an intolerable nuisance, to have to be the man who gives sentence. . . . [A]t one stroke the whole of the evil responsibility which man has arrogantly taken to himself is taken from him[.] . . . I am not the Judge. Jesus Christ is Judge."[32] This is "the basic sense for all that follows," and it has concrete implications for Christian ethics: "No man can judge another man's servant (Rom. 14:4)."[33] Barth does not pursue this, but it puts a question mark against the whole legal process as we have it. In some Reformation dispensations the judge was required to pray before sentencing as one who was also liable to judgment. The purpose of assize sermons was presumably to put human justice within this wider framework. It is not to say that the criminal justice system is impossible, as Herman Bianchi argues, but it is to say that we recognize its fragility.[34]

30. *CD* IV/1, p. 220.
31. Paul Ricoeur, *The Conflict of Interpretations: Essays in Hermeneutics,* ed. Don Ihde (Evanston, Ill.: Northwestern University Press, 1974), p. 429.
32. *CD* IV/1, pp. 233-34.
33. *CD* IV/1, p. 235.
34. "The ideas of punishment and punitive response to liability acts must wither away entirely. The very thought that one grown up human being should ever have a right, or a duty, to punish another grown up human being is a gross indecency, and the

Not only is there the ever present possibility of a miscarriage of justice, but we arrogate to ourselves that which belongs to God alone. In this connection the emphasis on "the majesty of the law," underlined in Britain by a liturgy of wigs, gowns, ushers, contempt of court, and the absolute authority of the judge in court, though it has obvious socio-logical reasons, is theologically extremely questionable. Dispensing judgment may be necessary, but it is a permission and carries with it the need to ask for forgiveness: its closest analogue is making war. It is an obvious evil that nevertheless must be pursued from time to time but that one can do only after much soul searching, as a last resort, and with a prayer for forgiveness. In no sense is it a good in its own right. In his dialogue with prison chaplains, Barth alludes to the majesty of the law and understands the preservation of order, and therefore law, as a task divinely laid on the state. However, legal right is not only estab-lished by divine grace but also kept within determinate limits *(begrenzt)* and its form established by it. The fact that it is grounded in grace is precisely what establishes punishment as care.[35] The very meaning of the law should be understood in terms of care.[36] In the criminal justice system we are dealing with human law, not divine law. To a questioner who wanted to say that God entrusts the exercise of justice to the state, he quoted Deuteronomy 32:35 and insisted that vengeance belongs to God.

The reconciling work of Christ here is to free us from the burden of judgment. As always, the nonsense of the opposition of supposed objective and subjective theories of the atonement is exposed. In Moberly's words, "the atonement was objective that it might become subjective in repentance, faith, and love." Barth extends and deepens this in his account of faith, love, and hope at the end of each of the vol-umes on reconciliation that we have. In terms of criminal justice we can say that, properly understood, what happens in Christ changes the structure of affect of societies that have heard the gospel from being primarily retributive to being primarily restorative. At this point we can note that Richard Snyder's allegation, in *The Protestant Ethic and the*

---

phenomenon cannot stand up to any ethical test" (H. Bianchi, "Abolition: Assensus or Sanctuary," in R. A. Duff and David Garland, *A Reader on Punishment* [Oxford: Oxford University Press, 1994], p. 341).

35. Barth, *Gespräche,* p. 65.

36. Barth, *Gespräche,* p. 77.

Spirit of Punishment, that Barth is amongst those who have contributed to the rise of the punitive ethos of our societies, is completely mistaken. Snyder argues that the punitive nature of Western societies is rooted in an understanding of grace that denigrates human beings as sinners. The failure to recognize grace inherent in creation has led to a functionalist attitude toward nature, and something similar has happened in regard to persons. "The classifications of 'fallen' and 'redeemed' — understood in reference to essential being and not simply in reference to behavior — serve as a way to divide the human race into persons and 'non persons.' This high doctrine of sin . . . results in what Tom Driver has called 'the latent Christian doctrine of the nonperson.' Some are unworthy, and evil, and others are graced. Some are alive; others are dead. Some are of God and some are of Satan."[37]

I am sure that Snyder is right that doctrines have social effects, and the analogy with Weber here is interesting, though I think Snyder has misidentified his target. In relation to Barth he unfortunately repeats the tired caricatures of the 1950s. Not only does Barth's doctrine of election, reiterated in the context of reconciliation in *CD* IV/2, make the division of persons Snyder refers to impossible, but, even more fundamentally, the emphasis throughout Barth's theology is not on judgment but on the "Yes" of God that led Berkouwer to allege that Barth gave undue emphasis to the "triumph of grace." "Joy" is one of the key words in the Barthian lexicon. The gospel is not gloomy, morose, and melancholy. On the contrary, a Christian is bright and merry "as one who has received the Yes of divine grace said also to him, who can therefore live personally by the power of this Yes in spite of the old man which still rumbles within him and the old world which still startles him, and who in virtue of the penetration of the vicious circle accomplished for him and not by him may take a few steps forward."[38] At every step Barth presupposes both solidarity in sin and redemption. That is why, I take it, he cheerfully went to preach in prison where, in one memorable sermon, he reminded his captive audience that all Christians line up behind the two *lestes* (Barth translates, "criminals") on the crosses on either side of Christ. It accounts, too, for the overwhelmingly positive tenor of his talk with prison chap-

---

37. T. Richard Snyder, *The Protestant Ethic and the Spirit of Punishment* (Grand Rapids: Eerdmans, 2001), p. 47.

38. *CD* IV/3.2, p. 662.

lains, in which Barth takes issue with those who suggest that some offenders are simply irredeemable.

Jesus as Judged

Barth's second exploration of the Judge judged in our place is that Christ accepts responsibility for what we do as sinners. Christ took our place as the judged. In taking our place our sin ceases to be ours: "His the accusation, the judgment and the curse which necessarily fall on us there. He is the unrighteous amongst those who can no longer be so because he was and is for them."[39] God's concern is to create order, to convert the world, and genuinely to reconcile it. "He did not, therefore, commit an act of arbitrary kindness — which would have been no help to the world."[40] The effect of this is that we always "see ourselves in Him as the men we are, [we] recognise ourselves in Him as the men for whom He has taken responsibility, who are forgiven."[41] In Barth's view this means that the freedom to do evil is removed from us. "The only possibility which is still open to us as we look at Him and at ourselves in Him is that of repentance, of turning away from the being and activity, from all that we have to see and acknowledge as guilty in Him, of readiness for this, of turning to what can be made of our evil case now that it is the case of Jesus Christ, now that He has undertaken to be responsible for it and to wrestle with it."[42]

This too has implications for ethics: "when we look at what Jesus Christ became and was for us, we cannot leave out some little love for our enemies as a sign of our recognition and understanding that this is how He treated us His enemies."[43] Love of enemies, Barth points out, destroys the friend-foe relationship, because if we love our enemy he or she ceases to be our enemy. "It thus abolishes the whole exercise of force, which presupposes this relationship, and has no meaning apart

---

39. *CD* IV/1, p. 237.
40. *CD* IV/1, p. 237.
41. *CD* IV/1, p. 241.
42. *CD* IV/1, p. 243.
43. *CD* IV/1, p. 244. George Hunsinger comments, "Enemy-love in Karl Barth's theology is the heart of the gospel" ("The Politics of the Nonviolent God: Reflections on René Girard and Karl Barth," in *Disruptive Grace: Studies in the Theology of Karl Barth* [Grand Rapids: Eerdmans, 2000], p. 35).

Timothy Gorringe

from it."[44] Hunsinger glosses this by speaking of "the renunciation of force *along with retributive emotions and attitudes.*"[45] Enemy love, in other words, undercuts the basis of retributivism and by the same token underwrites restorative justice. In his threefold discussion of the Word of Jesus in IV/2 Barth highlights peace as the heart of the good news. "And peace (εἰρήνη) includes what we mean by the term, but basically it is the equivalent of *shalom* in the comprehensive sense of salvation 'by Jesus Christ,' this name being underlined as the sum of all real peace."[46] If the command to love our enemies is the sign of the new order inaugurated by Christ, then this would work itself out in the field of criminal justice in terms of restorative justice, in terms of the restoration of *shalom.* David Garland notes that in the culture of control the offender's perceived worth tends toward zero and victims' interests expand to fill the gap. Tiny crimes are viewed cumulatively, and "the community" is the collective all-purpose victim. "How could this be?" he asks.

> How could offenders have been so thoroughly deprived of their citizenship status and the rights that typically accompany it? How could an overweening concern for "the victim" block out all consideration of the wrongdoer, as if the two categories were mutually exclusive? Perhaps because we have become convinced that certain offenders, once they offend are no longer "members of the public" and cease to be deserving of the kinds of consideration we typically afford to each other. Today's criminal justice state is characterized by a more unvarnished authoritarianism with none of the benign pretensions.[47]

Theologically, of course, the answer is that we have constructed a society without an effective understanding of either solidarity in sin or redemption.

Barth's claim that Christ has taken responsibility for us calls for comment, for responsibility is one of the key aspects of criminal justice. One of the main reasons for the return to retributivism in the 1970s was the worry that everything was becoming medicalized. Instead of there

44. CD IV/2, p. 550.
45. Hunsinger, "The Politics," p. 38, emphasis added.
46. CD IV/2, p. 197.
47. Garland, *The Culture of Control,* p. 181.

152

being criminals who take responsibility for wrongdoing, everyone was being offered therapy. This involved a failure to recognize responsibility for our actions as an intrinsic part of our humanity. To treat criminals or sinners simply as those who need therapy arguably fails to take the full measure of human dignity. C. S. Lewis argued that to be cured against one's will is to be put on the level of those who have not attained the age of reason.[48] Alternatively there is the danger that those who hold minority views can be held to be in need of therapy. You think war (or the market) is wrong? My goodness, see the psychiatrist! For these reasons we need to retain the idea of human responsibility. I take it that Barth is not arguing that Christ's taking responsibility for us means that responsibility is no longer an issue. On the contrary, to free us from responsibility would mean cheap grace — the act of arbitrary kindness that Barth condemns. What it does mean is that we are freed from the burden of guilt and thus enabled to think about the future.

Maintaining the idea of responsibility is also important in the development of the paradigm shift of the past thirty years in Europe and North America in the course of which the victim rather than the criminal has become our model. In earlier ages, as I noted, the criminal was everyman. Today, everyone is a victim: of their upbringing, their society, their genes, their gender, their sexuality, their education, or perhaps of God. If I am a victim I am not to blame: others are to blame. When I go off the rails it is their fault. They are to blame. Ultimately, God is to blame. The theological task is then not a theology of reconciliation but of theodicy. This refusal of responsibility is one of the key marks of the degenerative disease of our culture, the regression to babyhood. We create, effectively, a culture in the nappy stage. Barth would obviously have nothing to do with such a culture.

The claim that the freedom to do evil is taken from us must, obviously, be a case of Barth's "impossible possibility." As Barth illustrates in his wonderful accounts of pride, sloth, and the lie, we do in fact continue to commit evil, but this is a failure to recognize our new situation. Barth preferred to talk of Satan as "hypostatised falsehood," but he recognized that "the ancient foe . . . still has space to resist the Word of reconciliation, to hinder its understanding, acceptance and appropriation on the part of man" — not least under the guise of a false the-

48. C. S. Lewis, "The Humanitarian Theory of Punishment," *Twentieth Century* (March 1949).

ology.[49] The possibility of our doing evil remains therefore but has to be understood to be "absolutely subject to God."[50]

Jesus' Death as the Death of Sinners

Under the third heading, Christ judged in our place, Barth focuses on the suffering and death of Christ. Why was it necessary for Christ to suffer and die? In what sense is the passion also an action? For all his enthusiasm for Anselm, it is interesting to see how chary he is about the arguments of *Cur Deus Homo* here.

> My turning from God is followed by God's annihilating turning from me. When it is resisted His love works itself out as death-dealing wrath. If Jesus Christ has followed our way as sinners to the end to which it leads . . . then we can say with [Isa. 53] that He has suffered this punishment of ours. But we must not make this a main concept as in some of the older presentations of the doctrine of the atonement (especially those which follow Anselm of Canterbury), either in the sense that by His suffering our punishment we are spared from suffering it ourselves, or that in so doing He "satisfied" or offered satisfaction to the wrath of God. The latter thought is quite foreign to the New Testament.[51]

The "decisive thing" is not that Christ has borne my punishment but that "in the suffering and death of Jesus Christ it has come to pass that in His own person He has made an end of us as sinners and therefore of sin itself by going to death as the One who took our place as sinners."[52] Christ does not die out of any desire for vengeance or retribution on the part of God "but because of the radical nature of the divine love, which could 'satisfy' itself . . . only by killing him, extinguishing him, removing him. . . . He has done that which is sufficient to take away sin, to restore order between Himself as the Creator and His creation, to bring the new man reconciled and therefore at peace with Him, to redeem man from death."[53]

49. *CD* IV/3.1, pp. 261, 260.
50. *CD* IV/3.1, p. 261.
51. *CD* IV/1, p. 253.
52. *CD* IV/1, p. 253.
53. *CD* IV/1, pp. 254-55.

As we see, Barth steers cautiously around the motif of punishment here, but he still believes that although the concept of punishment does not occur in the New Testament, "it cannot be completely rejected or evaded."[54] Although he is not very happy with the idea of satisfaction, he still finds that the radical nature of the divine love needs the death of Christ. Here it seems to me he does not sufficiently acknowledge the difficulties implicit in the idea of punishment. The prison authorities profess three objects, wrote George Bernard Shaw: "(a) retribution (a euphemism for vengeance), (b) deterrence (a euphemism for Terrorism), and (c) reform of the prisoner. They achieve the first by simple atrocity. They fail in the second. . . . The third (reform) is irreconcilable with the first (retribution)." He then went on: "A punishment system means a pardon system: the two go together inseparably. Once admit that if I do something wicked to you we are quits when you do something equally wicked to me, and you are bound to admit also that the two blacks make a white. Our criminal system is an organized attempt to produce white by two blacks."[55] We could read this as a comment on Luke 23:34, "Father, forgive them." What God does in Christ is confront the ideological justification of violence in retributivism. The cross, as Colossians says, makes a public spectacle — unmasks the bogus and self-righteous pretensions — of the principalities and powers, which include retributive justice. Christ stands in the dock, is judged by the powers that be, is found guilty and executed: nothing could more finally expose them. In this way God delivers us from bondage to self-righteous legalized violence. The cross is "our only hope" because it reveals that God, the origin and end of all things, is made known in reconciliation and not, as so many philosophies, both religious and secular, suppose, in violence. In putting an end to us as judges it puts an end to the self-righteousness that generates violence. This seems to me a more convincing way of understanding the New Testament reflection on the significance of Christ's death than maintaining a residual place for punishment. Barth effectively recognizes this in his dialogue with prison chaplains. Part of the rationale of retribution is that offenders pay their debt to society, atone for their crimes. Barth absolutely disallows this possibility. Under no circumstances is punishment about expiation — that is something Christ has done for

---

54. *CD* IV/1, p. 253.
55. Shaw, in Webb and Webb, *English Prisons,* p. liv.

us and which we cannot do for ourselves.[56] In his account of punishment as care, Barth is effectively outlining a nonalienating form of punishment of the type tried in Barlinnie jail in Scotland, where high-risk prisoners were part of a trust circle and had to explain their misdemeanors within the group to each other. One of them, Jimmy Boyle, at one time dubbed "the most dangerous man in Britain," who had experienced every kind of punishment including isolation and brutal beatings, described this process of giving account as the toughest punishment he had ever experienced. In his case it led to his reformation and release: he is now a noted sculptor. Something like this is what Barth clearly has in mind.

From the perspective of criminal justice it is possible to do something more creative with the idea of satisfaction than Barth actually does. This was the idea, which we find in the Exodus law codes, as well as in Saxon societies, of settling the differences between victim and offender by the making of compensation. Like mediation, its aim is reconciliation between victim and offender. To some extent it is a symbolic process by which the offender does what is necessary *(satis facit)* to be included once more in the community.[57] To understand this within the context of God's reconciling work, we need to extend our understanding, as Barth does, to the role of the community, the church. In reparation thinking, the victim of an offense stands for the whole community that is damaged by crime. Reparation allows the offender to "give something back to society" and at the same time allows the community to make reparation to those offenders who have started life under handicaps.[58] Barth cheerfully acknowledged that offenders could follow Zacchaeus in this making amends — provided it was not thought of as part of punishment.[59] Salvation, says Barth, is "a living redemptive happening which takes place."[60] It was accomplished once for all on Calvary, but "it would not be our salvation if it did not create

56. Barth, *Gespräche*, p. 66.

57. Willem de Haan, *The Politics of Redress: Crime, Punishment, and Penal Abolition* (London: Unwin Hyman, 1990).

58. The means by which amends can be made include direct reparation, community service, but also such things as attending a drug treatment or alcohol treatment program, or even undergoing plastic surgery and taking speech therapy to overcome self-image problems.

59. Barth, *Gespräche*, p. 76.

60. *CD* IV/2, p. 621.

and maintain and continually renew the provisional representation in which it is to-day."[61] The form in which the church exists "can and must be to the world of men around it a reminder of the law of the kingdom of God already set up on earth in Jesus Christ, and a promise of its future manifestation. *De facto,* whether they realise it or not, it can and should show them that there is already on earth an order which is based on that great alteration of the human situation and directed towards its manifestation."[62] This is close, it seems to me, to the arguments of an Anabaptist like Howard Zehr on the role of the church vis-à-vis criminal justice: that the church offers an alternative, inclusive space to that of a society that operates according to the scapegoat mechanism. Here we can acknowledge the light René Girard throws on the whole criminal justice process, which is deeply scapegoating and, to the extent that it is retributive, rests on a systematic failure to acknowledge human solidarity.

Jesus as the One Who Acted Justly

Finally, Christ is the one who has acted justly in our place. "In the free penitence of Jesus of Nazareth which began in Jordan when He entered on His way as Judge and was completed on the cross of Golgotha when He was judged — there took place the positive act concealed in His passion as the negative form of the divine action of reconciliation. In this penitence of His He 'fulfilled all righteousness' (Matt. 3:15)."[63] Moberly exploited this insight, drawing on the image of criminal justice. He anticipates Barth in teaching that it is Christ's repentance that teaches us the heinousness of sin. It is the objective fact that makes subjective repentance, and therefore redemption, possible. In this argument, Moberly was seeking to bring objective and subjective theories of the atonement together. Barth does something rather different. He turns to an exegesis of the temptations and of Gethsemane in which he argues that Jesus "renewed, confirmed and put into effect, His freedom to finish His work, to execute the divine judgment by undergoing it Himself, to punish the sin of the world by bearing it Himself, by taking

61. *CD* IV/2, p. 622.
62. *CD* IV/2, p. 721.
63. *CD* IV/1, p. 259.

it away from the world in His own person, in His death. The sin of the world was now laid upon Him. It was now true that in the series of many sinners He was the only One singled out by God to be its bearer and Representative, the only One that it could really touch and oppress and terrify."[64] "Anyone who really talks of the Trinity talks of the cross of Jesus, and does not speculate in heavenly riddles."[65] This word of Moltmann seems to me the proper exegesis of this section of Barth's. God takes upon Godself the forces of death, undergoes the limits to which the creature is subjected, and, in "the Verdict of the Father," offers hope to humankind. Henceforth, as the whole New Testament witnesses, death cannot really oppress and terrify us. At the same time Barth still finds the need to speak of punishment and of this punishment involving death. If this is really the case, I cannot see how we avoid the divine underwriting of retributive justice. Paul Ricoeur has some profound words here. For Christianity, he argues, the logic of punishment is a shattered myth, a ruin, a memorial that belongs to the epoch of the law: "But now, without the law, the justice of God is made manifest . . ." (Rom. 3:21).

> Thus the memorial is a transcended past, on which one can confer neither the status of an illusion, from which one would be delivered, without relapse, by a simple movement of demythologization at the service of our thought, nor that of an eternal law of truth, which would find in the atonement of the Just One its supreme confirmation. Punishment is more than an idol to break and less than a law to idolize. It is an economy which "marks an epoch" and which preaching retains in the memory of the Gospel. If the wrath of God no longer had any meaning for me, I would no longer understand what pardon and grace signify; but if the logic of punishment had its own meaning, if it were sufficient unto itself, it would be forever invincible as a law of being; the atonement of Christ would have to be inscribed within this logic, and this would be the greatest victory, because it occurs in the theologies of "vicarious satisfaction," which remain theologies of punishment and not of gift and grace.[66]

64. *CD* IV/1, pp. 271-72.

65. Jürgen Moltmann, *The Crucified God,* trans. R. A. Wilson and John Bowden (London: SCM, 1974), p. 207.

66. Ricoeur, *The Conflict of Interpretations,* p. 376.

If Ricoeur is right, and I believe he is, then a more truly biblical direction than insisting on a final need for punishment is to try to understand what reconciliation might mean concretely for the criminal justice system. What Barth outlines as the ethical implication of the atonement has implications for criminal justice. As noted earlier, he highlights peace as the heart of the good news.[67] Barth also insists that love of our enemies is the sign of the new order inaugurated by Christ. These emphases, in my judgment, would properly work themselves out in the field of criminal justice in terms of restorative justice, in terms of the restoration of *shalom*.

Further Reflections

James Gilligan analyzes criminal justice through the lens of the health care system where there is primary, secondary, and tertiary care.[68] He argues that restorative justice is still primarily concerned with tertiary care — what happens in accident and emergency, patching things up after breakdown. It still focuses on one event that now defines all that matters of right and wrong. It leaves out the past and the social causes of the event. Theologically speaking, many accounts of the atonement, including Barth's at this point, think of the death of Christ in terms of tertiary care. Primary care, on the other hand, wants to develop healthy patterns. It focuses on the whole of society. It seeks to transform relationships in ways that support social justice and equality. It begins with the causes of crime. If we take a passage like Ephesians 2:15 ("He has abolished the law with its commandments and ordinances, that he might create in himself one new humanity in place of the two, thus making peace"), it seems to me clear that the author is not speaking about some future state, the new creation, but about concrete social realities here and now. The author is talking about a peace, *shalom*, which is a partial realization of the kingdom. It is something we can pray for and therefore work for. The early Christian communities understood themselves as a new people of peace. Citing Micah's prophecy that swords will be beaten into plowshares, Justin Martyr (ca. 150) commented, "That has now come about." This had implications for dealing

67. *CD* IV/2, p. 197.
68. Gilligan, *Preventing Violence*.

with offenders as well, for, following Paul's example in the Corinthian correspondence, how these communities dealt with offenses within their ranks by what the Australian criminologist John Braithwaite calls "reintegrative shaming." The key question for any Christian reflection on criminal justice is what the command to love our enemies means. The love of enemies, I take it, is a way of breaking the spiral of violence, of responding to harm without doing harm in return. It is, as Moltmann has said, a true ethic of responsibility, a way of extending our responsibility to our enemies.[69] Restorative justice processes such as mediation and reparation, when successful, issue in forgiveness. In terms of criminal justice this is problematic because states and courts cannot forgive; only victims can. Forgiveness as such cannot be part of the criminal justice system. On the other hand, what we can have is a less adversarial legal culture that seeks to facilitate reconciliation and so forgiveness.

The recurring suspicion of forgiveness is that it means people get off "scot-free." But forgiveness does not mean condoning crime. Forgiveness, we want to say, is costly — certainly one of the things we learn from the passion story, as Barth insists. It involves a struggle with grief, loss, and anger. It is the overcoming of these things. "Father, forgive them" is one thing as the cry of a dying man. It is another thing as an automatic reflex. Christian faith cannot mean that it should be that. At the same time, according to the Gospels, forgiveness is not conditional. In the Gospels the story of Zacchaeus, the crooked tax collector who has systematically defrauded people for a lifetime and accrued a fortune in doing so, is a story of acceptance rather than forgiveness (for Jesus is not one of his victims, except insofar as he is a member of the taxpaying public), but it illustrates the way in which forgiveness works. It is by his acceptance that Jesus enables Zacchaeus's penitence, that he enables him to address his past and to "become a new person," which is to say, change his behavior in the future. Just so does forgiveness work.

Like every aspect of restorative justice, the practice of forgiveness can only be learned in community. To use the most overburdened word in the language, forgiveness presupposes love. Only love can forgive, because only love is fully receptive to who somebody is. "In Christian love," says Barth, "the loving subject gives to the other, the object of

---

69. Jürgen Moltmann, *The Way of Jesus Christ: Christology in Messianic Dimensions*, trans. Margaret Kohl (London: SCM, 1990), p. 13.

love, that which it has, which is its own, which belongs to it. It does so irrespective of the right or claim that it may have to it, or the further use that it might make of it."[70] Restorative justice presupposes a vision of a society where people really know and respond to one another, a community that does not operate by exclusion, that recognizes there are less and more truly human ways of dealing with people, that seeks better practices of dealing with violence, of dealing with crime, and that is therefore passionately committed to social justice. At the root of restorative justice, in other words, is a community committed to *shalom*. The Christian, writes Barth at the end of *CD* IV/2, "is no heaven-storming idealist. But his interest is in the *ens realissimum:* the cause of God on earth; . . . His cause which is not a cause but His work, His kingdom, and in His work and kingdom He Himself, the living God, the living Jesus."[71] Practically speaking, he argues, loving one's neighbor means "guaranteeing in his own person the fact that God loves him too, and that he too is free to love God."[72] This guarantee is impossible without forgiveness, by which the community lives, which is, in a way, the rule of the community. It is a crucial part of its witness to God's reconciling work, what it is God has done and is doing to make and to keep human beings human.

I have concentrated on the short section "The Judge Judged in Our Place," but I have tried to set this in the context of Barth's wider account of reconciliation, including especially his pneumatology and his doctrine of the church. Taken together with his dialogue with prison chaplains, it seems to me that these far-reaching reflections on the gospel of reconciliation give us grounds for the construction of a different and less alienating system of criminal justice.

70. *CD* IV/2, p. 733.
71. *CD* IV/2, p. 794.
72. *CD* IV/2, p. 820.

9. For Us and for Our Salvation:
A Response to Timothy Gorringe

Katherine Sonderegger

This past year the United States passed the doleful mark of two million citizens imprisoned. This mark exceeds dramatically the numbers imprisoned in any industrial and postindustrial society. The death penalty, now held to be a violation of human rights by the European Union, was reintroduced in the United States in 1976; last year, thirty-seven prisoners were executed by the state. More striking still is the number of U.S. citizens on probation or parole: some five million. The integration of former prisoners into society, long a testing problem of the prison system, has eluded our nation again and again. U.S. citizens return to prison frequently, for longer sentences still. Since 1980, the number of prisoners and probationers has increased steadily and dramatically, and there appears no end in sight. Both men's and women's imprisonment rates have risen; both state and federal prisons hold more and more prisoners each year.[1]

Since the terrorist attacks of September 2001, the United States has forged another whole category of prisoner, the "enemy combatant." Immured in U.S. territory offshore, these prisoners have been deemed yet more dangerous and "alien" — to borrow Gorringe's phrase — than domestic criminals. They have been secluded, shamed, and tortured, under protocols euphemistically termed "enhanced interrogation techniques." Until recently they have been denied the bedrock of judicial freedoms, *habeas corpus*. Guantanamo Bay has not been consid-

---

1. These statistics are taken from the United States Department of Justice, Bureau of Justice Statistics, http://www.ojp.usdoj.gov/bjs/cp.htm#findings.

ered sufficient for the imprisonment of this new class of offenders: Navy brigs, secret prisons across the globe, and United States–administered prisons in Iraq have held, interrogated, and at times beaten, shamed, and tortured these offenders, for more than five years. Journalist Mark Danner terms shocking facts of this sort "frozen scandals": we have all seen the photographs from Abu Ghraib; we have all heard the statistics of rising imprisonment; we have all heard reports from military investigators of the violation of Army and Geneva Convention protocols; and we have watched the execution of domestic prisoners march steadily on, despite mounting legal challenges and moral doubts — yet nothing changes, and no one is to blame.[2]

Little wonder that Timothy Gorringe considers English and U.S. cultures "deeply retributive," mean-spirited, and driven by anger and fear. It is manifest that these are moral and theological failures, and we are in Gorringe's debt for unflinchingly exposing and assessing them.

In two books, *God's Just Vengeance* and *Crime,* as well as our essay, "Crime, Punishment, and Atonement," Gorringe explores the historical and theological roots of social punishment and, most especially, of the invention of the prison, not as a way station to trial and penalty — that is our modern-day jail — but as an end in itself.[3] The prison, at its very heart, is a deprivation and hiding away of criminals, intended to punish or, in more generous ages, to perhaps correct the offender. Gorringe argues that the Christian doctrine of atonement generated and shaped a "structure of affect" in Christian lands that sought to *punish* criminals; to make them pay. Gorringe holds that Latin doctrines of the atonement provide the furniture of the Western, punitive mind in two ways: we cannot accept that forgiveness can be issued without first exacting a penalty — a little death — or death itself, and we identify punishment not with restoration or integration but rather with isolation and exclusion. These themes Gorringe traces to Anselm, though with several careful qualifications, and in the end to Reformed, Puritan theologies, which teach that Christ suffers on the cross the divine wrath against sin, and takes in our place the punishment that would be our lot.

2. Details of Guantanamo Bay prison, CIA secret renditions, Abu Ghraib, and other Iraqi prisons and the U.S. policy on torture — the "torture memos" — are contained in Mark Danner, *Torture and Truth* (New York: New York Review of Books, 2004).

3. Timothy Gorringe, *God's Just Vengeance: Crime, Violence, and the Rhetoric of Salvation* (Cambridge: Cambridge University Press, 1996); Timothy Gorringe, *Crime* (London: SPCK, 2004).

This doctrine, often styled the "penal substitutionary doctrine of atonement," forms the bedrock — the "structure of affect" — in English-speaking Protestantism; hence it is to England and the United States that Gorringe turns his spotlight. The U.S. thirst for imprisoning, seemingly unquenchable, corresponds, Gorringe argues, to the Calvinist relish for "sacred violence": the taking in and taking up of punishment into Christ's own person and work. In our essay, Gorringe frames his thesis more cautiously: "Tracing intellectual causality is always problematic, as the forty-year debate about Lyn White's claims regarding Christian responsibility for the ecological crisis shows."[4] Yet his underlying conviction remains constant: "[T]he Anselmian understanding of the atonement did influence Western structures of affect in a retributivist direction" (pp. 136-37).

Now, it might appear from this summary that Gorringe would oppose imprisonment, shaming, penalty, and punishment altogether. But not so. Gorringe's books are filled with examples of horrendous crimes, committed against persons — so called "street crime" — and against society as a whole — "white-collar crime." Gorringe thinks there may be some people who simply must be sequestered for the sake of society; some might be shamed publicly as penalty for crime; others might pay restitution; still others might be punished. In our essay Gorringe adduces the case of Jimmy Boyle, "the most dangerous man in Britain," who underwent a form of public shaming and punishment — recounting his crimes before fellow prisoners in the Barlinnie jail — and came out a changed man (p. 156). Here a "nonalienating form of punishment" aims at rehabilitation of the prisoner (p. 156). It may not be Gorringe's ideal response to crime, but it worked, and he is pragmatic enough to recognize a good practice in its fruits.

Gorringe is also surprisingly caustic about the growing British and U.S. attention to the victims of crime: "Today, everyone is a victim: of their upbringing, their society, their genes, their gender, their sexuality, their education, or perhaps of God. If I am a victim I am not to blame: others are to blame. . . . This refusal of responsibility is one of the key marks of the degenerative disease of our culture, the regression to babyhood." He concludes icily: "We create, effectively, a culture in

---

4. Timothy Gorringe, "Crime, Punishment, and Atonement: Karl Barth on the Death of Christ," p. 136 above. Hereafter, page numbers for Gorringe's essay are incorporated into the text.

the nappy stage" (p. 153). Hand in hand with this cold-eyed glance at crime victims is Gorringe's skepticism about the social roots of crime. In *Crime,* Gorringe notes the eagerness, from the nineteenth century onward, to find the cause of criminality in society itself: poverty and broken families and futility lie at the heart of crime. Not so, Gorringe says. The majority of working-class people are law abiding, he notes, and when wealth increases, crime rates do not fall. Indeed, the very notion of "white-collar crime" depends on wealth creating, not inhibiting, the impulse to defraud and harm. Gorringe concludes that crime is an enigma, a puzzle no single theory can capture or solve.[5] These complexities do not discourage Gorringe from proposing a radical reworking of our response to crime; far from it. They all lead to a proposal Gorringe and others have called "restorative justice."

In our essay, Gorringe describes restorative justice this way: "[C]rime is viewed primarily as a breakdown in relationships rather than as a breach of the law. Justice, in turn, is the restoration of relationship, something that cannot be decreed by statute but only decided by debate and negotiation" (p. 143). Gorringe cites the United Nations definition as a general summary of this movement: restorative justice is a "process in which the victim, the offender and/or any other individuals or community members affected by a crime actively participate together in the resolution of matters arising from the crime" (p. 143). Now, Gorringe finds the primary warrant for this form of response to crime in an alternative doctrine of atonement and a characterization of the kingdom of God as a community of healing, of peace, and of restoration. It is to these theological reconsiderations that this essay will shortly turn — but not without a quick glance at these formal definitions of restorative justice.

A Christian who examines this movement must be struck immediately by the arm's-length treatment of the law in this process of restoration. Gorringe deepens our suspicions by his skeptical tone in describing law courts, judges, and rulings. He writes, almost as an aside, in a longer section on Karl Barth: "[T]he emphasis on 'the majesty of the law,' underlined in Britain by a liturgy of wigs, gowns, ushers, contempt of court, and the absolute authority of the judge in court, though it has obvious sociological reasons, is theologically extremely questionable" (p. 149). Twinned with this ironic glance at judicial "lit-

5. Gorringe, *Crime,* chapter 4 (especially pp. 65-72).

urgy" is Gorringe's conviction that judges in ancient Israel — should they sit in the gate judging right — concerned themselves exclusively with defending the poor and powerless. Rendering verdicts impartially, assessing penalties according to code and precedent, prosecution and advocacy: all these, Gorringe says, are the legacy of modern law courts and prison systems. True justice emerges from the community — the "alternative, inclusive space" of the church, or the local gathering of offender and victims — as they deliberate, negotiate, and forgive. The love of one's enemies is the communal test of justice, Gorringe claims, and this, he observes, is not a matter of society or of law. Not surprisingly, Gorringe buttresses these comments on justice with a Pauline-style opposition to the law. He cites Ephesians 2:15 — long a centerpiece in theological antinomianism — to underscore the kingdom of God as an extra- or translegal community of peace. "[I]t seems to me clear," Gorringe says, "that the author [of Ephesians] is not speaking about some future state, the new creation, but about concrete social realities here and now. The author is talking about a peace, *shalom,* which is a partial realization of the kingdom" (p. 159). Christians have reason to be wary of such conclusions.

One reason is more topical and centers on a theological assessment of social justice. Recently a gathering of specialists in international law noted the danger posed to human rights, civil liberties, and the rule of law in the U.S. response to the 2001 terrorist attacks. The time has come, they urged, for the U.S. government and judiciary to suspend these infringements of constitutional protections: "We have been shocked by the damage done over the past seven years by excessive or abusive counterterrorism measures in a wide range of countries around the world," Arthur Chaskalson, a member of the International Commission of Jurists, said. "Many governments, ignoring the lessons of history, have allowed themselves to be rushed into hasty responses to terrorism that have undermined cherished values and violated human rights." Mary Robinson, a former president of Ireland, concluded, "Seven years after 9/11 it is time to take stock and to repeal abusive laws and policies enacted in recent years. . . . Human rights and international humanitarian law provide a strong and flexible framework to address terrorist threats."[6]

---

6. Kevin Sullivan, "Jurists Decry Loss of Rights; International Panel Says 'War on Terror' Has Diluted Principles," *Washington Post,* February 18, 2009, p. A8.

At the heart of the U.S. treatment of "enemy combatants," I believe, lies a conviction and a fear that the rule of law, from the Bill of Rights to the Geneva Convention, no longer applies in our day; "the gloves must come off." Of course, Gorringe finds the treatment of U.S. prisoners in Guantanamo Bay and Iraq abhorrent. Everything in his essays and books argues against such cruel punishment and torment. Yet we cannot overlook the *formal* similarities here. Those who have argued for suspension of constitutional rights and international conventions have relied on an underlying assumption that the *community* must decide the rules, not the law court, and those rules must alter as the situation alters, especially in the face of danger. Fear has dominated U.S. political and social culture, and the demand for security has driven leaders and citizens to find legal protections "quaint and antiquated" and the rule of law malleable — perhaps dispensable — in a world defined by terror. In my view the rule of law, and the respect for law, are the bedrocks of a human and humane society. There is no substitute for commandments, statutes, and precepts, and for the determination, from elite to the least, that these laws apply to all, in all cases, and that no one is above them. In my judgment Christians, who have particular instruction to protect, visit, and pray for prisoners "as though they were in prison themselves," have a heightened obligation to teach and honor the rule of law, and to advocate justice within a society governed by it.

But there is another reason to be wary of Gorringe's construal of restorative justice. We may well question his theological exegesis of the law of Israel and its place in Pauline soteriology. It will come as no surprise to students of the New Testament that the apostle Paul's attitude toward the Torah of Israel is delicate, complex, and deeply rooted in the Mosaic and prophetic books themselves. Yet Gorringe appears to favor a more schematic and polarized reading of Paul's account of law and gospel. Relying on Paul Ricoeur, Gorringe ties retributive punishment to the "epoch of the law" (p. 158). Romans 3:21 — "But now, apart from the law, the righteousness of God is revealed" — serves as the "Reformation verse," this time a reformation of justice from the "logic of punishment" into a theology of "gift and grace."[7] Now, to be sure, Gorringe is

---

7. Paul Ricouer, *The Conflict of Interpretations* (Evanston, Ill.: Northwestern University Press, 1974), p. 376 (cited by Gorringe in "Crime, Punishment, and Atonement," p. 158).

not offering a New Testament exegesis here, and we should not push too hard on his brief allusions to the apostle Paul. Yet Christians should pause before this instinctive reaching behind the law for a gospel of grace.

Reading across the Pauline corpus, we should rather say that the apostle found the Mosaic law good and salutary and God-given; it forms part of the glorious heritage of Israel, and marks out Jesus as well as Paul as "sons of the covenant." They are born under the law; they are not Gentile sinners. In a famous and much controverted verse, Paul declares that "Christ is the end [*telos*] of the Law" (Rom. 10:4). I believe we should read: Christ is the goal of the law, its summary, or to use theological idiom, its fulfillment, and for that reason the Apostle to the Gentiles stands himself "under the Law of Christ."

This is not the whole story on Paul's attitude toward Israel's law; of course, we must take into account Paul's willingness to speak of "curses" in the law, its occasions for sin, and the dangerous place of "works of the law" in the search for justification before God. But neither these sections nor Paul's powerful teachings on grace undermine the fundamental conviction that law itself is the good gift of Israel's God, and that obedience to temporal rulers manifests respect for God, from whom all authority flows. Indeed, Romans 13 itself combines a high doctrine of the "majesty of law" with a meditation on Israel's law as summed up and obeyed in the Levitical commandment to love the neighbor. Not in contradiction but rather in continuity with this meditation is Paul's concluding exhortation to "put on the Lord Jesus Christ, the armor of light" (Rom. 13:14), so that we should not be damned but be found as those who walk according to the light. Judgment, trial, and statute are far from being set aside, either in Israel — think of the Lord's prosecution of Israel in Isaiah — or in the apostle Paul. Rather, they are exemplified, obeyed, and fulfilled in Israel's deliverer, Jesus Christ, the righteousness of God from faith to faith.

And so we are brought to Jesus Christ, his person and atoning work. These are after all the heart of Gorringe's essay, the very heart of the Christian life. And here Gorringe turns explicitly to Karl Barth. In our essay Gorringe adds a note missing from *God's Just Vengeance:* the place of Karl Barth in the "Western structures of affect" that Gorringe spies behind our punitive courts and prisons (p. 137). Barth represents a kind of mixed genre for Gorringe. On one hand, Barth is an unmistakable Reformed theologian, a member of the theological movement that adopted and radicalized "Anselmian" atonement doctrine, transforming it into "penal substitutionary doctrine of atonement." Yet on the other hand, Barth hardly warms to Anselm's central argument in *Cur Deus Homo,* and more striking still, he underscores his solidarity with prisoners by his preaching in the Basel jail and teaching prison chaplains that all imprisonment should be a *"form of care (Fürsorge)"* (p. 136), all chaplaincy a witness to our redemption, sinners all, in Christ.

Barth's doctrine of atonement, especially as laid out in *CD* IV/1, "The Judge Judged in Our Place," represents for Gorringe a test case of the relation of "vicarious satisfaction" to the "theologies of punishment" — to borrow Ricoeur's language once again. Indeed, in the opening of his essay, Gorringe sets out his reading of Barth as a dilemma: "I am going to suggest that [Barth] nevertheless follows an unreconstructed understanding of punishment, one not in line with his understanding in his meeting with prison chaplains. Followed through consistently, this could have led to a different approach to offenders than the one we actually find, or alternatively he could have modified his account of the death of Christ" (p. 137). After a careful overview of Barth's larger doctrine of reconciliation and an attentive reading of prominent themes in §59.2, Gorringe concludes his essay on a milder note: "I have concentrated on the short section 'The Judge Judged in Our Place,' but I have tried to set this in the context of Barth's wider account of reconciliation, including especially his pneumatology and his doctrine of the church. Taken together with his dialogue with prison chaplains, it seems to me that these far-reaching reflections on the gospel of reconciliation give us grounds for the construction of a different and less alienating system of criminal justice" (p. 161). It may well be that Gorringe, like so many of us, finds Barth more attractive, complex, and in the end, more persuasive, the more we read and read closely the real grit of the *Church Dogmatics.* Again and again in his essay, Gorringe notes how Barth's particular doctrinal position holds great potential for transforming our treatment of crime and criminals. Yet the criticism remains. The heart of his objection, I believe, lies here: "Barth still finds the need to speak of punishment and of this punishment involving death. If this is really the case, I cannot see how we avoid the divine underwriting of retributive justice" (p. 158).

Against this threat of "sacred violence," Gorringe sets his own account of the passion of Jesus Christ. Taking Luke as his primary Gospel witness, Gorringe focuses on divine forgiveness as the heart of Christ's teaching, the heart of his death at the hands of a corrupt judiciary. He writes:

> What God does in Christ is confront the ideological justification of violence in retributivism. The cross, as Colossians says, makes a public spectacle — unmasks the bogus and self-righteous pretensions — of the principalities and powers, which include retributive justice. Christ stands in the dock, is judged by the powers that be, is found guilty and executed: nothing could more finally expose them. In this way God delivers us from bondage to self-righteous legalized violence. The cross is "our only hope" because it reveals that God, the origin and end of all things, is made known in reconciliation and not, as so many philosophies, both religious and secular, suppose, in violence. In putting an end to us as judges it puts an end to the self-righteousness that generates violence. (p. 155)

Now this is a doctrine of atonement that is broadly Socinian in character. In *God's Just Vengeance,* Gorringe defends the Socinian recasting of traditional atonement doctrine, a recasting that has long been rejected by descendants of the magisterial Reformers.[8] Gorringe is not much impressed by the traditional criticism of Socinianism, first voiced by Mosheim, as a bare rationalism, nor even less by the charge that it understands nothing of the gravity of sin. Still, Gorringe does allow that Socinus realizes nothing of the "vicariousness of all life," and it is this failure that "makes his theology seem thin and superficial."[9] But Gorringe is drawn to Socinianism for other reasons. He highlights Socinus's progressive social ethics against Grotius's punitive Calvinism in which "the purpose of religion is bound up with justifying the law-governed, and property-owning, community."[10] Indeed, a rehabilitated Socinus appears as the forerunner of restorative justice: "Socinianism, both in its roots in humanism and in Anabaptism, is opposed to the death penalty and wary of magistracy. As a 'vector' of tolerance (to use E. P. Thompson's term) it prepares the way both for Quakerism and for the Deist humanism of the following cen-

8. Gorringe, *God's Just Vengeance,* chapter 6 (especially pp. 142-55).
9. Gorringe, *God's Just Vengeance,* p. 146.
10. Gorringe, *God's Just Vengeance,* p. 154.

tury, which championed Montesquieu and Beccaria against those who believed in judicial severity."[11]

Central to Gorringe's defense of Socinianism — indeed, to the argument of the book as a whole — is the link Gorringe finds between an exemplarist doctrine of Christ's passion and a merciful and humane response to criminals and crime. The death of Christ properly exemplifies, shows, and shows forth a gracious love and pardon; it awakens in us a mercy toward others and instructs us on a peaceable society. Twinning Socinus's doctrine of the passion to Münzer's, Gorringe asks if "the question arises whether a *theology of life under the cross* does not take the place of a theology of satisfaction."[12] Gorringe's vision of Christ's death as the exposure of the cruelty and folly of retributive justice, and the revealing of God's sole and sovereign will for reconciliation, tells us clearly that the answer to his question is yes. Christ dies not to satisfy a wrong, still less to suffer a punishment prepared for others, but rather to judge and shame the rulers of this age, and teach those who live under the cross that such retribution must end; forgiveness is the new banner of the kingdom.

Against this vivid backdrop, Gorringe invites us to view Barth's atonement doctrine as all too Anselmian in character, bent on satisfaction, penalty, and vicarious death. He focuses our eyes on Barth's insistence that the sinner must die, the old self be put off, truly and permanently, and Christ alone stand as the One elected for rejection. Gorringe of course sees that Barth's atonement doctrine ranges over far greater territory than this, and he knows full well that Barth's deep instinct in the doctrine of reconciliation is one of expiation, not propitiation,[13] of Christ bearing and bearing away the sins of the world. Gorringe affirms Barth on this point: "Christ does not die out of any desire for vengeance or retribution on the part of God" (p. 154). He cites Barth approvingly: "We must not make this a main concept . . . of the doctrine of the atonement . . . [that] He 'satisfied' or offered satisfaction to the wrath of God. The latter thought is quite foreign to the New Testament."[14] Yet punishment, and more tellingly, punishment unto death, remains an indispensable element of Barth's account of the

11. Gorringe, *God's Just Vengeance,* p. 154.
12. Gorringe, *God's Just Vengeance,* p. 144.
13. If indeed that distinction itself holds water — Gorringe notes the difficulty conceptually and historically in separating the two in *God's Just Vengeance,* pp. 36-40.
14. *CD* IV/1, p. 253.

world's salvation: "It cannot be completely rejected or evaded."[15] Gorringe concludes that, for Barth, "the radical nature of the divine love needs the death of Christ" (p. 155). It is here that Gorringe sees most closely the Anselmian character of Barth's whole doctrine. Not *Cur Deus Homo* (Why did God become human?), but rather, Why did Christ die? That is the central question for Gorringe, the vital question that haunts him from the pages of the *Church Dogmatics*.

Barth answers simply, "for us and for our salvation." Now, despite Gorringe's extensive commentary on this "fourfold 'for us,'" in *CD* §59.2, he does not in my view express or accept the fundamental axiom on which this doctrine of representation rests. Barth holds — properly, I believe — that Christ's death is a *transaction,* an *event* in which God in Christ works our salvation, a passion that is the one true, lively, and vital action for the world's redemption. We have to do with God *(negotium cum Deo),* Calvin solemnly teaches in the *Institutes.*[16] But even more true is the proclamation that God has to do with us: he brings about in the death of the Beloved the liberation, atonement, pardon, and judgment that is the world's deliverance. That Christ's death is "sufficient in itself," that it needs no completion by a sinner's conversion or by a believer's response in a loving heart, is Barth's formal expression of a dogmatic truth that Christ's dying, in the act itself and by its own power, brings about a new state of human life, a new creation.[17] Of course, it also teaches and guides. But Christ's death takes our place in a visceral and dynamic sense: it crowds us out, as Barth says over and over; it replaces us and leaves us nowhere to stand. It brings it about that we sinners are now extinguished, annihilated, dead. The event of our judgment, the verdict against us, and white-hot purifying fire of God's No against sin: these are *realized* in the death of Christ, his going outside the city wall for us and for our sake.

Thus, for Barth, Christ's passion is an event that already includes all of us. And here, I think, we see the greatest divide between Barth's instincts in the doctrine of reconciliation and Gorringe's. For Gorringe the carrying out of Christ's work lies ahead of us all. We must proclaim and begin to live the community of *shalom,* to oppose cruelty and vio-

15. *CD* IV/1, p. 253.

16. Cf. John Calvin, *Institutes of the Christian Religion,* trans. Ford Lewis Battles, ed. John T. McNeill (Louisville: Westminster John Knox, 1960), p. 212 n. 2 (1.17.2; 3.3.6; 3.3.16; 3.7.2).

17. *CD* IV/1, p. 318.

lence, to restore and reconcile, to integrate sinners, remembering that we are sinners ourselves. We are all in this sense vicars, representatives; we all live for others, because so much has been given us. Of course, these themes are not absent in Barth. But they are radically reworked by the effective and gracious exchange that is atonement. For Barth — again, rightly so, I believe — the death of Christ must put an end to us: our ways are the paths of death and curse and wandering in a land that is waste. For just this reason Christ accepts the baptism of John and becomes the great penitent of the Bible. God pronounces death to the first sinners; Moses sets forth the way of life and the way of death; and the judgment of God rests upon us all in the representative Israel, "for all have sinned and fall short of the glory of God" (Rom. 3:23). This death must not be merely represented, though to be sure it is that. It must rather be carried out, exacted. And Christ does do that. The mercy of God is seen in this annihilating of the old self, the sinner. What is unjust, what is wrong, what is cruel and cold and malicious, what is against God and neighbor — this is removed, and removed effectively from the earth. Barth has no brief for an atonement doctrine that is merely "forensic." For all his judicial imagery, Barth rejects a doctrine that merely "declares" us righteous before God. No, Christ's obedience unto death *makes* it so. God's right over the creature has been vindicated; already in Christ our new obedience began. This is the justice only God can create, restore, and defend. For this reason it is a work of mercy. God is for us in just this sense: he does this work while we were dead in our sins.

Now, does this teach retribution? Is this atonement doctrine simply a new and stunning example of an old and punitive "structure of affect," one that sends more and more citizens to prison and torment and death? Have we learned meanness at the foot of the cross? Gorringe, I believe, would answer yes. But I believe strongly that our answer must be no. But of course, it is no easy thing to say why we should respond no, nor what warrants we can muster for such a response. Gorringe is quite right, I believe, to stress that "tracing intellectual causality is always problematic"; a fortiori with a doctrine that teaches our universal sinfulness, including our intellect and will. But we might point to two elements, one historical and one dogmatic, that might lend confidence to our support of Barth's doctrine of vicarious atonement.

One is simply the example of Barth himself. Far from representing the dilemma Gorringe sets out at his essay's opening, Barth rather exemplifies how Christ's atoning work, for us and in our place, properly gives rise to a Christian humanism; a solidarity in sin, but even more in grace. I believe a fuller study of the history of the church, and particularly of the saints, would yield many more exemplars of the merciful word of Christ's gracious death, to sinners, prisoners, criminals all. And the other, more dogmatic and so the more persuasive, is the record of Scripture itself.

The passion of Christ stands at the heart of the gospel, the good news of our salvation; the Gospels, the letters of the apostle Paul, and the revelation to John are unthinkable without the cross as the event of our deliverance, the gracious act of God for the unrighteous. The evangel is not about punishment or penalty or cruelty, but rather freedom and mercy and hope. But this is not because we have discovered a righteousness of our own — a new way of life, a new social order or practice — but rather because Christ has *become* our righteousness, by taking our sinful selves to himself and to his death, and in place of our death giving us life, his resurrection life, for us and for our salvation.

Timothy Gorringe has raised our sights from an abstract commitment to prisoners to a concrete wrestling with crime and sentencing, and even more, to the relationship of the death of Christ to our relish for punishment and incarceration. This is as it should be. Christ is the world's Lord; there is no dimension of worldly life that is not under his sway or remains untouched by his sovereign and unique work. To defend Barth's account of the atoning work of Christ is not to seal it off from its social effects; far from it. Rather, it is to underscore how the power, efficacy, and radicality of Christ's person and work remain his, and his alone. Only God can save: the force of this dogmatic truth can never be exhausted. God alone can assess — judge — the sin of the world, its cruelty, meanness, and heartlessness; God alone can take this sin to himself, not only to assume it but to break it, to consume and end it. The covenant with Israel, and through it, with the whole world, is sealed in Christ's blood not because a testimony has been given there about the travesty of injustice, but rather because in the lifeblood of the Son of Man, poured out for the many that day on Golgotha, a rupture had been broken open in the lawlessness of the world. Christ made there the turning point of the cosmos: the old burned up, consumed, and put away, the new enacted, given, bestowed. This is a perfect work. There is no repetition of it, no imitation or application of it that completes or realizes or carries forward this work. Christ's death cannot be "exemplarist" in this sense. Rather, the "curse" of the law, visited on transgression; the wrath against sin; the defense of the helpless sinner, plunging into the death that is godlessness — all this horror can be seen and borne and conquered by God alone, once, for all. This is why the doctrine of atonement is good news. Christ has taken our place, crowded us out, in the very darkness and death and cruelty that is our second nature. He alone stands there, the tortured criminal. And we, the prisoners of sin, are delivered, broken free, sent on our way. This is the new world Christ made that day. May we and the whole world live now as the liberated, for that is what we are.

10. Barth and the Economy of Grace

Kathryn Tanner

I

Barth in a 1949 article at the start of the Cold War, "The Church between East and West," famously advocated a "third way" between the two.[1] Rather than align himself as a Christian with one side or the other in a situation of escalating tensions between world powers, he eschewed blanket judgments of simple condemnation or praise for either side, offering instead more measured judgments of relative strengths and weaknesses, properly attentive to the good and bad on both sides. In keeping with Barth's repudiation of hidebound consistency to inflexible principle, a repudiation he thought necessary to respect the freedom of God's Word, the grounds for such a third way were situation-specific and pragmatic. The humanitarian goals of Soviet-style communism — a state dedicated in principle to the material well-being of all its citizens — might hold greater attractions for Christians than Western promotion of a laissez-faire, merely formal freedom — a sink-or-swim-at-your-own-risk-freedom of individual self-determination. But the often ruthlessly inhuman means taken in the East to further those humanitarian ends ruled out any strong Christian advocacy of the Soviet cause. To a church situated in the West, the strength of the West's opposition to the East on such grounds might seem obvious. But for that very reason Barth counseled churches there

1. Karl Barth, "The Church between East and West," in *Against the Stream: Shorter Post-war Writings, 1946-52,* ed. Ronald Gregor Smith (London: SCM, 1954).

to avoid simply swimming with the tide of Western sympathies. Doing so would merely confirm the self-righteous blindness of the West to the deficits of its own cause, and render hypocritical any call for churches in the East to keep an appropriate distance from their own Soviet-style states.

Were circumstances different, Barth implies, the search for a third way would be less urgent. It was proper for Christians to align themselves without significant reservation against National Socialism, for instance. Indeed, this sort of relatively unequivocal taking of sides in an already established conflict is appropriate, Barth suggests, against any movement like this where both goals and means are thoroughly inhuman and where opposition means swimming against the stream at significant cost and therefore hardly conveys sympathetic confirmation of self-righteously held popular sentiments. Barth clearly intends in this essay — and in other writings around the same time — to defend a significant circumstantial difference between cases, and in that way justify variation in the sort of stance that Christians should take toward political movements of their day: what held for National Socialism, in short, need not hold for the Eastern Bloc.

To the extent search for a third way means critical freedom of judgment vis-à-vis available social options, it is always, however, the appropriate stance for Christians to take — as so many of Barth's fundamental theological moves make clear from the time of his early reservations about religious socialism on. Upholding "a third way" in this sense simply signals the need to maintain a distinction between God's kingdom and any human claimant. God's kingdom, Barth reminds us, is found already complete in Christ, and therefore one needn't turn to the church or any trajectory of human history in search of it. And, though we are called to respond appropriately to that event in all our provisional, fallible, indeed sin-filled acts, its implications for us will be finally achieved in human history by Christ and not by us. Any social arrangement that we work for remains at its best a mere parable or analogy *(Gleichnis)* of the kingdom, having some correspondence *(Entsprechung)* to it, in virtue of what we must assume to be Christ's own lordly influence there, within a more fundamental, never expungeable relation of nonidentity. The third way represents in this respect the "third possibility" of neither *being* God's righteousness nor totally *unlike* it, insofar as human action is determined by the event of the achievement of the kingdom in Christ in ways human action can neither give itself nor escape.[2]

Understood along the lines I've been suggesting, Christian insistence on a third way becomes the constantly applicable rebuke to any power, human movement, or trajectory in the world purporting to be lordless, hoping, that is, to exempt itself from judgment in light of that history of God's dealings with the world that has its beginning and end in Christ. Upholding a third way means that no political or social movement can address us as an ineluctable absolute or inexorable fate. It is to say what Barth in *CD* IV/2 claims that church law ideally should say to those outside the church: "that worldly law, in the form in which they regard it as binding, and outside which they believe that they cannot know any other or regard any other as practicable, has already ceased to be the last word and cannot enjoy unlimited authority and force; that there are other possibilities, not merely in heaven but on earth, not merely one day but already, than those to which [the world] thinks that it must confine itself in the formation and administration of its law."[3]

If the third way amounts to this sort of exercise of free judgment with respect to every human way, the gospel itself in its claim on human life must be what instigates it, Barth is suggesting. It is because the gospel makes its own claim on human life that Christians are freed to judge every other claim in critical fashion. The effort to follow after, to correspond to the gospel's own claim on human life, would lie behind Christian independence from all extant proposals for the proper arrangement of human life, what stands in the way of identification of the Christian cause with any of them, and prevents the simple substitution of any such proposal for the content of the Christian cause.

In keeping with Barth's repudiation of a two-kingdoms doctrine as that works itself out in his understanding of the relation between law and gospel, the gospel of God's action with and for us in Christ cannot be viewed as leaving the world to any independently formulated law. The world is not left by Christ to its own devices apart from him. Instead, the gospel is itself a message about human action in proper correspondence with the history of God's actions with and for us as those actions have their beginning and end in Christ. It pro-

2. *CL*, p. 266.
3. *CD* IV/2, p. 721.

claims the good news that God in Christ has fulfilled this covenant of correspondence in action between God and us even on our side by taking our place in Christ, to be as we should be, the now for once faithful and obedient human partners of God. What God has asked of us, God has performed in Christ for us and apart from us, in a way that only on that basis comes to include us. Consequently, the law is always itself a word of grace — in its fulfillment by Christ as in its origination in God's unilateral decision to be in Christ a God in covenant with us. But the content of the gospel for all its graciousness, through and through, retains the form of law determining comprehensively the course of all further human action in conformity with it. One cannot therefore serve two masters — the law and Christ, the law some of the time, in the temporal sphere; Christ in spiritual matters in the time that remains — but only Christ in all that one does, whatever the sphere of that service.

> [T]he community of Jesus Christ has a very inadequate view of its Lord, the King of Israel who is also the King of the world, if it is not prepared to recognise that even world-occurrence outside takes place in His sphere and under His governance, or if it tries to imagine that in this occurrence we are concerned either with no God at all, or with another God, or with another will of the one God different from His gracious will demonstrated in Jesus Christ, and therefore with another kingdom on the left hand directed by God to another end and in another spirit.[4]

> The Lord of the [Christian] community . . . is also the Lord of world-occurrence generally. . . . Therefore in the latter case no less than the former the Christian can be obedient to Him. . . . [The] decision [in Christ] was made for all men and for the whole world, and therefore in the case of the Christian for the totality of his being in all its dimensions. This means that he is claimed [by Christ] not only in the religious sphere but also in the secular; not only in the spiritual but also in the physical; not only in the ecclesiastical, but also in the political and economic and academic and aesthetic.[5]

4. *CD* IV/3.2, p. 686.
5. *CD* III/3, p. 256.

II

Because the gospel takes the form of a law with this kind of comprehensive scope, Christians have a distinctive basis for political and social judgment in the good news of God's gracious being with and for humanity in Jesus Christ. They have their own place to stand when making judgments of the sort that everyone else must make — judgments about the proper course of action in political, economic, and social spheres. They have a third way that is their own way, as that 1949 article maintains[6] — the way of the gospel that includes a rule or order for human living in correspondence to the history of God's actions toward us.

For this reason Christians are never simply telling the world what it is already inclined to say. What indeed would be the point of that? "It is really not worth while repeating again in Christian terms what is being said *ad nauseam* in every newspaper in secular terms."[7] In virtue of its grounding in the gospel of Jesus Christ, there is indeed always something fundamentally revolutionary behind all the small reforms of those countermovements with which Christians, as full participants in the world, come to align themselves in ultimately provisional, conditional fashion. The basis for those alignments — the hope behind them, what they witness to — is the revolution of God, which is fundamentally and at its root the qualitative overturning of all this world's sinful schemes, a movement of God's light into our darkness, the ending of the old and the coming of the new beyond the old's powers and imaginings, the total revolution that no human party or movement can tell of or give itself.

In their confidence in God's own victory in Christ over the powers of this world, Barth never tires of telling us, Christians are freed for definite actions, their own small steps, concrete decisions that can lead them, at least on occasion, to side with one social or political movement over another. But even in this apparent coincidence with what others think and say, there should be a quite different dimension to their allegiances, one that comes out in their freedom to decide differently another day: "after a short external agreement with what is said by others it points away in what is for them a strange direction. For there is a great difference between the same secular matters as seen

6. Barth, "The Church," p. 132.
7. Barth, "The Church," p. 142.

from the standpoint of the kingdom of God and as seen from a supposedly inherent logic, metaphysics and ethics."[8]

When that difference is not apparent for some time, when, that is, Christians align themselves rather unambiguously with one movement or another in an extended struggle, as Barth says is their right in the appropriate circumstances, Christian freedom in relation to its political coalition partners becomes a function primarily of the properly Christian basis of their judgments. The Christian cause is never simply identical with a political or social movement, however close its alliance with it, because the grounds of that alliance remain Christ's actions with and for us. This lack of identity in the grounds of judgment is to be made clear in the irreversibility of the associations that Christians make between the kingdom and any particular social movement, such as socialism. Just as God is love does not mean love is God, God's kingdom may be the basis for a Christian identification of socialism with it without that implying that socialism on its own merits is to be identified with the kingdom.

This irreversibility is no more than assertion, however, unless one can materially show the way the gospel message suggests of itself something like socialism, unless one can demonstrate that the gospel contains within it definite direction of some sort or other for Christian political decision in particular circumstances. One has to turn one's attention to dogmatics, in short, as the starting point for distinctively Christian political judgments, if the claim of irreversibility is to hold water.

And this would seem to be at least one intent of the whole project of the *Church Dogmatics* after its aborted start:

> I am firmly convinced that, especially in the broad field of politics, we cannot reach the clarifications which are necessary to-day, and on which theology might have a word to say, as indeed it ought to have, without first reaching the comprehensive clarifications in and about theology which are our present concern. I believe that it is expected of the Church and its theology — a world within the world no less than chemistry or the theatre — that it should keep precisely to the rhythm of its own relevant concerns, and thus consider well what are the *real* needs of the day by which its own programme should be directed.[9]

8. *CD* III/4, p. 511.
9. *CD* I/1, p. xvi.

Only by proceeding in this way can one prove that Christianity offers on political questions anything more than "the secret power of giving to man the inward capacity to seek and attain the aims and purposes which he has independently chosen."[10] If the goals, content, and direction of human action are not to appear to be imported from elsewhere for simple Christian ratification, if they are not to seem to be based on an autonomous, and what Barth would judge to be sinful, estimation of our own about how to distinguish good from evil, right from wrong, then the substance of the Christian position on political questions has to be thoroughly grounded theologically.

III

And here is where I begin to part company with Barth. Barth does not seem to me to carry through on this project with sufficient rigor in keeping with his otherwise quite marked — and to me quite proper — Christocentrism. The gospel message is of much more direct social and political consequence than the ethical portions of the *Church Dogmatics,* at least as we have them, imply.

Take for example Barth's criticism of capitalism — economics in particular will be my focus in this essay. In the unfinished lectures in *CD* IV/4 where reconciliation in Christ is the direct matter for discussion, the criticism of capitalism remains almost entirely formal. Under the rubric of "Mammon" — "material possessions, property, and resources that have become the idol of man"[11] — capitalism is criticized as a lordless power that in its independence from judgment by Christ turns against the very human beings who have rendered it so, subjecting them now to its own absolute dominion irrespective of human ends. In the very attempt to be masters of their own fate apart from God, people find that the forces and powers they have unleashed turn unchecked against them. Unmastered by God, those forces and powers exalt themselves, as well, beyond the human; all human ends and purposes are subordinated to, dragged beneath, their heartless, unfettered sway. Criticism of capitalism along these lines — as an idol to which humans must bow down, an ineluctable fate of near demonic propor-

---

10. *CD* I/2, p. 336.
11. *CL,* p. 222.

tions — is, one should say, well taken. And perhaps today more than ever, given the apparent demise, since Barth's time, of state socialism as a viable economic option and the resurgence of capitalism in extreme neoliberal forms. Capitalism has become the lordless power par excellence in our day, by seemingly exhausting the field of economic possibility and by conforming to the neoliberal ideal of markets completely unconstrained by any governmental or social regulation that might subordinate their workings to the ends of human well-being. But this kind of critique remains purely formal in that it has nothing specifically to do with capitalism. Any power can — and will in a sinful world — become lordless in Barth's sense, and assume thereby a destructive capacity. Mammon is simply one example among others here. As a result we are given very little hint of what it is about capitalism, besides its lordlessness, that is particularly problematic, the features specific to capitalism that should fall under Christian rebuke. Were capitalism in particular to fall under the Lordship of Christ, what would happen to it?

It seems from *CD* IV/4 that it would simply lose its inhumanity. Lordless powers are "inhuman . . . powers . . . hostile to man. . . . They disrupt his life. . . . The lordship of these powers, which are all of them no more than exponents of the rebellion that separates man from God, is synonymous with the destruction and ruin of both the individual and society."[12] The material problem with capitalism, then, is that it is not *for* humanity in proper correspondence with the way Christ was. It does not have at its heart, as Christ did, the effort to "serve . . . the cause of man . . . his right and worth."[13] But if mere inhumanity is the charge, the "proper correspondence to Christ" violated here seems indistinguishable from what capitalism was said to violate in *CD* III/4: the basic form of humanity as a creature made for covenant with God in Christ, expressed paradigmatically in the human need to be with and for one's fellows. "[T]he unrighteousness of the fall of people from God . . . ineluctably carries with it their fall from one another, the changing of their being with one another, which corresponds to their being with God, into a general being without and against one another."[14] "Man's alienation from God [in the setting up of lordless powers] at once car-

12. *CL,* p. 233.
13. *CL,* p. 267.
14. *CL,* pp. 211-12.

ries with it his self-alienation: the denaturalizing of the humanity and fellow humanity of his own existence, the contradiction of the determination, inalienably given to him as God's creature."[15] And there is nothing specifically christological about that: the basic form of humanity put at risk here is merely the external presupposition within human life generally for the specific relations achieved in Christ with God and other human beings. The rule of Christ as reconciler, which Barth is supposed to be telling us about now, the kingdom of Christ's grace in particular, seems in this way to be collapsed in its wider import — beyond, that is, the sphere of the church, its proper worship and prayer, so much emphasized in *CD* IV/4 — into the rule of Christ as creator. As Christians we are to pray for God's own kingdom in Christ to come again, and not merely to pray but to act, in making our own little steps for relative improvements in the disordered world we live in.[16] However, Barth declines to tell us much of anything about that kingdom to come in its own specifications for human life, about what "the institution of [God's] perfect lordship in human relations and interconnections" might look like, the shape of its own "salutary order in human life and fellowship" as a directive for Christian witness on those fronts.[17] The kingdom of God to come as a kingdom on earth remains purely mysterious and incomprehensible in *CD* IV/4[18] — quite deliberately so — despite the fact that it has already come in Christ, in the new relationships between God and humanity and among human beings that have already been set up, achieved in him.

Moreover, in *CD* IV/4 no advance is made beyond what Barth already offered in *CD* III/4 in the critical treatment of capitalism's specific features on the grounds of inhumanity — if anything, the complaints are only vaguer. In *CD* III/4 we heard too about the inhumanity of an economic system that looks past humanity altogether in its self-propelling dynamism to amass and multiply possessions, a system that forces people, under threat of starvation, into work, however degrading or alienating, "in the service of a sinister and heartless and perpetually ambiguous idol."[19] But we also heard more specifically about how fundamentally competitive relations among workers and between employ-

---

15. *CL*, p. 213.
16. Cf. *CL*, p. 271.
17. *CL*, p. 212.
18. Cf. *CL*, pp. 237-38.
19. *CD* III/4, p. 532.

ers and employees might disturb the basic form of our fellow humanity in lives of pure "self-concentration and self-centredness," under the illusion of self-sufficiency rather than mutual need.[20] Remedied in *CD* III/4 is the vague generality of *CD* IV/4 where Barth limits his complaints to the fact that, under the reign of Mammon, "[a]s people are estranged from God, so they are from themselves and their neighbors, alienated from God and themselves and their fellows. As the powers tear apart the individual, so — because there are so many of them and in such competition — they tear apart society also."[21] Despite its basis in apparently free labor contracts, we hear in *CD* III/4 more specifically of Barth's suspicion of the way private ownership of the means of production enables employers to exploit the weakness of those desperate for work to extract more value out of them than they are paid.[22] Those wage workers, moreover, Barth tells us in this earlier volume, should not work to earn their daily bread in "abstract isolation" from others, but in "a social act involving association and comradeship."[23] "Fundamentally, we can work aright only when we work hand in hand. The nourishing bread to be gained from work can only be the bread broken and shared with the fellow-worker."[24] The vital claims of each for his or her daily bread must be coordinated with that of all others in ways that seem incompatible with competition with others for jobs or simple exclusive ownership of what one has earned. Inhuman, because in violation of our fellow humanity, is that competition based on contest in which "one aims to be better off than the other simply for the sake of being better off than the other," in which "[b]y doing better, he hopes to secure easier and ampler access to that for which the other also strives," where one works for one's "own advantage, and therefore inevitably to the disadvantage of the other and at the cost of the partial or even perhaps the total exclusion of the other from that which both desire."[25]

To make my criticism of Barth's efforts here even more pointed, I might suggest that these are the very same criticisms of capitalism he offered in his very early 1911 article, "Jesus Christ and the Movement for

20. *CD* III/4, p. 478.
21. *CL*, p. 233.
22. Cf. *CD* III/4, p. 542.
23. *CD* III/4, p. 537.
24. *CD* III/4, p. 537.
25. *CD* III/4, p. 540.

Social Justice."[26] They occur in the *Church Dogmatics,* it's true, without the easy equation of socialism with the kingdom to be found in that article, but also without any obviously better theological foundation for them either. If anything, the earlier article more clearly bases its judgments directly on the gospel — ironically enough. For example, quoting a socialist who maintains that "the real original sin . . . is self-seeking . . . that bourgeois society depends upon the self-seeking distinction between 'mine' and 'yours,' on the social war, on competition, on the defraudation and exploitation of the one by the other," Barth can venture to say, yes, "Jesus' view of property is this: [private] property is sin, because property is self-seeking. What's mine is absolutely not mine!"[27]

IV

A major unanswered question to pose to the *Church Dogmatics* is then this: Can one criticize the competitive features of capitalism, which Barth singles out, on more highly developed theological grounds with a specifically christological focus? I believe one can do that without great difficulty, and that Barth himself might have done so, if he had moved from capitalism's violation of fellow feeling, moved from the external basis and circumference of God's work in Christ — which is fine as far as it goes — to the central meaning of God's work in Christ himself: "'God with us' at the heart of the Christian message . . . means the redemptive grace of God. It is this which constitutes, factually, the singularity of the event [and] marks [it] out [from] within the whole history of the togetherness of God and man, [from] the creating, preserving and over-ruling of created being, . . . God gives to created being what can only be given to it and what can be given only by Him . . . : Take what is mine — this final, supreme, unsurpassable gift; take it, it is meant for you."[28] How might the dogmatic heart of Barth's theological outlook, as expressed here, have been developed in its socioeconomic implications? Doesn't it have some rather obvious ones — in line spe-

26. Karl Barth, "Jesus Christ and the Movement for Social Justice," in *Karl Barth and Radical Politics,* ed. and trans. George Hunsinger (Philadelphia: Westminster, 1976), pp. 19-37.

27. Barth, "Jesus Christ," p. 32.

28. *CD* IV/1, pp. 8-9.

cifically with that early 1911 article's attack on private property and simple self-seeking?

I'm not Barthian enough to want to do this along strictly Barthian lines, so I'll do it on my own terms as a theologian. But the bottom line will be the same: God's relations with us as those have their beginning and end in Christ contain in themselves a critique of competitive relations. They point in and of themselves to an otherwise unimaginable reworking of the noncompetitive relations of mere fellow humanity, which Barth seems unable to move beyond; they must do so just because, as Barth says, grace in Christ is so much more than mere creation or preservation or overruling in world history generally.

If the beginning and end of all God's ways is Christ, then one can say that in and through the whole history of God's relations with us, as that history spans creation through redemption, God intends to give us the good of God's own life, a good that God is and remains even as we are to come to enjoy it. In Christ God comes into quite intimate relationship with us, to take on our very humanity as God's own, in order to give us what we cannot give ourselves, God's own very life in all its unaltered goodness in so doing. This is the point and culminating moment of all God's ways with us. If so — if this is what is achieved in Christ and it is the key to our entire history with God — then lodged within the whole compass of Christian dogmatic concepts, I'd like to argue, is a very odd account of relations between owning and enjoyment by others — an alternative noncompetitive economy of sorts, brought to its completion in Christ. When we are incorporated into this economy of God's dealings with us in and through Christ, human fellowship as we know it should be thoroughly reworked in the process, in unexpected fashion.

What is odd about the relations between owning and enjoyment in the Christian story of God's relations with us as they have their beginning and end in Christ is that competition in property and possession seems absent. Something can be one party's property at the same time as it is another's; having something in one's possession for one's own use need not lessen the degree to which it is enjoyed by others.

In God's relations with the world, what is provided to others remains one's own property and possession because property relations here are not in any usual sense exchanges or transfers. Unlike goods that are bartered, traded, or sold, unlike even pure gifts on a contemporary Western understanding of that, goods in this history are not being alienated, taken out of the possession of one party and handed over to others, in ways that make them no longer the property of the first. Nor, as in loans, do goods remain one's property while being transferred out of one's possession for use by others. And the degree to which one enjoys the use of them is not lessened by one's giving others the use of them. Nothing is transferred, as if these gifts involved the moving of material goods from one site to another; therefore one can retain full possession of one's own property in providing others with it.

One sees this lack of competitive exchange or transfer, for example, in God's creating of us. The conditions for competitive transfer are lacking for very peculiar reasons here. There is nothing to us, prior to God's creating of us, to receive such a transfer of possession or delivery of property. We as a whole are the gift, rather than being the gift's already existing recipients. And in creating us, God is not portioning out or alienating God's own property to us, but originating from the ground up, out of nothing, a distinctly created, nondivine version or reflection of the goodness that God retains in full.

But the usual theological reason for the absence of competitive sorts of transfers or exchanges (the reason that underlies even their absence when God creates us) is that there is no need for competitive sorts of transfers or exchanges. What one has becomes the other's own, without the need for any transfer that would lessen one's ownership or possession of it, because of a closeness in relationship to that other. Others are attached to or one with you, and you to them. And therefore what you have becomes theirs, and what they have becomes yours. As the father says in the parable of the prodigal son: "Son, you are always with me, and [therefore] all that is mine is yours" (Luke 15:31).

One can think of this "with" — "you are always with me" — in either a physical or a personal/moral sense; the terms at issue here — "closeness," "attached to," "one with," etc. — have multiple associations in that way. Think, first of all, of a physical analogy — say, a lit blowtorch set next to a lead pipe. In virtue of their physical closeness, the pipe gains the basic properties of the flame — it becomes hot, it glows — without the flame's loss of them — the flame still burns, for example, at the same degree Fahrenheit. Or, in the second place, think of a closeness of personal identification or intense political solidarity, which needn't have anything to do with physical proximity. In that case, the sufferings or doings of others might also be felt as one's own;

what happens to others or what they do becomes a part of one's own story as well. Or think of a close moral or legal relationship: crimes that others carry out might be attributed to you, they become your own in a legal or moral sense that obligates your making restitution for them too, in virtue of your identification, your close association, with the group that committed them.

Analogies of both personal and physical closeness like this figure heavily in theological cases of noncompetitive property and possession. The persons of the Trinity share all the qualities that make God God because there is no separation in their relationships with one another. Their relationship is so close that it is like three overlapping suns, burning together indissolubly. What the first person of the Trinity has the second and third also have, because in all of them the very same thing is found repeated in different modes. The persons of the Trinity therefore are only offering to one another what they have and hold in common.

Similarly on christological topics which are at the heart of the Christian story of these odd property relations: in Jesus, what humanity has becomes the Word's own and the reverse. This time not because the very same concrete thing is found repeated in both in different ways (as in the Trinity) but because the Word assumes to itself, unites with, becomes one with what is so very different from itself — the humanity of Jesus suffering under the sins of the world. In virtue of the Word's identification with the humanity of Jesus, the Word acquires all the property of that humanity, appropriates it, so to speak; it now belongs to the Word as much as it belongs to that humanity. All that the humanity of Jesus accumulates over the course of his life — all that accrues to the humanity of Jesus in virtue of what he does and suffers — one can also now say that the Word does and suffers. Because all that happens to that humanity is in this way its shared or common property, the Word is able to give the gifts of its own property to that humanity. For example, the immortality that the Word continues to enjoy is given to that suffering humanity of Jesus so as to raise it up, resurrected and healed. To summarize what is going on here in a kind of Pauline way, taking off from 2 Corinthians 8:9: by becoming one with us in Christ, the Word, while remaining rich, acquires our poverty and neediness, just for the purpose of giving to us thereby what we as mere creatures do not have or own by nature — the very riches of God's own life, its holiness and incorruptibility.

V

Just as these relations of noncompetitive property and possession take a different shape or mode depending on whether the Trinity or Jesus is under discussion, so will they assume a distinctive form in relations among human persons, as human relations are made to conform to Christ, in and through him. Extending the relations between humanity and divinity in Christ into human relations in an appropriately distinctive way, one might say the following. In contrast to the relationship in Christ between a divine Word that is absolutely rich and a humanity ever poor in what divinity has to offer, in human society everyone is bound to be only relatively rich in some respects and relatively poor in others. The roles of giver and recipient could therefore properly shift back and forth (you'd have at least a two-way street here) depending upon the particular goods of human life involved; one would be talking in that case about persons establishing relationships of common property for the purpose of their *mutual* fulfillment in community. And, unlike the case of the unsurpassable good of Jesus' own divinity, the goodness of the gifts in human relations could presumably grow as what everyone does with them for their own good is shared among givers and receivers: gifts are enhanced as they are used by others for their own good and thereby enrich the givers; my enjoyment of what I have and give to others grows as theirs does. But the basic shape that noncompetitive property and possession takes in the relation between humanity and divinity in Christ would still hold here in relations among human persons. Identifying with others in a joint pursuit of universal benefit, those who are rich (in certain respects) should make the poverty of others (in those same respects) their own property; they should consider the poverty that others suffer to be something that is happening to them. The point of so closely identifying with others in their poverty is just to make, in turn, the good things one richly has the property of those poor in them, so as to alleviate their poverty. The lives of the poor are to be materially transformed by their being able to draw upon, as their very own property, what one continues to enjoy. The result is the possession and enjoyment of the very same goods in common: what we have for our own good is also the property of others from which they too benefit. We all benefit from the same things at the same time with the same right; the goods are at that point no more mine than yours.

More like the case of the Trinity than the case of Christ, in non-competitive property and possession among humans the goods that are the natural properties of the providers are also natural to the recipients, since all the parties are human. But the greater similarity remains here, not with the Trinity, but with relations between humanity and divinity in Christ, with the way God relates to us for our benefit in Christ. Like what happens in Christ, one is to take to oneself what is different from oneself, one is to make one's own, for example, those lacking what one has, for the specific purpose of alleviating their need. One makes a gift to them only if they don't already have what one is offering to them, in contrast to what happens in the case of gift giving within the Trinity. There, in the Trinity, one person makes a gift to the others in the sense of its being superfluous to them, something they don't need, a kind of redundancy. One doesn't have in human relations that self-sufficient communing of same with same that the common property of the Trinity suggests. Instead, when one gives, one has everything to do with what is unlike oneself — those who are not in one's own circumstances, not in one's same economic class or social bracket. Gift relations are not established with those who already have what you have in virtue of similar customs, a shared corporate group, family allegiance, or national affiliation, and so on; but with those who don't. As a provider of goods one identifies oneself very closely with all those one would not naturally resonate with or feel sympathy for because of their cultural and social differences from one.

To get a little better sense of what noncompetitive property and possession might be all about here, let's come at the idea from the other way around, from the side of the recipients of goods rather than from the side of providers. We have what we have only in a relationship with those who are providing it to us, and therefore our property is always theirs too; having those things for one's own does not make them less the property and possessions of these others. This is true of what creatures have from God. Creatures have their own existence and qualities, it is true, as a kind of exclusive property in that what they have is natural to them and not to God: what they have is proper to them, for example, insofar as they are finite, and God is not finite. But all this property, which is ours as creatures in this very strong sense, is never simply ours in that it remains inseparable from God's giving of it. God's provision is never a finished fact, with an end product that goes its own way, giving completed in the given. Instead, we remain constantly dependent upon God for all that we are and have as creatures. We exist and have what we have as creatures only as God continues to hold all this up into existence, so to speak, only to the extent that God continues to give us all those things. In a new twist on the same non-competitive relations, we genuinely have the gift of eternal life in Christ — it is ours to enjoy — but not in and of ourselves as some kind of new "supernatural" human property that we have acquired for ourselves. Eternal life, as a divine property, just cannot become a natural property of human beings in that way. We have eternal life only insofar as we are one with Christ, in a close relationship with him that allows us to draw upon what is proper to Christ as the divine Word incarnate. In sum, our coming to be and to act independently of God is never the ground of our becoming ourselves and making things our own. We are our own and have for our own only as both what we are and have remain God's own.

On this noncompetitive understanding of things, being ourselves as the persons we are and having all that we have for our own good should not come, then, at the expense of our being our fellows' own in community. Word and Spirit are themselves, and are replete in their own fullness, just because they are the Word and Spirit of the first person of the Trinity. We are ourselves, and have all that we have for the good as creatures, just to the extent we continue to be God's creatures, ever receiving from the Father's hands of Word and Spirit. What the humanity of Jesus has, beyond its created capacities, is its own only as the Word makes that humanity the Word's own by assuming it to itself. What we have in Christ for our perfection and elevation becomes our own only as we are Christ's own. Following the same noncompetitive trajectory into human relations, our lives as individuals should be constituted and enhanced in their goodness as we share our lives with others in community, identifying ourselves thereby as persons in community with others and not simply as persons for ourselves. We perfect one another in community as our efforts to make the most of our own gifts and talents enter into and supplement the similar efforts of others in a combined venture for goods otherwise impossible.

One's sense of self should be expanded in the process beyond anything simply one's own. One includes others, incorporates them, so to speak, within one's sense of self (which doesn't mean confusing them with oneself — any more than God and the human are to be confused in Christ). One does so out of a recognition that the life one lives is essentially constituted by relations with others, to one's own benefit. One thereby comes to identify with others in the way that noncompetitive forms of property and possession require from providers. Knowing that we have ourselves as gifts from God and from all those others in whom we are in a community of mutual benefit, we now give to others, rather than withhold from them, rather than hold what we have simply as our own.

VI

Now what I have just described conforms, I think, to what Barth recommends: a Christ-centered dogmatic foundation for ethics. The gracious dealings of God with us as they center in Christ amount to a gospel with the form and fashion of a law claiming human beings in their free agency as social beings. As Barth recommends, so here:

> The one Word of God which is the revelation and work of His grace is also Law. That is, it is a prior decision concerning man's self-determination. It is the claiming of his freedom. It regulates and judges the use that is made of this freedom. As the one Word of God, which is the revelation and work of His grace, disposes of man, it is also the impulse directing him to a future that is in keeping with this "disposing." As the one Word of God which is the revelation and work of His grace reaches us, its aim is that our being and action should be conformed to His.[29]

But in my proposal, in contrast to Barth's own procedure in the *Church Dogmatics,* the direction offered to human living remains fully integrated in the gospel message of God's gracious dealings with us as they center in Christ; the question of the proper ordering of human life is taken up only as part of that story, as that story itself suggests the proper lines for considering the question of human life together. The basis for judgment here — the starting point and foundation of theological judgment concerning human life — is no longer the basic form of humanity, humanity itself, as that might be considered on its own, in at least relative abstraction from the specific shape of God's dealings

29. *CD* II/2, pp. 511-12.

with and for us as they have their beginning and end in Christ. Barth's reservations about general anthropology as the basis for such judgments now extend — I think appropriately — to theological anthropology, at least as a subject matter with implications of its own for human life that one might explore in relative independence of God's claim on us in Christ. That anthropology has its place, but now quite clearly it has second place.

God's dealings with us are certainly of revolutionary import here; they would involve the transformation of human association, root and branch, in ways we could not have expected on the basis of our own experience and suppositions regarding economic life. The final import of God's dealings for us — if we were really to follow their shape — seems nearly unimaginable. What economic system could this possibly be in which, for example, property is shared in such utterly noncompetitive ways?

And yet we are given some definite direction about the new character of human life to come in Christ, in ways that don't simply leave the question of application up to us. Direction is given *to* us, as I hope I have shown, by the specificity of the very treatment of the history of God's dealings with us as they have their beginning and end in Christ. Those ways of God, with the same quite definite form, differentiate themselves across the span of their operation — in God's own life, in creation, covenant, redemption in Christ — depending on the way we are made a part of them. They make, in short, their own application to us in and through Christ. It is, indeed, hard to see how God's kingdom could provide any direction of its own as the mere mystery it remains in *CD* IV/4. The fact that the character of God's own dealings with us is rendered concrete in the story I have given does not mean it must fall into our hands, as Barth fears, to become "a tolerably well-known magnitude, a sum of dogmas, forms of life, ideals and hopes" that the church might consider "an object" to be "surveyed and . . . weighed against the demands of the general spiritual or other situation of a given age, translated into the language and concepts and philosophy and practical notions of this age, and both critically and positively interpreted, reduced, explained, deepened and applied . . . [in] complete freedom in this respect, namely, [by] a cheerful . . . application of the well-known text, a critical reworking and handling of the well-known object."[30] Rather

30. *CD* IV/3.2, p. 818.

than leaving us with the task of producing something analogous or like it in our own lives through some process of freely self-empowered imitation, on my way of telling, God's way of dealing with us in Christ includes us and therefore naturally extends its sway over us; it makes its own application to us by continuing to incorporate us, in all the specificity of our particular situations, within it. That whole ongoing process, which I have tried to trace, far from being some dead repetitive system under our own control in its very predictability, is the situation-specific event of application of God's kingdom brought about by God himself in ways uncontrollable by us. As Barth suggests, God draws near to us in Christ and incorporates us in all our active agency within that history; it is this very action of Christ that brings about a correspondence in action on our part to it.[31] Drawing out the implications of this in a way Barth doesn't quite, one could say: what we then do in any such corresponding form of action neither is God's kingdom nor simply unlike it — in short, a mere parable or analogy of God's kingdom — because what we do *is* God's kingdom in Christ properly *altered* as it extends itself to include our ongoing lives.

However clear the directives we are given on economic matters, they nevertheless remain unidentifiable with any extant economic claimant of the day. We have here I think a genuinely third way between available economic options — between, say, capitalism and state socialism. In the first place this is so because these economic directives have a distinctively Christian basis. But this independence of foundation also becomes manifest in clear material differences from other economic options. Because it espouses a fundamentally noncompetitive vision of relationships, this third way is certainly not capitalistic. Exclusive property rights and getting ahead at the expense of others — the fundamentals of capitalism — fall under opprobrium. Because it proposes a community dedicated to the good of all its members, and a more corporate sense of self, this third way might seem quite close to socialism in its basic presuppositions about individual and social life. But more is at stake here than simple cooperative effort for the sake of mutually enjoyed profits — the root of socialism.

No more in human life than in the relations of God with us is a distinction between competitive and cooperative forms of existence ultimate. God doesn't compete with us if God gives us all that we are. But

31. Cf. *CD* IV/3.1, pp. 183-84, 190-91, 193, 220.

for the same reason, God doesn't cooperate with us either. We don't each do our little bit in some joint venture for ends neither of us could achieve alone. God doesn't just do God's own part but in some strong sense — as that is realized to the utmost in Christ — gives us what is asked of us. What we think of as competition and cooperation are both, then, competitive from a theological standpoint in that they both involve a kind of inverse proportion between the achievements of the partners to relationship: the more the one has or does, the less the other has or does.

To see the parallel for human economies — why the difference between competitive and cooperative isn't ultimate there either — it is important to understand the way in which ownership and simple fairness in the distribution of a given pie are not the crucial matters for this third, Christian-grounded, economic way. What matters instead of ownership is equal access and enjoyment. The distinction between private and common ownership that divides capitalism from state socialism is thereby rendered moot; free use makes the question of private or state ownership irrelevant in this third way. Even socialism is dependent on partitive forms of distribution that are competitive at bottom: the more there is for me, the less there is for you; we'll only be all satisfied if there is enough to go around. Excess capacity and profits are therefore the prerequisites for society-wide opportunity and fulfillment under socialism. Competitive conditions of scarcity are its underlying limit too; it therefore hardly escapes what capitalism makes the inevitable fact of economic relations even in times of plenty — I'll get what's mine at your expense. In the third way, to the contrary, the very same things are enjoyed equally by all; whatever there is, in whatever amount, all take a full share.

Both points about ownership and partitive distribution can be understood better once one sees the odd parallel between our third way and the economic category of public goods. A public good is something that, if one person benefits from it, everyone can. And this generally means it is not possible to charge for access to it. A lighthouse is an example; one cannot limit the boats that enjoy its benefits to those willing to pay for the help they receive. This fact of free, unfettered access is what makes the ownership question moot. The state might own the lighthouse — if the economic system is socialistic. Or it might be privately owned, under a capitalist regime. Who owns the lighthouse is irrelevant when enjoyment is unrestricted. The lighthouse is as much mine as yours on the only matter that counts: enjoyment of the benefits of it. The ultimacy of the distinction between capitalism and socialism — at least as that is based on the importance of the difference between privately and commonly owned property — is in this way undercut.

Public goods are also not enjoyed by partition or division, and for this reason they are not subject to the scarcity concerns that make economies competitive either explicitly in the case of capitalism or implicitly in the case of socialism. Public goods are not divided up as they are appropriated by individuals, and therefore are not progressively depleted as more and more people take their share. It is the whole of the good that everyone enjoys in the case of a public good such as a lighthouse; there is the same amount to go around no matter how many people partake of it. Everyone is able to use a public good, it seems, without using it up.

Indeed, public goods are simply not individually appropriable in any way that might mean the exclusion of others from what one enjoys oneself. My enjoying of the whole — say, the entire arc of illumination thrown by a lighthouse onto the sea — doesn't prevent your enjoying it at the same time. Instead we all benefit from the very same thing at the very same time. My use of a public good therefore does not rule out yours in the way private ownership by definition excludes others from use of what one owns oneself. But surpassed too is the way individual use of commonly owned property is also necessarily exclusive: the state might own the tractor but when I'm on it, you're not. In a way that neither capitalist nor socialist economies make much of, use by one person of a public good does not diminish to any degree the amount of that good available for others' use. In accord, then, with a theological affirmation of noncompetitiveness in relationships, in the case of a public good one need never be in the position of having to benefit at the expense of others nor need they ever benefit at your expense.

What an entire economy organized along these same lines might look like remains unimaginable. But the real world example of public goods makes clear that a Christian account of grace has no exclusive monopoly on the hope for it. Given the commonplace fact of public goods — what could be more ordinary, even quaint, than the building of a lighthouse? — the specifically Christian hope for noncompetitive relations is not simply a pipe dream for the fellow humanity we share with all others.

11. Karl Barth on the Economy: In Dialogue with Kathryn Tanner

Christopher R. J. Holmes

I

To think *theologically* about late modern economic arrangements and to describe the extent to which they are held captive by the powers of sin and death is no easy thing. This is so precisely because the temptation is ever present to proceed toward a theological articulation of the economy and to proscribe ways in which it can be rendered more humane in a fashion that is utterly inattentive to the gift economy of the triune God. Much of modern theology sets a poor example for us by working with the assumption that the God of the gospel is *not* prophetically present and at work in Word and Spirit in relation to our current economic arrangements, calling the Christian community to become participant in his work of humanizing them. Fortunately, however, such an incipient naturalism that fails to take seriously God's economy is challenged in the thought of the most important Protestant theologian of the twentieth century, Karl Barth, and in the work of one of the most creative and rigorous theological voices to have emerged in English-language theology of the early twenty-first century, namely, that of the University of Chicago theologian Kathryn Tanner.

The task of this paper is to describe the ways in which Barth's basic dogmatic vision funds an account of the economy that is deeply informed by the redemptive activity of the triune God as it impinges on all forms of human economic arrangements. To do so I will proceed in the following twofold manner. *First,* I will rehearse Tanner's reading of Barth on the economy, attending to the points at which she is appreciative of Barth, and why at other points she finds it necessary to move beyond Barth — namely, because of Barth's formalism. Tanner is a premier conversation partner in the exploration of Barth on the economy, not only because she has carefully written on Barth and the economy and is generally appreciative of and sensitive to his concerns, but also because her criticisms of Barth help his readers to better appreciate his own determination to map all our actualities in relationship to the one reality, the covenant of grace that finds its center in Jesus Christ. *Second,* having noted why Tanner thinks it necessary to move with and *beyond* Barth, the paper will identify the ways in which Tanner's insightful criticisms help us to better appreciate Barth's own sense of the concreteness of God's economy. Her criticisms clarify why Barth is so allergic toward the positing of the kinds of applicatory principles that Tanner deems necessary if the divine economy is to be given concrete specification in the human economy.

My contention, then, is that Barth understood the rule of God as possessing inherent practical significance and therefore does not need to be further specified by a series of principles or programs, whether that be in the social, political, or economic sphere. Jesus Christ's proclamation and enactment of the rule of God is concrete in and of itself, argues Barth; concreteness is indeed ingredient in it. Exploration of the character of that concreteness as it impinges upon the economy will be the paper's concern.

II

It is necessary to begin the fulfillment of this twofold purpose by surveying Tanner's constructive proposals, most especially as they come to the fore in her book *Economy of Grace* and in her essay "Barth and the Economy of Grace."[1] Tanner's reading of Barth and her constructive proposals in relation to Barth are appreciative of both the eschatological import of his theology and of his intention to provide a genuinely theological account of human action as action in correspondence to God's own saving self-disclosure. As concerns the eschatological import

---

1. Kathryn Tanner, *Economy of Grace* (Minneapolis: Augsburg Fortress, 2005); "Barth and the Economy of Grace," pp. 176-97 above. Hereafter, page numbers for Tanner's essay are incorporated into the text.

of Barth's understanding, Tanner rightly describes Barth's anxieties regarding the inability of political, social, and economic arrangements to
be immediately transparent to the kingdom of God. For Barth, God's
rule is a rule that always remains over and above human arrangements
of any kind, not in an abstract sense, but rather in the sense that God, as
the active agent and Lord over them, continually summons them
through his Word to become ever more permeable to his reign. In
Barth's judgment, one can never draw a straight line from any form of
political, social, or economic arrangement to the gospel itself. Tanner
writes, "Just as God is love does not mean love is God, God's kingdom
may be the basis for a Christian identification of socialism with it without that implying that socialism on its own merits is to be identified
with the kingdom" (p. 181). Neither socialism nor capitalism, nor any
other economic program for that matter, can be identified with the
kingdom. The kingdom resists domestication of any kind whereby a
particular prescription for economic life, drawn up independent of the
gospel and its claim, is thought to be continuous with the gospel itself.

As concerns Barth's efforts to describe human action as action in
correspondence, Tanner ably demonstrates the extent to which God's
economy is generative of a certain kind of human economy, "a rule or
order for human living in correspondence to the history of God's actions toward us" (p. 180). Indeed, her account is sensitive to Barth's
overarching concern to demonstrate that Christ claims all facets of human existence, thereby setting them upon a path of correspondence, albeit provisional, to his life-giving rule.

Although Tanner clearly appreciates the eschatological and humane character of Barth's writings on the economy, she parts company
with Barth, for the very basic reason that he does not adequately press
home the "direct social and political consequences" of his own
Christocentrism, especially as it appears in the ethical portions of the
Church Dogmatics. More specifically, Tanner argues that Barth's criticism of capitalism in *CD* IV/4 §78.2 "remains purely formal. . . . As a result we are given very little hint of what it is about capitalism, besides
its lordlessness, that is particularly problematic, the features specific to
capitalism that should fall under Christian rebuke. Were capitalism in
particular to fall under the lordship of Christ, what would happen to
it? It seems from *CD* IV/4 that it would simply lose its inhumanity"
(p. 183). What Tanner seeks of Barth, in short, is that he extend his criticism of capitalism by providing more "specifications for human life. . . .

The kingdom of God to come as a kingdom on earth remains purely mysterious and incomprehensible in *CD* IV/4" (p. 184). In other words, the gospel itself, for Tanner, orders human life in more focused and direct ways than Barth himself allows. The responsible reader of Barth must thus move beyond him. His theology does not enable the church to know how to best respond in a concrete fashion to the lordless powers of our day — in this case, capitalism.

When one examines Tanner's writings on this subject, one notices the extent to which her account of the divine economy aims to give *concrete* direction to the human economy. In a manner that transcends the antinomies of both socialism and capitalism, she argues for an alternative way wherein "the very same things are enjoyed equally by all; whatever there is, in whatever amount, all take a full share" (p. 196). Such enjoyment of goods by all is made possible by the unbridled generosity of God and God's gift of grace. "Making what one has the root and impulse of giving to others is simply the summary story of God and the world on my telling of it. . . . Our lives participate in that divine mission and thereby realize the shape of God's own economy by giving that follows the *same principle:* self-sharing for the good of others."[2] God's story thus makes possible another kind of human story and thus an alternative economy governed by sharing. It is an economy that works according to the specific contours of the divine economy wherein the principle of noncompetition — among people themselves and also in relation to God — reigns.

This result is, for Tanner, a kind of economic third way. Thus, unlike many on the theological left, she does not do away with the idea of economic growth or with capitalism per se, as both can be reimagined in accordance with the theological principles of unconditional giving and noncompetitive possession.[3] "First, there is the capitalist ideal of a mutually beneficial competitive equilibrium. . . . Second, there is the capitalist interest in avoiding mutually destructive economic spirals and in fostering complementary or virtuous ones."[4] The benefit of such a construal is that it allows profit to be used for capital invest-

2. Tanner, *Economy of Grace,* p. 85, emphasis added.
3. "[L]odged within the whole compass of Christian dogmatic concepts, I'd like to argue, is a very odd account of the relations between owning and enjoyment by others — an alternative noncompetitive economy of sorts, brought to its completion in Christ." Tanner, "Barth," p. 187.
4. Tanner, *Economy of Grace,* p. 106.

ment and passed on to workers for their benefit, thereby allowing "a virtuous spiral of mutual benefit, which the snowballing effect of capitalism also presumably allows."[5]

One of the most striking features of Tanner's proposals and modifications regarding current forms of laissez-faire capitalism — designed as they are to move the conversation beyond Barth's formalism in the direction of an account that provides more directives than does Barth's — is the ubiquity of the language of "principles." What Tanner is after is indeed a set of theological principles of economy — chiefly that of noncompetition — that take their cues from God's saving economy. The articulation of such principles is a necessary corrective and alternative to Barth's christological formalism.

One of the difficulties associated with describing the character of Barth's antipathy toward the language of principles in relation to human action as its pertains to the economy is that he has not written anything on the economy per se. One must scour many passages in the *CD* as well as in other more occasional pieces such as "The Christian's Place in Society" (September 1919) to ascertain in a more systematic fashion what Barth's thoughts on the economy might be. In my judgment, the best place to begin the exploration is in §49.3 of *CD* III/3, where Barth offers a description of the nature of God's rule in the *hic et nunc*. His account of the character of the divine rule provides us with a basis for determining what form(s) of economic life might best attest God's kingdom as enacted in the life, death, resurrection, and ascension of Christ in fulfillment of the promises made to Israel.

The first thing to be said regarding the divine rule, for Barth, is that Israel's God is "the King of all occurrence . . . [which] is an idea that is practically significant in itself. It determines human existence."[6] Barth is adamant that God's kingship is not a theoretical or speculative idea. Rather, God's Lordship is absolutely decisive for all of life; its practicality is ingredient in itself. The Lordship of God gives, in other words, direction to all of life. But it is the *manner* in which it gives direction for all of life that is the issue for Tanner. Again, for Tanner, Barth is short on specifics; his account is, according to her reading, by and large devoid of reflection on the kind of human economy the divine economy engenders. Perhaps the difference is best stated in these

5. Tanner, *Economy of Grace,* p. 113.
6. *CD* III/3, p. 192. The page numbers in the following paragraphs refer to *CD* III/3.

terms: both are concerned with concreteness but seek to account for that concreteness rather differently.

Regarding concreteness, Barth writes: "We at once find ourselves in a concrete relationship with this concrete act of [divine] government as the act which is decisive for all events and therefore for our own life and existence and activity" (p. 194). It is Barth's judgment that God's activity of world governance, most fully disclosed in Jesus Christ, possesses its own inner concreteness. As such, it is concrete governance: God concretely governs and lays claim to us and to our world in Jesus Christ. "[I]f the King of Israel is the Lord of the world, He is also our Lord, and therefore He is thinking of us and laying claim upon us" (p. 194). The divine world-governance, in Barth's mind, is therefore "concrete and actual and true in all its parts," and as such possesses "immediate practical significance" (p. 195).

When one reads Barth with a view toward Tanner and her concerns, it cannot be argued that he is not concerned with the very practical character and significance of God's governance of the world in Christ. But what Barth does not do, as a function of his basic conviction that God's world governance in Christ is a "formative economy and disposition" (pp. 194, 195, 196, 198), is prescribe in the form of principles or programs the implications of what God's economy might mean for our economic life. To make such a move would, for Barth, be to suggest an *inertness* on the part of the active agent of that economy, that is, the triune God who creates, establishes, and fulfills covenant fellowship with the creature. For this reason Barth is allergic to the idea of application, the idea that God's work must somehow be applied in order for it to be rendered concrete. For Barth, God's action possesses a concreteness in itself; it need not be further concretized via principles, for it *is* concrete and possesses its own inner clarity and perspicuity.

Barth's chief concern in the ethical portions of the *CD* is to emphasize the context in which we act as that of the one covenant of grace whose center is Jesus Christ. "It is in this fact that we find true economy and disposition" (p. 195). If the Christian church is to have anything to say that is Christian about the shape of our economic life, it can do so only inasmuch as it attends to the divine economy that is ever present and active in all our presents, calling and enabling us to become participants in itself. As a consequence, "we can no longer think of world occurrence generally as a raging sea of events which has neither form nor direction" (p. 196). It is indeed God's governance that gives direction to world occurrence, argues Barth. What is at issue, however, is the *way* in which it gives direction. For Tanner, Barth's account of God's governance via his saving economy does not give enough definite direction to our economy. That is not to say that Tanner wants to "simply leave the question of application up to us." But it is to say that the kingdom, according to Tanner's reading of Barth, cannot provide any direction of its own, for it in the end remains a "mere mystery."[7] The issue, I suspect, boils down to this: Does Barth's insistence that there cannot be any ontological correspondence between human (economic) activity and God's activity necessarily fund a formalistic approach? Tanner would seem to think so. I want to argue, contra Tanner and with Barth, that the latter's hesitancy to apply principles derived from the divine economy and to posit them in relation to our economy does not necessarily lead to abstraction or formalism. Rather, such a hesitancy is itself a bulwark against abstraction and formalism. Stated somewhat differently, Barth refuses to speak of the ethical correlates of God's activity in applicatory terms precisely because he fears that such a move detracts from the decisive and definitive significance of the divine economy itself.

The economy of redemption is definitive per se because it is reality. It is not only the basis of all reality but that which continually establishes reality, thereby calling all our actualities to correspondence with itself. There is in fact only one economy. Hence, in response to the question of whether God's Lordship enacted in the covenant of grace is "a provisional arrangement, an economy, beside which there can perhaps be other economies," Barth answers a resounding *no*.[8] But is that then to say that God's economy is only an economy that disrupts and casts down all forms of human economic life? Is there only a negative note to be heard in all of this? Certainly not. But what is to be heard, is that at the core of human history there lies the redemptive economy of the triune God, and not other economies, and that God's economy cannot simply be united with any old form of human economy. Barth is insistent on this point because he is all too aware of the pernicious character of modern ideologies and the naturalistic impulses that animate them. For example, in relationship to "historical materialism" Barth offers the following scathing criticism:

7. See Tanner, "Barth," p. 194. The comment is directed toward *CD* IV/4.
8. *CD* II/1, p. 46.

In face of the modern development of community, historical materialism is 1. the affirmation in which the child at last acquires a name, namely, that the whole history of mankind at its core is the history of human economy or economic history, and that everything else, the achievement of civilisation, science, art, the state, morality and religion, are only phenomenal accompaniments of this one reality, expressions of the current relations of economic forces, attempts to disguise, beautify, justify, and defend them, occasionally perhaps even expressions of its discontent, instruments of its criticism, means of its alteration, but at all events secondary forms or ideologies from which economics is differentiated as true historical reality.[9]

Barth is exceptionally critical of all attempts to reduce human history or "economic history" to "economic forces" themselves, precisely because it is not "economic history" but rather God's history via his establishment of covenant fellowship with humanity in Jesus Christ that is at the core of human history. Indeed, Barth is opposed to any form of economic life that would alienate men and women from the fulfilling of God's commandment, which is the act that is proper to them as men and women of the covenant.[10]

What animates Barth's weariness with respect to the language of principles is the strongly eschatological focus and orientation of his theology. It is this focus, present throughout Barth's corpus, that funds his resistance to the kinds of principles of application that Tanner thinks are necessary if the rule of God is not to degenerate into a "mere mystery." What then to make of statements like the following from the "early" Barth, statements that are, I would argue, in essential agreement with his more mature dogmatic vision: "But do not expect me to provide a solution [to the Christian's place in society]! None of us may boast a solution. There is only one solution, and that is in God

---

9. *CD* III/2, p. 387.

10. I am indebted to Professor Jane Barter Moulaison of the University of Winnipeg for drawing this point to my attention. She describes Barth's critique of Reformation views of work and also the extent to which Barth relativizes the importance of work and thus "the ethos of work that prevails in modern bourgeois culture." In short, work for Barth "is to be undertaken for the sake of life's preservation, and is taken on so as not to be a burden to others." See "Barth on Work" (paper read at the annual meeting of the Canadian Evangelical Theological Society, Vancouver, B.C., May 2008).

himself"?[11] Hence, the only points Barth thinks he can offer on the basis of such a belief are *"points of departure."*[12] Barth is keenly aware of the need to articulate such points, even as he is also all too aware of the fact that such an eschatological focus can be construed as denoting the annulment of our creatureliness and a lack of concern for the connection of the covenantal activity of God with our social and economic life. So Barth: "The Divine is something whole, complete in itself, a kind of new and different something in contrast to the world. . . . It does not passively permit itself to be used: it overthrows and builds up as it wills. . . . Where then has the world of God any available connection with our social [and economic] life? How do we come to act as if it had?"[13] The last two questions are also Tanner's questions. But is it enough to say in response, as does Barth, that the only solution is "God himself"? Well, yes, if one understands, with Barth, that God is living, active, and communicative, lending us thereby his "motion." And God's motion is positive: even as it negates the purported autonomies of creaturely life, it seeks to recast them and to build them up. It does so by resisting our human tendency to identify the kingdom of God as it pertains to certain economic reform movements or economic revolutions. God clearly wills to possess our economic order(s). "God could not redeem the world if he were not its Creator. Only because it *is* his possession can it *become* his possession."[14] Barth's account, then, proceeds on the assumption that the Christian church, in seeking to witness to and to demonstrate a more humane set of economic arrangements in society, will do so only inasmuch as it recognizes and commits itself to the following notion: the world the church serves and in which it seeks to become a participant in what God is doing in the world to humanize the world, is not a world without God.

It is precisely at this point, Barth argues, that the language of applicability breaks down. It does so because it assumes a priori a kind of independence or autonomy on the part of the human economy, rather than understanding the economy — despite its very real inhumanity — as being that to which God is redemptively present. In other words, the ethical heart of Barth's dogmatic work, even from very early on, does

11. Karl Barth, "The Christian's Place in Society," in *The Word of God and the Word of Man,* trans. Douglas Horton (Boston: Pilgrim Press, 1928), p. 282.
12. Barth, "Christian's Place in Society," p. 282.
13. Barth, "Christian's Place in Society," p. 277.
14. Barth, "Christian's Place in Society," p. 299.

not need to be developed along the line of principles, simply because socioeconomic implications are already ingredient in it.

Barth's exegesis of Matthew 6:25ff. in §64.3 ("The Royal Man") further develops his aversion to the deriving of applicatory principles or programs from the divine economy so as to provide direction to the economic order. Barth writes: "But this is what Jesus says ['take no thought for the morrow'] in words which are strangely illuminating and pregnant and penetrating — who can escape their truth and comfort and inspiration? — even though they obviously do not give to the community in which the Gospels arose any directions as to their practical realisation, and have a final validity even though they are exposed from the very outset to the accusation that they are incapable of practical realisation."[15] The point Barth is pressing home is that of a strengthened appreciation of the christological content of the economy. That is, the economy Jesus inaugurates and establishes is, despite its impracticality, nonetheless valid. His economy's validity is rooted in its radical questioning of all human economies and its penetration of them. The new thing that God in the royal man Jesus is doing is "penetrating to the very foundations of economic life in defiance of every reasonable and to that extent honourable objection."[16] One could easily add "practical" too, in that the very unsettling of all programs and principles by the royal man displays and demonstrates his freedom. The demonstration of his freedom, relativizing as it does the limit(s) and frontier(s) of the economy, is "all the more powerful in its lack of any direct aggressiveness."[17] And herein lies the key: the words and works of Jesus — whom Barth calls "the incomparable revolutionary" — are amazingly free to penetrate "the very foundations" of our economic order. In so doing the power of the one who makes all things new is seen and understood to be that much more powerful and humanizing.[18]

III

Let us examine, then, in greater detail the ways Barth's allergy toward principles helps one to better understand his mature account of the

15. *CD* IV/2, p. 178.
16. *CD* IV/2, p. 178.
17. *CD* IV/2, pp. 178-79.
18. *CD* IV/2, pp. 178-79.

nature of God's rule in the world, and how that rule actively opposes and judges the "lordless powers," capitalism being but one of them.[19] Even though Barth does not directly engage the topic of economy in §78, "The Struggle for Human Righteousness," his comments on this struggle are very instructive for what his critique of late modern Western economic arrangements might look like. Indeed, the lordless power that is most pronounced in our day and age — as of that of Barth's — is that of mammon, the hypostatization of which is constitutive for current economic arrangements. In accordance with the spirit of the world, mammon seeks "self-absolutization."[20] Mammon seeks, in other words, to become an end in itself, an idol — a false God — which alienates us from God and one another. "The lordship of these powers, which are all of them no more than exponents of the rebellion that separates man from God, is synonymous with the destruction and ruin of both the individual and society."[21] Accordingly, the economy can be said by Barth to participate in the same rebellion that separates humanity from God, a rebellion that destroys the individual and collective well-being of humanity. The economy is deeply enmeshed in the sin of our first parents in which we and it freely participate. To be healed and emancipated, the economy needs to be mortified and vivified by the person and work of the Son of God.

Furthermore, what is crucial to notice in Barth's treatment of the "lordless powers" in §78 is not simply the way he describes how human economic arrangements have been taken captive. Simply put, he does not merely describe what is wrong with current arrangements. Instead, he also indicates what *shape* Christian resistance to the Babylonian captivity of them is to take. Perhaps what most distinguishes Barth's account from Tanner's is most evident at this point, in that Barth's account of the ethics of the kingdom is replete with language of God's active agency, how God has not left it up to us to put into practice his rule, but rather is making it possible by his Spirit for us to become participant in his rule. This is a kind of participation that manifests itself no doubt in certain forms of human economic arrangements.

One of the particular human actions suggested by Barth, which is in accord with his emphasis on Christ Jesus' setting of "all [economic]

---

19. *CL*, p. 222.
20. *CL*, p. 222.
21. *CL*, p. 233.

programmes and principles in question," is service of the poor, service
to and among those with whom Jesus freely identified himself. This is a
kind of Christian decision made in correspondence to God's activity in
Jesus Christ that is not an idea or program, but rather is inclusive of a
direction that ought to be recognized and which itself contains
imperatival force. I say so on the basis of Barth's description in §64.3 of
the royal man himself. "But again, we do not really know Jesus (the Jesus of the New Testament) if we do not know Him as this poor man, as
this (if we may risk the dangerous word) partisan of the poor, and finally as this revolutionary."[22] There is a kind of economic direction
contained in Christ's enactment of the reign of his Father, and it is perhaps best expressed in terms of economic policies that reflect partisanship with the poor and by a church that cares for the poor.

If such an economic direction is the case, however, is it possible or
necessary to speak of the Christian community's *decisive* action in relation to the lordless powers? "The decisive action of their revolt against
disorder, which, correctly understood, includes within itself all others,
is their calling upon God in the second petition of the Lord's Prayer. . . .
The kingdom of God is God himself in the act of normalizing human
existence."[23] The economy, as with all other principalities and rulers in
the present age, needs to be normalized. A normalized economy enjoys
a kind of "transitory validity" precisely because it acknowledges its
conditionedness by God as its limit and frontier. But of the form of
that normalization Barth is hesitant to speak, precisely because doing
so would obviate the need for the most decisive action of all, the calling
upon God. It is therefore somewhat difficult to fully accept Tanner's
criticism that Barth's treatment is formalistic, precisely because Barth
does in fact offer an account of the kinds of human activities most appropriate to God's kingdom that has come and is coming. This is human activity that, if undertaken, would effect the community's will to
see and to struggle for more just human economic arrangements that
attest to God's rule of plenty that encompasses all in Christ Jesus.

We are, says Barth, to rise "up to fight for human righteousness
and order in the midst of disorder and in opposition to it."[24] The fight
for human righteousness is inclusive of the fight for economic righ-

22. *CD* IV/2, p. 180.
23. *CL*, p. 212.
24. *CL*, p. 213.

Christopher R. J. Holmes

teousness, as with moral, civil, and societal righteousness — interdependent as they are. But the fight Barth encourages is of a very particular kind: it is a fight rooted in witness; indeed, the fight of the Christian community over and against the lordless powers takes shape as witness. The category of witness is thus crucial to Barth. Without the language of witness, the responsibility of the Christian community to participate in God's humanizing activity could very well inculcate despair and inaction on the community's part, or else take on a very Pelagian form. This is because of Barth's sober assessment of the power of the rule — albeit circumscribed — of the lordless powers. "People who know God's will — and Christians should be such people — cannot in any circumstances accept this plight as an unalterable reality, even though no people, not even Christians, can overcome it or rescue humanity from the pressure of its rule."[25] Barth's point is simply that it is God in Christ who through the power of the Spirit overcomes the lordless powers and therefore "their provisional and relative character . . . their secret fallibility."[26] Hence the profoundly inhumane character of late capitalist economic arrangements can only be overcome — as they have already been — by the God who has enacted his rule in the life, death, and resurrection of Christ in fulfillment of the promises made to Israel. That they have been overcome, even as the Christian community rebels against them and their plight, and thereby enters into conflict with them, is what gives the community's rebellion and plight its character as witness. The community's rebellion does not take place in a vacuum. It is rebellion that corresponds — albeit frailly and inasmuch as it calls upon God — to the revolution of God in Christ whose cause is reconciliation for all in both a vertical and a horizontal sense. "For human life [economic, political, moral, etc.] as it emerges in this activity of Jesus is really like a great hospital whose many departments in some way enfold us all."[27]

Thus the Christian community does not fight against people per se. Rather, the community fights against the "plight which is caused by all, for which all are responsible, and which oppresses all."[28] Indeed, within this plight "there can and may be no reconciliation or peace." In

---

25. _CL,_ p. 211.
26. _CD_ IV/2, p. 172.
27. _CD_ IV/2, p. 221.
28. _CL,_ p. 221. Parenthetical page numbers in the following paragraphs refer to _CL._

210

greater detail Barth describes this plight as one of "disorder." This disorder "arises and consists in the unrighteousness of the fall of people from God which as such ineluctably carries with it their fall from one another" (p. 211). What can possibly oppose and thereby overcome such disorder? Simply this: a hearing of the "proclamation of the righteousness of God and in and with it the proclamation of the order of right, freedom, and peace which is given to man" (p. 212). It is at points such as this that the eschatological focus of Barth's treatment of the rule of God comes to the fore. That is, the righteousness the gospel proclaims includes within itself an order, an order of righteousness, freedom, and peace. The form of this order is never a form given in advance, however. Indeed, the Christian community, in correspondence to the royal man, is to display a kind of freedom in relation to the orders positively or negatively contested around it. This freedom is expressed by and in the freedom to conform to God's rule enacted and made manifest in Christ, the royal man.

When it comes to the economy, one can see how such a stance hardly encourages Christians individually or corporately to articulate in advance how a human economy in correspondence to God's economy might look. For Barth, such a move would be far too speculative and thus inattentive to how the rule of God continually brings itself to bear each day anew on human existence, thereby normalizing it. This is not to say that Barth would have the community embrace a fatalistic view of the way things are or defer to a kind of quietism that is indifferent to the groans of the suffering and oppressed. By no means. Barth is arguing that God himself has taken the decisive action, and having done so wills that we, his children, take decisive action too. Our most decisive form of action is, once again, to call upon God. This action, the ultimate act of revolt, "includes within itself all others" (p. 212). Accordingly, the Christian community is to fight against economic unrighteousness, and for that matter, unrighteousness of all kinds. Indeed, unrighteousness — disorder — is to be opposed. And that to which the Christian is to be directed is righteousness. But righteousness is not a value or a principle but rather is ingredient in him who is righteous and who creates righteousness within human communities that call upon God and are ordered by God's Word and Spirit.

It would seem that Barth's vision of the Christian community's activity in the world with respect to the current form of the economy is more ad hoc than Tanner's. I say ad hoc because Christians for centuries have existed in diverse economic arrangements and landscapes, some more righteous, others less. Barth would have the church, regardless of its social and economic location, recognize, in faith, that God, in coming to the world in Christ, created and is creating righteousness, including economic righteousness. He calls the church to rise up and to partake in what God is creating through the fight for righteousness and order in the midst of profound economic disorder. This fight will — God willing — establish economic orders of life and value that enjoy a kind of transitory reality, precisely because they acknowledge God as their limit and frontier, and God's Son as the royal man who penetrates the very foundations of economic life. Indeed, the Lord precedes our witness and is the one who always gives rise to it among those who "have fallen wholly and utterly under the lordship of the lordless powers" (p. 237). The rule of God — inclusive as it is of economy — "is the great new thing on the margin" (p. 237). To be sure, the Christian community's prescriptions for what ails us economically may relate to this reality and truth. "It is as well for us if they do. In and of themselves, however, they are all empty shells" (pp. 237-38). This is not to condone apathy or inactivity, but it does serve as a salient reminder that our concepts and prescriptions, while not in vain, are "real only as God himself comes as King and Lord, establishes righteousness in our relationship to him and to one another, and thus creates peace on earth" (p. 237).

V

In her *Economy of Grace* Tanner offers a noncompetitive account of God's economy in relation to the human economy. She does so via a series of prescriptions that would render our economy more humane. I suspect that her proposals do indeed relate — quite thoroughly — to the God who comes as King and Lord, establishing righteousness. That said, I wish Tanner's detailed specifications would include a far richer account of God's agency and the extent to which the contemporaneity and communicative agency of God would differently shape such specifications. Indeed, we do not commit ourselves to the world without God, a world that is enclosed by God in Christ. The Christian community's task via the economy of our day is thus neither uncritical affirmation nor activist denial. It begins, rather, with a sober assessment made possible by the reign of God's grace. "We must honestly confess, even when we seek to comprehend our situation from the viewpoint of God, that we know the element of tragedy in it better than that element of sovereignty which might reconcile us to it."[29]

Viewing our economy from the viewpoint of God's saving activity will certainly make us more profoundly aware of the extent to which it does not conform to the gospel imperative to love God and love neighbor as oneself. But even as we make such an assessment, Barth would have us be cognizant of the fact that our own work for renewal "is also disjunct from . . . the work of God."[30] However, Barth does *not* denigrate the impetus for the work of witnessing to a more humane economic order that must necessarily take place. It is *not* to say that the Christian community is to defend the status quo of current economic interests and forms. But it is to say that even as the Christian community goes on the attack, "from a naïve acceptance to a criticism of society," it cannot do so with the understanding that its work — even its critical work — is utterly transparent to God's work. Yet work it must: "We must enter fully into the subversion and conversion of this present and of every conceivable world, into the judgment and the grace which the presence of God entails."[31] It is precisely the Christian community's affirmation of the world as a world that God is *for* in Christ, that generates its resistance to the world — in this case, the economic world — which falls so radically short of the reign of God that is advancing even now.

I suspect the reason Barth is short on "specifics" has far more to do with his confidence in the reign of God that interrogates and "is all the more powerful in its lack of any direct aggressiveness" than with his attention to the actualities in which we find ourselves.[32] I am afraid that were we to receive from this impinging reign propositions whereby we could correspond to — or more problematic, enact — this reign, we would no longer focus upon calling on the impinging reign itself. Instead, we would focus on the propositions that are meant to provide concrete specifics as to how the reign is taking shape. "We believe there is an inherent meaning in relations already existent and we believe also

29. Barth, "Christian's Place in Society," p. 311.
30. Barth, "Christian's Place in Society," p. 312.
31. Barth, "Christian's Place in Society," p. 318.
32. *CD* IV/2, pp. 178-79.

in evolution and revolution, in the reform and renewal of relations, and in the possibility of comradeship and brotherhood on our earth and under our heaven, *for the reason* that we are expecting wholly other things; namely, a new heaven and a new earth."[33] Perhaps the move toward principles and programs would lead to a domestication of the hope for "wholly other things," to an obscuring of the direction and line contained in the hope itself — Jesus Christ. Perhaps it would also denote a settling down of the community in relation to the hope to which it is called, precisely because the community would have realized that hope already, rather than adopting a posture of active waiting before the consummation of that hope. Christian hope, while concrete, is never concrete in such a way as to do away with the necessity of following after and of becoming participant in all circumstances in the one in whom we hope — the Lord Jesus Christ, prophetically present in Word and Spirit — and what he is *now* doing.

The concern for practicality is no doubt sound and laudable. But Barth refuses to offer the kinds of prescriptions Tanner thinks necessary because he thinks it is God who, as the community calls upon him in the power of the Spirit, evokes the kind of practical reforming and renewing activity proper to a community that hears and waits upon the Word in faith and in obedience. "When we look toward the 'wholly other' *regnum gloriae* . . . both our Yes and our No, fall into *right practical relation to each other in God*."[34] Barth is not so much concerned with articulating "practical" economic prescriptions precisely because he is focused on the coming kingdom of God that points to new ways of addressing the economic challenges besetting us. The witness Christians bear and the economic goals for which they work are never separate from the hearing and the hoping that is new every day and to which the Holy Spirit gives rise.

As noted at the outset, to write an article on Barth and the economy is a difficult thing to do. It is difficult because Barth's own way of doing theology — as concretely biblical, christological, and therefore eschatological as it is — resists giving an answer to the question of "What ought we then to do?" without first deferring to the commandments of God themselves, especially the command to call upon God.[35] What

---

33. Barth, "Christian's Place in Society," p. 323.
34. Barth, "Christian's Place in Society," pp. 324-25.
35. Barth, "Christian's Place in Society," p. 326.

ought we then to do as Christians about our participation in an economy that exacerbates the gap between rich and poor and privileges economic "growth" at all cost? Barth might not seem, according to a rudimentary reading, to have provided any answers to the question. Yet when one takes Barth on his own terms, that is, in accordance with "the fundamental Biblical answer we have given," there is indeed only one thing possible.[36] "But it is just that one thing which *we* do not do. What can the Christian in society do but follow attentively what is done by *God?*"[37] God is at work, on the move, present, and redemptively so. Christian resistance toward the current form of the economy as well as its witness to a more humane form of economic existence is a matter of it following the God who is at work. This God effects witness among men and women to his work that is making all things new, and calls them through his Word and Spirit to become participant in it. That God will, as part of that calling, raise up women and men who will speak prophetic words regarding a more just form of economic life and exchange is our hope, a hope the community has every reason to believe will be brought into being through the One who is indeed making all things new.

36. Barth, "Christian's Place in Society," p. 327.
37. Barth, "Christian's Place in Society," p. 327.

12. Barth and the Christian as Ethical Agent: An Ontological Study of the Shape of Christian Ethics

Paul T. Nimmo

In the course of this essay I hope to locate Barth's thinking about the Christian as ethical agent — and correspondingly his understanding of the theory and practice of Christian ethics — within the ontological context to which it belongs. In one sense, then, I intend to explore some of the contours of what John Webster calls "moral ontology," the kind of ethical field that Christians believe themselves to inhabit.[1] In another sense, however, I wish to explore the ontological foundations of that ethical field, in the being in action of the eternal and triune God. In both senses, this essay will aim to exposit something of what Barth calls the "very definite order of being" that Scripture makes manifest in its witness to divine revelation.[2]

To offer a focused understanding of this potentially vast topic, I propose to engage Barth's understanding of the Christian as ethical agent by means of a pattern of *exitus* and *reditus* — of moving out and of coming in. But, in an inversion of what is sometimes the order pur-

---

1. John Webster, *Barth's Moral Theology: Human Action in Barth's Thought* (Edinburgh: T. & T. Clark, 1998), pp. 151-53.
    2. *CD* I/2, p. 5.

My thanks are due to those who read through and commented upon prior drafts of this paper and to those who gave such helpful feedback on it at the conference. In particular, I would like to register my debt in respect of the former to Tom Greggs, and in respect of the latter to Nigel Biggar, Jesse Couenhoven, David Demson, and Kathryn Tanner. I would also like to thank Daniel Migliore for his gracious invitation to speak at the conference.

sued, I want to begin *not* with God, moving out to the ethical agent and her ethical context, and then returning to God, but in the *reverse* order. For the purposes of this essay, then, I will start with the ethical agent, move outward (and perhaps upward) to consider God, and then return to the ethical agent once again.[3]

This essay proceeds in four sections, followed by a brief conclusion. In the first section, I will consider the Christian who finds herself encountered by the Word of God. This theme will lead us to think not only about the Word of God as law and gospel, but also about the origin of that Word in the divine decision and act of election. In the second section, I will investigate the doctrine of election a little further, considering in particular the relationship between Jesus Christ and the being of the God who elects. At this point, I fear I will go against any desire to keep theological ethics at the level of the economic Trinity and, following Barth, will delve into the ethical dimensions of the immanent Trinity. In the third section, I will move from the sphere of inner-Trinitarian relationships to the history of Jesus Christ, the God-human in divine-human unity. At this point, I will particularly consider the way Barth derives his understanding of Jesus Christ as an ethical agent in relation to God by means of the *analogia relationis,* and will seek carefully to make explicit certain connections in Barth's work that remain implicit in the original. In the fourth section, I will return to Barth's understanding of the Christian as ethical agent, and demonstrate how the obedience to which the Christian is called is grounded in the eternal divine act of determination to constitute God's essence to be for us in Jesus Christ. This, as I will show, has particular and significant ramifications for the shape of the Christian life. Finally, in a brief conclusion, I will explore the telos of the ethical activity of the Christian.

The Election of the Christian: A First Word

For Karl Barth, the Word of God is spoken by God, but it is not an abstract word spoken into a vacuum. Rather this Word is spoken to a re-

---

3. The ordering of the material in this paper has been selected for heuristic purposes, and should not be taken to endorse any particular methodological or hermeneutic commitments.

cipient, and it is spoken in a specific time and place and situation. On encounter with the Word of God, the Christian hears clearly that the Word has a twofold dimension.

First, the Word of God is a word of gospel. This gospel, however, is not any good news: this word is the good news of *election*. This good news has two aspects. On the one hand, this word of gospel is such that God has *elected* Godself to be gracious toward humanity, to be its Lord and Helper.[4] This means that humanity is not only created and claimed and governed by God, but that it is also loved by God.[5] Indeed, God loves humanity so much that God gives Godself in Jesus Christ to and for the creature. This is the glory of God revealed in Jesus Christ and is, for Barth, "the sum of the whole doctrine of God."[6] On the other hand, the word of gospel is such that God has *elected* humanity to witness to this glory of God.[7] The fundamental purpose of the human being, and indeed of the whole creation, is that the ethical agent witnesses in her life — in her being and her action — to the glory of God. This is not primarily a function of ability, obligation, or necessity, though all these are clearly relevant; this is primarily a function of permission.[8] Under the word of gospel and through the gift of divine grace, the human being is given the freedom to glorify God.

Second, however, the Word of God is also a word of law, a command that renders the Christian responsible and demands obedience. In response to the divine act of election, to the prior self-determination of God to be for her in Jesus Christ, there arises the question of the self-determination of the ethical agent. There therefore arises the question of her responsibility and her decision, her obedience and her action.[9] In contrast to the word of gospel, where permission was the primary dimension, it seems that we have here precisely to do with ability, obligation, and necessity. The word of law cannot be avoided or replaced. It requires our active recognition, it demands our active obedience, and, as the criterion of good or evil, it submits us to judgment.[10] It is important to recognize, however, that this word of law is not the law of sin

---

4. *CD* II/2, p. 510.
5. *CD* II/1, p. 671.
6. *CD* II/1, p. 671.
7. *CD* II/2, p. 510.
8. *CD* II/1, p. 672.
9. *CD* II/1, p. 511.
10. *CD* II/2, p. 632.

and death; rather, this is the law of the Spirit of life, "the true Law of God, revealed again in its proper substance as Law of grace, and made effective again in spite of its perversion by sin."[11] This construal of the Word of God as law clearly reflects the commitment in the Reformed tradition at large (in face of Lutheran opposition) to the validity of the third use of the law — the law in and for the Christian life. This word of law — precisely for and to *the Christian* — expresses the will of God.

It is important to recognize that the Word of God is always found in this twofold dimension — as gospel and as law, as grace and as command. The Word of God is both together and both simultaneously: Barth writes that "In its content, it is Gospel; in its form and fashion, it is Law."[12] Indeed, it seems to me that we only really understand Barth's ethics when we see this twofold aspect of the Word of God: it is "not only a communication but a challenge, not only an indicative but as such an imperative."[13] While gospel and law are certainly inseparable, for Barth, they are not without hierarchy. On this point there is no equivocation: the Word of God is "first Gospel and then Law."[14] What this means for the Christian is that her self-determination worked out under the word of law cannot ever jeopardize her determination by the word of gospel. No matter how sinful or evil her actions may be, they cannot undermine her status as elected by God — as a person created by God, reconciled in Jesus Christ, and redeemed by the Holy Spirit. While an individual may be disobedient and lost to herself, she is never lost to her Creator,[15] for she has not "fallen lower than the depth to which God humbled Himself for [her] in Jesus Christ."[16] This mention of the humiliation of God for humanity in Jesus Christ brings us to the doctrine of election, and the second section of the paper.

---

11. *CD* II/2, p. 592.

12. *CD* II/2, p. 511.

13. *CD* III/2, p. 165. The classic treatment of this issue in Barth remains "Evangelium und Gesetz. Zugleich vom Verhältnis von Dogmatik und Ethik," by Eberhard Jüngel, found in *Barth-Studien* (Gütersloh: Gütersloher Verlagshaus Mohn, 1982), pp. 180-209.

14. *CD* II/2, p. 511. It is entertaining to note here Barth's riposte to his Lutheran critics, as he draws upon texts from Luther himself that he reads as supporting his own position (*CD* IV/3.1, pp. 370-71).

15. *CD* III/2, p. 197.

16. *CD* IV/1, pp. 480-81.

The Election of Jesus Christ and the Immanent Trinity

The individual Christian is not, for Barth, the direct and proper object of the divine election of grace. Nor, indeed, is the direct and proper object of divine election a collection of individuals. Instead, Barth writes, it is "one individual — and only in Him the people called and united by Him, and only in that people individuals in general in their private relationships with God."[17] The original object of election, then — which is to say the original human being in whom God has elected to be gracious toward humanity and whom God has elected to be the witness to this glory of God — is Jesus Christ.

What is, of course, unique about Jesus Christ is that he fulfills the law of God. As Jesus Christ is elected by the grace of God, he is concerned simply with obedience. In all his acts, he is subject simply to the will and command of God. When confronted by this will and command of God, Jesus Christ simply obeys. We — that is, the rest of humanity — are elect only *in* Jesus Christ: he is the original ethical agent, the original responsible human person. Rather than the fulfillment of the law of God in and by Jesus Christ rendering it redundant for Christians, however, it is precisely in this fulfillment of the law by Jesus Christ that there is found, for Barth, the basis of the validity of the law for the Christian. He writes: "God orders and only orders on the basis of the fact that He Himself has given and realised and fulfilled what He orders."[18] In Jesus Christ, the elect human being, posits Barth, it is not only that "God has acted rightly towards us" but also that "in the same person man has also acted rightly for us."[19] Again and even in the person of Jesus Christ, then, there is no separation of gospel and law: it is precisely in the history of Jesus Christ that the command of God is not only revealed, but is also established and fulfilled. The commanding grace and gracious command of God lead Jesus Christ ultimately to crucifixion, however, and we will have to ask below what that commanding grace and gracious command mean for Christians as ethical agents and for the shape of Christian ethics.

For the moment, however, we need to continue moving out from the ethical agent further. Thus far, we have seen how the Word of God

---

17. *CD* II/2, p. 43.
18. *CD* II/2, p. 565.
19. *CD* II/2, p. 539.

that encounters us as gospel and law reaches us as a result of our election, and how our election is rooted in the election of Jesus Christ. We now need to consider how the election of Jesus Christ relates to the being of God.

In his doctrine of election, Barth posits that Jesus Christ is not only the object of election — the one who is elected — but also the subject of election — the one who elects. At the point where the elect human is revealed, then, "just as truly there is revealed at that same point the electing God."[20] Indeed, Barth asks rhetorically, "If Jesus Christ is only elected, and not also and primarily the Elector, what shall we really know at all of a divine electing and our election?"[21] Hence Barth writes: "[E]lection is obviously the first and basic and decisive thing which we have always to say concerning . . . [the] presence of God in the world, and *therefore* concerning the eternal decree and the eternal self-determination of God which bursts through and is manifested at this point."[22] In contrast to the majority of the Reformed tradition that followed Calvin, in which a *decretum absolutum* — an absolute decree — stands at the heart of the doctrine of election, Barth's theology insists that Jesus Christ himself takes the place of the *decretum absolutum*.[23] "Jesus Christ is the electing God. We must not ask concerning any other but Him. In no depth of the Godhead shall we encounter any other but Him. There is no such thing as Godhead in itself. Godhead is always the Godhead of the Father, the Son and the Holy Spirit. But the Father is the Father of Jesus Christ and the Holy Spirit is the Spirit of the Father and the Spirit of Jesus Christ. There is no such thing as a *decretum absolutum*."[24] This insistence that Jesus Christ is the electing God has profound ramifications for Barth's doctrine of the Trinity, not only in its economic sense, but also in its immanent sense.

How Barth construes the relationship between the being of God and the act of election, and with which directionality, is a matter of some contention in Barth studies at the present time.[25] My own under-

20. *CD* II/2, p. 58.
21. *CD* II/2, p. 105.
22. *CD* II/2, p. 54, emphasis added.
23. *CD* II/2, p. 75.
24. *CD* II/2, p. 115.
25. For two of the more recent contributions to the ongoing debate, see Bruce McCormack, "Election and the Trinity: Theses in Response to George Hunsinger," *Scottish Journal of Theology* 63, no. 2 (2010): 203-24, and George Hunsinger, "Election and the

standing of this relationship will become clear in due course. But I wish to stress at the outset that my primary motivation in exploring the relationship between Barth's doctrine of election and Barth's doctrine of the Trinity at this juncture is *ethical* — to determine how that relationship impacts upon Barth's understanding of the Christian as ethical agent and upon his conception of the shape of Christian ethics. As a result, I wish now to turn to a part of Barth's doctrine of reconciliation where all three of these matters — the being of God as Trinity, the act of election, and the shape of Christian ethics — are simultaneously investigated by Barth.[26]

The relevant passage is in volume IV/1 of the *Church Dogmatics,* where, in §59.1, Barth tackles the key christological question *quo iure Deus homo* — by what right did God become human? Right at the outset of his consideration of this issue, Barth inquires whether, in the event of the incarnation, "we have to do with a *novum mysterium* [a new mystery] . . . , with what is noetically and logically an absolute paradox, with what is ontically the fact of a cleft or rift or gulf in God Himself *(ontisch mit dem Faktum einer Kluft, eines Risses und Abgrundes in Gott selber),* between His being and essence in Himself *(Sein und Wesen in sich)* and His activity and work as the Reconciler *(seinem Tun und Wirken als Versöhner)* of the world created by Him."[27] What Barth is asking is whether we have in Jesus Christ to do with God in a way that is somehow ontically different from the way God is in Godself. Does God undergo change to become incarnate? Does God become somehow different to God, and does there correspondingly somehow arise a conflict at this point within the being of God?

Barth's answer to these questions is a resounding "No." For Barth, indeed, to answer in any other way would be supreme blasphemy. Instead, Barth notes that in the incarnation "God gives Himself, but He does not give Himself away. He does not give up being God in becoming a creature, in becoming man. He does not cease to be God.

Trinity: Twenty-five Theses on the Theology of Karl Barth," *Modern Theology* 24, no. 2 (2008): 179-98.

26. At a number of points in what follows, I will include citations from *Die Kirchliche Dogmatik,* the original German text of the *Church Dogmatics,* in order to reference the underlying terminology that Barth invokes in the course of his writing. (Cf. Karl Barth, *Die Kirchliche Dogmatik* [hereafter *KD*], 4 vols. in 13 parts, 5th ed. [Zürich: Evangelischer Verlag, 1947-67].)

27. *CD* IV/1, p. 184 (*KD* IV/1, p. 201).

He does not come into conflict with Himself."[28] Indeed, claims Barth, not only is it the case that the being of God in Christ does not come into conflict with the being of God in itself, but, moreover, that God in the incarnation has "done and revealed *that which corresponds to* His divine nature ([er] *hat . . . das seiner göttlichen Natur* Entsprechende *getan und sichtbar gemacht*)."[29] In the act of incarnation, then, God is genuinely true to Godself, as God puts "into effect the freedom of His divine love, the love in which He is divinely free."[30] So, while the incarnation may represent a "new mystery" for us, indeed, while it may be in contradiction to all human ideas about divine nature, it is no "new mystery" for God. Barth writes: "He is amongst us in humility, our God, God for us, as that which He is in Himself, in the most inward depth of His *Godhead* (*in der innersten Tiefe seiner* Gottheit). He does not become another God. In the condescension *(in der Kondeszendenz)* in which He gives Himself to us in Jesus Christ He exists and speaks and acts as the One He was from all *eternity* and will be to all *eternity (als der Eine, der er von* Ewigkeit *her war und in* Ewigkeit *sein wird)*."[31] It is not that God is still God *despite* humiliating Godself for us in Jesus Christ; it is that God is *precisely* God in the humiliation for us in Jesus Christ that incarnation brings.

Barth calls this idea — that God is in the humility of the incarnation what God is in Godself — the "second and outer moment" of the

---

28. *CD* IV/1, p. 185.

29. *CD* IV/1, p. 187 (*KD* IV/1, p. 204), emphasis added to the English translation in accordance with the emphasis marked in the original text of the *Kirchliche Dogmatik*. Similar emphases will be added to the translations below — where particularly significant — without further comment, and in each case will be accompanied by the original German text to show where Barth himself felt that the emphasis in the relevant passage should lie.

30. *CD* IV/1, p. 187. In his doctrine of election, Barth relates the divine love and the divine freedom, which ground the event of the incarnation, explicitly to the eternal divine act of election: "In so far as God not only is love, but loves, in the act of love which determines His whole being God elects. And in so far as this act of love is an election, it is at the same time and as such the act of His freedom" (*CD* II/2, p. 76).

31. *CD* IV/1, p. 193 (*KD* IV/1, p. 211). Again, this view finds its roots in Barth's doctrine of election, where he writes: "It is undoubtedly the case . . . that the election does in some sense denote the basis of all the relationships between God and man, between God in His very earliest movement towards man and man in his very earliest determination by this divine movement. It is in the decision in favour of this movement, in God's self-determination and the resultant determination of man, in the basic relationship which is enclosed and fulfilled within Himself, that God is who He is" (*CD* II/2, p. 52).

mystery of the deity of Christ.[32] However, this second moment is grounded in something deeper — what Barth calls "the first and inner moment of the mystery of the deity of Christ."[33] Barth reasons that if the humility of the incarnate Jesus Christ is not simply an attitude of the human being Jesus of Nazareth, then there must be a humility grounded *within* the being of God. If this is the case, then the self-emptying and self-humbling of God in the incarnate Jesus Christ — as an act of obedience — cannot be alien to God in Godself. Barth posits: "We have not only not to deny but actually to affirm and understand as essential to the being of God *(als dem Sein Gottes wesentlich)* the offensive fact that there is in God Himself *(in Gott selbst)* an above and a below, a *prius* and a *posterius,* a superiority and a subordination . . . that it belongs to the inner life of God *(zum inneren Leben Gottes)* that there should take place within it obedience."[34] What this means is that it is not only that the incarnate Jesus Christ is free and able to render obedience, but that there is also in Godself a freedom and an ability to render obedience.[35]

This fact may seem somewhat troubling: it might be feared that it not only compromises the unity of the divine being but also jeopardizes the equality of the divine being. On the one hand, however, Barth insists that we have here to do with a divine unity that consists precisely in the fact that God is in Godself both One who is obeyed and Another who obeys. This unity is dynamic and living, not dead and static, and therefore the application of any "mean and unprofitable concept of unity" to God is to be abandoned once and for all.[36] On the other hand, meanwhile, Barth posits that there is no need to conclude from the existence of an Above and a Below in God that there is any trace of a gradation or a degradation or an inferiority in God, as if the very *homoousion* itself were threatened. Taxonomy in the Trinity does not necessarily imply ontological hierarchy, contra all-too-human ways of thinking. In respect of both fears, the key — according to Barth — is to allow our thinking about the divine nature to be governed not by human modes of thinking and conceptualities, but by the revelation of God in Jesus Christ. When this occurs, Barth writes, "we cannot avoid

---

32. *CD* IV/1, p. 192.
33. *CD* IV/1, p. 192.
34. *CD* IV/1, pp. 200-201 (*KD* IV/1, p. 219).
35. *CD* IV/1, p. 193.
36. *CD* IV/1, p. 202.

the astounding conclusion of a divine obedience."[37] Indeed, Barth contends, "we cannot refuse to accept the humiliation and lowliness and supremely the obedience of Christ as the dominating moment in our conception of His *divinity (den Gehorsam Christi als das geradezu beherrschende Moment in unsere Vorstellung von seiner* Gottheit)."[38] Our understanding of God, then, can only be subsequent to observing the actual history of God in Jesus Christ.

Having observed that, for Barth, the concept of obedience is to serve as the dominating moment in our conception of God and that there is no ontic distinction between the being of God in the incarnation and the being of God in eternity, we are still left with compelling questions concerning divine freedom and divine necessity. In other words, does there have to be obedience in God? And, if so, is God thereby no longer free?

For Barth, the freedom of which God makes use in his action as the incarnate Reconciler of the world does not demonstrate an arbitrary freedom.

> [God] does not make just any use of the possibilities of His divine nature, but He makes one definite use which is necessary on the basis and in fulfilment of His own decision *(Er macht von den Möglichkeiten seiner göttlichen Natur nicht irgend einen, sondern einen bestimmten, den auf Grund und im Vollzug seiner eigenen Entscheidung notwendigen Gebrauch)....* What takes place is the divine *fulfilment* of a divine *decree (die göttliche* Verwirklichung *eines göttlichen* Dekretes). It takes place in the freedom of God, but in the inner necessity of the freedom of God *(in der inneren Notwendigkeit der Freiheit Gottes)* and not in the play of a sovereign *liberum arbitrium.* There is no possibility of something quite different happening.[39]

This passage of the *Church Dogmatics* is very important. First, it is clear that Barth recognizes that the divine nature may or might have had other possibilities than obedience and incarnation. He never speculates on them or investigates them — after all, on what basis could he do so? — but he recognizes that they are (or, perhaps better, were) there. Second, he affirms that God makes use of one possibility, and that God

---

37. *CD* IV/1, p. 202.
38. *CD* IV/1, p. 199, translation altered (*KD* IV/1, p. 218).
39. *CD* IV/1, pp. 194-95 (*KD* IV/1, pp. 212-13).

does so in the divine freedom, and that God is thus unequivocally free from external compulsion or constraint. The freedom of God is not to be compromised. Third, and perhaps most significantly for our purposes at the present moment, Barth determines that the possibility of which God does make use is necessary "on the basis and in fulfilment of His own decision."[40]

If obedience and incarnation rest upon a decision, however, and if that obedience and determination for incarnation are intrinsic, no — to use Barth's word — *essential,* to the divine being, not only in time but also in eternity, then that leads to the tentative conclusion that, for Barth, God is Lord over God's own being. In other words, God determines God's own being in eternity, and God does this in determining Godself to be for humanity in Jesus Christ in the divine and gracious and free act of election. It is after this fashion that I would understand how Barth can write that in the saving event of the incarnation "we do not have to do with one of the throws in a game of chance which takes place in the divine being, but with the foundation-rock of a divine decision which is as we find it divinely fulfilled in this saving event and not otherwise."[41] Again, it is along this line of interpretation that I would understand how Barth can later refer to "the ontological necessity *(die ontologische Notwendigkeit)* in which this Father has this Son, and this Son this Father, . . . the self-evident fulfilment of that determination of a son to his father, the actual rendering of a perfect obedience *(die tatsächliche Leistung eines vollkommenen Gehorsams),* the ceaseless unity of the One who disposes and the One who complies, the actual oneness and agreement of that which they will and do."[42] Clearly, there was and is (and will be) no external compulsion on God to do anything. God remains free. Yet Barth indicates that, precisely on the basis of the *freedom* in which God eternally determines God's own being in election, there arises a certain and very particular *necessity* in respect of what will transpire in the history of Jesus Christ.

The history of Jesus Christ is an eternal history, for, as Barth notes, "The self-positing God is never apart from Him as the One who is posited as God by God."[43] However, it is precisely as an Above and a

---

40. *CD* IV/1, p. 194.
41. *CD* IV/1, p. 195.
42. *CD* IV/1, pp. 209-10 (*KD* IV/1, p. 229).
43. *CD* IV/1, p. 209.

Below that God has Self-posited and posited the divine being in eternity.[44] By way of this eternal Self-determination, God in his mode of being as the Son fulfills the divine subordination, in obedience, and God in his mode of being as the Father fulfills the divine superiority, in commanding. And Barth insists that the Father and the Son are never without the Holy Spirit, who is the bond of their mutual love.[45] Indeed, for Barth, God is Father and Son in perfect unity precisely because God is also "a Third, the One who affirms the one and equal Godhead through and by and in the two modes of being, the One who makes possible and maintains His fellowship with Himself as the one and the other."[46]

We have reached the furthermost point of our journey out from the individual human being in time. We find ourselves here right at the heart of the being of the God who is Trinity, and here we find obedience, not only in time, but also in eternity. The Father commands the Son and the Son obeys the Father, all in the communion of the Holy Spirit and without compromising either the unity or the equality of God. This is what God has determined to be the Trinitarian essence of the divine nature in the eternal decision of election. Lest we seem to have strayed from our ethical path, it is time to begin our journey back toward understanding the Christian as a responsible ethical agent, on which route we find ourselves once again confronted by the incarnate God-human Jesus Christ.

The Election of Jesus Christ and the Economic Trinity

We have just been exploring the inner-Trinitarian relationship between the Father and the Son. We have seen that this relationship, resulting from the eternal divine act of election, is identical in content to the relationship between God and Jesus Christ in time. In the *Church Dogmatics,* Barth expresses the connection between these two relationships —

44. *CD* IV/1, p. 200.
45. *CD* IV/1, p. 209.
46. *CD* IV/1, pp. 202-3. Barth continues, "In virtue of this third mode of being He is in the other two without division or contradiction, the whole God in each. But again in virtue of this third mode of being He is in neither for itself and apart from the other, but in each in its relationship to the other, and therefore, in fact, in the totality, the connexion, the interplay, the history of these relationships" (*CD* IV/1, p. 203).

between the relationship between Father and Son in eternity and the relationship between God and Jesus Christ in time — in terms of an *analogia relationis,* an "analogy of relations." Already in his doctrine of creation, Barth had written that "in [the] decision of the Creator for the creature there arises a relationship which is not alien to the Creator, to God as God, but we might almost say appropriate and natural to Him *(die ihm, wenn man so sagen darf, angemessen, natürlich ist).* God repeats in this relationship *ad extra* a relationship proper *(eigentümlich)* to Himself in His inner divine essence *(in seinem inneren göttlichen Wesen).*"[47] The relationship between Father and Son in the "inner" divine being in eternity is therefore repeated and reflected in God's eternal covenant with humanity as it is revealed and operative in time in the humanity of Jesus Christ, the God-human in divine-human unity.[48] Between these two relationships, there is, Barth observes, "a correspondence and similarity *(eine Entsprechung und Ähnlichkeit).*"[49]

It is important to recognize explicitly that this is not "a correspondence and similarity" of *being,* some sort of *analogia entis,* but a correspondence of *relationship.*[50] This correspondence, this *analogia relationis,* is conceived by Barth in the following manner: "the freedom in which God posits Himself as the Father, is posited by Himself as the Son and confirms Himself as the Holy Ghost *(die Freiheit, in der Gott sich selber setzt und durch sich selber gesetzt ist als der Sohn und sich selber bestätigt als der Heilige Geist),* is the same freedom as that in which He is the Creator of man, in which man may be His creature, and in which the Creator-creature relationship is established by the Creator."[51] This presentation of the *analogia relationis* is phrased in terms of one dimension of the basic divine perfection — freedom. Barth proceeds, however, to provide a further formulation of the *analogia relationis* in terms of the other dimension of the basic divine perfection — love: "The correspondence and similarity of the two relationships consists in the fact that the eternal love in which God as the Father loves the Son, and as the Son loves the Father, and in which God as the Father is loved by the Son and as the Son by the Father, is also the love which is addressed by God to man."[52]

47. *CD* III/2, p. 218 (*KD* III/2, p. 260).
48. *CD* III/2, pp. 218-19.
49. *CD* III/2, p. 220 (*KD* III/2, p. 262).
50. *CD* III/2, p. 220.
51. *CD* III/2, p. 220 (*KD* III/2, p. 262).
52. *CD* III/2, p. 220.

The relationship of freedom and love between God and humanity in time is thus grounded in the eternal relationship of freedom and love between Father and Son. These relationships of freedom and love are themselves determined in the divine event of election, in which God determines Godself in eternity to be for humanity in Jesus Christ.

On the basis of the previous section, however, it is possible and indeed helpful to supplement these expressions of the *analogia relationis* in terms of freedom and love by introducing the concept of obedience. It has been seen already that the obedience that Jesus Christ renders to God in time is grounded in the eternal obedience that the Son renders to the Father. This would allow for a further formulation of the *analogia relationis,* one that appears to me to be implicit in the work of Barth himself but is never made explicit. This would run along the following lines:

> The correspondence and similarity of the two relationships consists in the fact that the eternal obedience which God as the Father commands of the Son, and as the Son renders to the Father, and in which God as the Father commands the Son and as the Son obeys the Father, is the same obedience which God demands of the creature, which the creature may render to God, and in which the relationship between God and the creature is established by God.

In common with Barth's own formulations of the *analogia relationis,* this "correspondence and similarity" would be grounded in the divine act of election in eternity and would be effected and revealed in time in the person of Jesus Christ. And corresponding to the *analogia relationis* expressed in terms of "freedom," the "creature" referred to here would be — at least in the first instance — Jesus Christ.

What this new formulation adds to Barth's understanding of the *analogia relationis* is a sense of the directionality inherent not only in the event of the incarnation in time, but also in the event of election in eternity, a directionality that leads freely, but also necessarily, to the cross. Though it is not brought out explicitly in connection with the *analogia relationis,* this directionality is clearly present in Barth's own work. For example, in the section of the *Church Dogmatics* we considered above — answering the christological question *quo iure Deus homo?* — Barth writes:

> [Jesus Christ] realises perfectly the ὑπακοή [obedience] and ὑποταγή [submission] and τιμή [honor] which correspond to the perfect lordship of God as its necessary complement. He sets up the lord-

ship of God and reveals it in the quite free but quite necessary *(in der ganz freien, aber auch ganz notwendigen)* decision, in the determination which is native to Him and therefore utterly natural *(in der ihm von Haus aus eigenen und darum von innen heraus natürlichen Bestimmtheit)*, to go the way of the servant of God, the way downwards, to lowliness and finally to the cross.[53]

What this passage elucidates is that the complement of the Lordship of God in this world, which the world could not have produced of itself, is the decision for a life of obedience in humility. In this decision, we see that Jesus Christ *freely* sets himself on the road to death on a cross in abandonment, but we now see also that this road is *necessarily* determined for (as well as by) him in the eternal divine decision of election — it is a determination that is *"von Haus aus"* and *"von innen heraus"* "natural" to him. And thus Jesus Christ travels this road of obedience "self-evidently, naturally, in His own freedom, and therefore perfectly *(selbstverständlich, natürlich, in seiner eigenen Freiheit und gerade darum vollständig)*."[54] To return to (but to reverse and perhaps even subvert) our language above, Jesus Christ performs the will of God, not only in heaven but also on earth. In his obedience and humility, Jesus Christ fulfills the law, not only eternally but also temporally. Obedience is therefore a fundamental dimension of the *analogia relationis,* and deserves to come to expression as such.

The consequence of the *analogia relationis* as expressed in these three formulations — freedom, love, and obedience — is that the being and action of the incarnate Jesus does not arise by accident or caprice. Instead, Barth insists, it "follows the *essence,* the inner being of God *(folgt dem* Wesen *Gottes, seinem inneren Sein)*."[55] Barth therefore contends that "[t]he humanity of Jesus is not merely the repetition and reflection of His divinity *(die Wiederholung und Nachbildung seiner Divinität),* or of God's controlling will; it is the repetition and reflection of God Himself *(die Wiederholung und Nachbildung Gottes selber),* no more and no less. It is the image of God, the *imago Dei.*"[56] It is here, in the person of Jesus Christ, that we see that the humanity of Jesus Christ — the cohumanity of Jesus, his being *for* humanity — is the direct correlative

53. *CD* IV/1, p. 208 *(KD* IV/1, pp. 227-28).
54. *CD* IV/1, p. 208 *(KD* IV/1, p. 228).
55. *CD* III/2, p. 220 *(KD* III/2, p. 263).
56. *CD* III/2, p. 219 *(KD* III/2, p. 261).

of his being *for* God.[57] It is in the person of Jesus Christ that there is revealed the true image of God.

This construal of the *imago Dei,* based on the *analogia relationis,* has corresponding implications for Barth's theological anthropology. For Barth, the "ontological determination of humanity is grounded in the fact that one man among all others is the man Jesus."[58] At the same time, however, and correspondingly, the ethical determination of humanity — the determination of the Christian as ethical agent — is also determined by this fact. This mention of the ethical determination of humanity in Jesus Christ moves us into the final stage of our exploration of Barth's understanding of the Christian as ethical agent, in which we move from Jesus Christ and his obedience to consider the Christian herself as a responsible individual before God.

The Election of the Christian: A Second Word

For Barth, in the Word and work of God in Jesus Christ "the right action of man has already been performed."[59] As we saw above, however, there is no room for Christian antinomianism or passivity at this point: that Jesus Christ has fulfilled the law does not remove us from the claim and judgment of the law but instead validates the law and its claim of and judgment on us. Thus Barth writes that because Jesus Christ has already performed this right action, it "waits only to be confirmed by our action."[60] Consequently, Barth posits: "In the one image of Jesus Christ we have both the Gospel which reconciles us with God and illumines us and consoles us, and the Law which in contradistinction to all the laws which we ourselves find or fabricate really binds and obligates us."[61] It is precisely in the light of the gospel, then, that there exists a claim on our obedience. It is precisely because in Jesus Christ the eternal covenant between God and humanity is established and the law is fulfilled that there arises for us the ethical question: "What does it mean to be a [human being] now that this decision has been reached by the grace of God?"[62]

57. *CD* III/2, p. 220.
58. *CD* III/2, p. 132.
59. *CD* II/2, p. 543.
60. *CD* II/2, p. 543.
61. *CD* II/2, p. 539.
62. *CD* II/2, p. 558.

Paul T. Nimmo

We can begin to understand what it means by pursuing the implications of the *analogia relationis* that we explored in our last section for theological anthropology. We noted that there was an analogy between (on the one hand) the relationship between the Father and the Son and (on the other hand) the relationship between God and the human Jesus. For Barth, however, there is a further analogy, namely, between these Trinitarian relationships and the relationship between Jesus Christ and us. Barth states explicitly that the ethical agent is created by God "in correspondence with [the] relationship and differentiation in God Himself: created as a Thou that can be addressed by God but also as an I responsible to God."[63] Indeed, he suggests, "the history between Him and us is primarily and properly the representation, reflection and correspondence of the life of God Himself."[64] In other words, the Christian ethical agent is posited in a relationship with God whose contours are defined by the *analogia relationis* revealed in Jesus Christ: a relationship, therefore, in which she is called to freedom and to love and — we must now explicitly mention — to obedience.

To answer the ethical question of what it means to be a responsible Christian in light of the gracious decision of God in election, then, we are directed to Jesus Christ, the royal man who is described by Barth as "the pattern of Christian existence."[65] We are summoned by this Word of God to obedient action in freedom and love, which action — in all its humanity and thus dissimilarity — is nevertheless by the power of grace similar, parallel, and analogous to the act of God in Jesus Christ. In short, we are summoned to "do in [*our*] circle . . . that which God does by Christ in His circle."[66] Barth writes: "Our aim must correspond to the distinctive aim of our Father in heaven, who meets both the good and the evil with the same beneficence. It must be a readiness to forgive one [another], to be compassionate, to bear one another's burdens and to live and help one another. It must be persistent kindness even towards persecutors of the faith. It must be a humility in which we do not look at our own things, but at the things of others. It must be a love which is directed even — and especially — to our enemies."[67] It is thus in Jesus Christ that there is revealed and embodied

63. *CD* III/1, p. 198.
64. *CD* IV/2, p. 347.
65. *CD* IV/2, p. 835.
66. *CD* II/2, p. 579.
67. *CD* II/2, p. 578.

the obedience, the submission, and the honor that correspond to the perfect Lordship of God as its perfect complement.[68]

There is at this point an obvious connection to be made with the long-standing Christian tradition of the *imitatio Christi* — the imitation of Christ. It is noteworthy, however, that Barth dismisses late medieval and certain evangelical traditions of the *imitatio Christi* as something one "must not waste time describing and criticising."[69] For Barth, a true conception of the *imitatio Christi* has nothing to do with a formulaic repetition of the life of Christ: he contends that one could "try to copy everything that Jesus demanded and that [the disciples] did, and yet completely fail to be disciples, because we do not do it, as they did, at His particular call and command to us."[70]

Barth is determined here to insist upon the specificity, the concreteness, and the particularity of the divine command as it is given to and heard by the individual Christian in encounter with the Word of God. The result is that the command of God cannot be fixed or formulated into general ethical principles or rules, whether in Scripture or elsewhere; we are never called or commanded by a brute rule. We are, however, called in and by Jesus Christ, and his purpose remains that out of our lives should come "a repetition, an analogy, a parallel to His own being — that [we] should be conformable to Christ."[71] In the event in which this happens, we correspond by grace in our being and in our action to our election in Jesus Christ and we become by grace the image of God.[72] As the ethical agent as a being in action conforms to the pattern of Jesus Christ in freedom and love and obedience, then, she both realizes her own true self-determination and conforms to her determination in Jesus Christ — in short, she becomes also under the law what she already is through the gospel.

68. *CD* IV/1, p. 208.

69. *CD* IV/2, p. 533. Barth comments that it is precisely the arbitrariness of *all* imitation that is its weakness: "Just what imitation really intends, imitation cannot achieve" (*CD* I/2, p. 276).

70. *CD* IV/2, p. 553.

71. *CD* I/2, p. 277.

72. *CD* II/2, p. 575. Barth notes elsewhere once again that this correspondence is not an *analogia entis* but an *analogia relationis*: "As God is free for man, so man is free for man; but only inasmuch as God is for him, so that the *analogia relationis* as the meaning of the divine likeness cannot be equated with an *analogia entis*" (*CD* III/1, p. 195). Moreover, this image is, for Barth, "such that, as the *analogia relationis,* it can never cease to be God's work and gift or become a human possession" (p. 201).

The question arises at this point, however, as to the connection between the ethical instruction found in the New Testament and the word of law encountering the Christian in the present. After all, if the New Testament commands or the actions of Jesus Christ are not to be taken to apply to us in any immediate imperative sense, then what purpose do they have in Christian ethics and what relevance do they have for us? In answer to this question, Barth argues that what the New Testament stories about the following of the disciples really preserve are "certain prominent *lines* (*gewisse große* Linien) along which the concrete commanding of Jesus, with its demand for concrete obedience, always moved in relation to individuals, characterising it as His commanding in distinction from that of all other lords."[73] Though the commanding of Jesus Christ is not identical for every time and place and person, then, nevertheless it will always move along one or more of these "prominent lines." These "lines" indicate a pattern of Christian life that Barth presents in some detail, a pattern that involves the renunciation of material attachments and social status, the promotion of practical pacifism, the relativization of family relationships, and the condemnation of false religiosity.[74]

There is, moreover, one further "prominent line" to consider. Barth believes that the final and most decisive "line" of Christian discipleship indicated in the New Testament is the direction of Jesus Christ to take up one's cross. For Barth, Christians always already stand under the sign and direction of the cross of Jesus Christ.[75] However, Barth is adamant that Christians do not thereby stand under the *shadow* of the cross, because the "cross is for them light and power and glory and promise and fulfilment, present liberation and the hope of that which is still to come, the forgiveness of sins, and here and now eternal life."[76] Indeed, in taking up the cross for herself, a cross similar to but not identical with the cross of Jesus Christ, the Christian points to God, to the will of God for the world, to the future revelation of the majesty of God, and to the glory in which Jesus Christ already lives and reigns.[77]

73. CD IV/2, p. 547 (KD IV/2, p. 619).
74. CD IV/2, pp. 547-52.
75. CD IV/2, pp. 263-64.
76. CD IV/2, p. 263.
77. CD IV/2, p. 606. Barth unfolds his understanding of this "prominent line" of discipleship in a section of his doctrine of reconciliation entitled "The Dig-Cross," CD IV/2, §66.6, pp. 598-613.

The fact remains, however, that this remains a life under the sign and direction of the cross. Correspondingly, Barth notes that the shape of the Christian life attested in Scripture involves lowliness of mind, a bowing beneath the law of humility, and condescension, self-denial, and self-abasement; it requires a life of bearing each other's burdens, of subjection, obedience, and submission, of fellowship with the life and the sufferings of Christ, and of following his example; it calls for taking up the cross and for patience in its sufferings, for love of our enemies and for prayer for our persecutors.[78]

One final question remains, however: Why is there such a radical downward directionality to the shape of Christian discipleship, both as attested in Scripture and as experienced today? Barth formulates the question thus: "What is it that gives to New Testament ethics this direction, this tendency, this dynamic, this pull which in experience has again and again been found to be dominant and exclusive and irresistible, setting aside all pretexts and excuses, the pull from the heights to the depths, from riches to poverty, from victory to defeat, from triumph to suffering, from life to death?"[79] Barth addresses this question in the midst of the remarkable passage we explored above in the doctrine of reconciliation, in which he draws out the *ethical* consequences for Christian individuals and for Christian ethics of his *ontological* understanding of God.

For Barth, the downward trend in New Testament ethics and in Christian discipleship results from the eternal divine decision of election in which God determined Godself to be for humanity in Jesus Christ. According to the New Testament, God does not only love those who love God in return; God does not have to be exalted, but can also be lowly; God does not have to be alone or among friends, but can also be abroad among enemies; God does not have to judge only, but can also forgive; in being lowly, God is exalted.[80] When the "law" of humility and obedience that leads toward the cross applies in the first in-

---

78. *CD* IV/1, pp. 188-90.

79. *CD* IV/1, p. 190.

80. *CD* IV/1, pp. 190-91. When Barth later expresses the ways in which the activity of the incarnate Jesus Christ corresponds to God, he offers the following answer: "[Jesus Christ] resembles God in His unpretentiousness in what seems to be His world to human eyes; in His corresponding partisanship of those who are lowly in this world; in the revolutionary character of His relationship to the established orders; in His positive turning to man as he exists and is and is oppressed in this world" (*CD* IV/2, pp. 248-49).

stance to Jesus Christ,[81] then it does so not as a matter of divine caprice or blind chance. By contrast, as was discussed above, this "law" pertains to him *ontologically,* as a result of the gracious decision of God to be this God. It is, in Barth's words, precisely as "this God, in this divine nature," that God is "the Father of Jesus Christ, the One who in Him reconciles the world to Himself."[82]

To take the final step, however, this cruciform "law" of humility and obedience applies not only to Jesus Christ, but also to those who are elect in him, to the community of Jesus Christ and its constituent individuals. "This God" is therefore also, according to Barth, "the Law-giver and Himself the law for those who know Him in Jesus Christ."[83] At this juncture, Barth once again posits that "we must disperse any remaining appearance of chance or arbitrariness with which the whole phenomenon might be enshrouded."[84] Crucially, Barth writes: "If in fellowship with Christ Christians have to be μιμηταὶ θεοῦ [imitators of God] (Eph. 5:1), if the τελειότης [perfection], the fulfilment of the being and essence [*die Ausrichtung des Seins und Wesens*], of their heavenly Father is the measure and norm of their own τελειότης [perfection] (Matt. 5:48), then in its original and final authority and compulsion the demand addressed to them is necessarily this and no other."[85] Two things are important to observe in this statement. First, Barth maintains that the ethical demand upon the Christian — as attested in the New Testament witness — *necessarily* has this downward shape. In the New Testament passages that advocate Christian obedience and humility, then, we do not have to do with chance or arbitrariness but "with a reflection of the New Testament concept of God,"[86] of the God for whom it is as natural to obey as to command, to be humbled as to be exalted. Second, this downward trend not only reflects the activity of the Father, to which we are called to correspond, but also the fulfillment of the being and essence of our heavenly Father. On the one hand, this contention of Barth once again confirms the view expressed above that the very essence of God is determined for this obedience and humility, and that this determination occurs in the eternal divine act of election. On the other hand, this conten-

81. *CD* IV/1, p. 189.
82. *CD* IV/1, p. 191.
83. *CD* IV/1, p. 191.
84. *CD* IV/1, p. 190.
   D IV/1, p. 190 (*KD* IV/1, p. 208).
   D IV/1, p. 190.

tion of Barth also indicates that the Christian as ethical agent is determined for this obedience and humility ontologically. In other words, as Barth later explicitly notes, that we stand under the sign and direction of the cross is "not so much a matter of morals as 'ontology' *(Es geht nicht um Moral, es geht viel eher um 'Ontologie'!)*."[87]

The result is that, in correspondence with the essence of God, humility is "not to [Christians] something strange or remarkable, an ideal which is quite impracticable in its strict sense," but is rather "necessarily that which is natural to them."[88] We do not have the option to choose whether to exalt or abase ourselves, whether to save our lives or lose them, whether to take up our cross or to leave it, whether to hate our enemies or to love them, whether to accept suffering in the discipleship of Christ.[89] We are not — to use one of Barth's favorite images — Hercules at the crossroads with a *liberum arbitrium*. There is no general principle or symbol of the cross about which we can deliberate and choose.[90] Instead, we stand under the sign and direction of the cross because that cross is the cross of Jesus Christ and because God in Jesus Christ stood there first, in obedience and humility. We stand there because Jesus Christ is both the subject and the object of the election of God and because we are elect in him. Moreover, this existence under the cross is, for Barth, not a yoke of servitude that the Christian must bear because God wills it. It represents rather God's call "into the freedom of the children of God, into a following of the freedom and the work in which God Himself is God."[91] It is only because Jesus Christ is the electing and elected Son of God who suffers and dies in love and freedom and in obedience and humility that we are "called and empowered in fellowship with Him to choose the ταπεινο-φροσύνη [humility] which is natural to the children of God."[92]

The shape of the Christian life of discipleship and its downward directionality that is actualized in the command of God is therefore not a matter of divine arbitrariness or ethical caprice. Rather the call of Jesus Christ to correspond to our true being in humility and obedience is grounded in his very own being and action and in the very being and action of God, not only in time, but also in eternity. This is what it

87. *CD* IV/2, p. 264 (*KD* IV/2, p. 292).
88. *CD* IV/1, p. 191.
89. *CD* IV/1, p. 191.
90. *CD* IV/1, pp. 191-92.
91. *CD* IV/1, p. 191.
92. *CD* IV/1, p. 192.

means for the Christian as an ethical agent to live under the Word of God: to face the daily challenge to live, by grace, in freedom under the sign and direction of the cross, and thereby to correspond to her calling in Jesus Christ.

Conclusion

We have traveled some way with Barth in the course of this essay: from the ethical agent to God and back again, picking up some humility and obedience along the way. It remains perhaps only to say a very brief word about the purpose of the ethical action of the Christian, about the telos of the obedience of our being in action.

When the Christian *is* obedient, she corresponds in her action — which conforms to the law — to her being — which is declared in the gospel. She acts as one created, reconciled, and redeemed by God. In this obedient correspondence of being and action, of being in action, her human self-determination by grace corresponds to her divine determination. In the exercise of her true freedom in this vocation, the Christian reflects the activity of the God who determined Godself in eternity to be both humble and exalted, both Below and Above, for her sake. The goal of this event of correspondence, for Barth, is a double glorification. On the one hand, there is a glorification of God by the human being, and on the other hand, there is a glorification of the human being by God. This glorification takes place as an event, and on the creaturely side it is provisional and limited and transient. Nevertheless, it is a real glorification: the Christian in obedient humility receives "a part in the genuine divine *gloria,* and the divine *gloria* is not ashamed to dwell in it and to shine through it."[93] This is the telos of the life of the Christian, and it is in humility and obedience that it is reached.

The Word of God that confronts us as gospel and law thus both proclaims the permission to glorify God and issues the command to glorify God. It is as the Christian glorifies God in this way that she herself participates in the divine glory, that the will of God for her is fulfilled, and that her being and her action, determined in the eternal divine act of election, fulfill their telos. This may not happen often, but — by the grace of God — it can and does happen. Alleluia.

II/1, p. 669.

13. Karl Barth's Conception(s) of Human and Divine Freedom(s)

Jesse Couenhoven

In Paul Nimmo's helpful description of Karl Barth's understanding of the Christian as ethical agent, he considers Barth's concept of the correspondence of relationship *(analogia relationis)* between the being and action of "the inner being of God,"[1] and the incarnate person Jesus Christ — and therefore between God and humanity. His discussion, like Barth's own, leads me to wonder how Barth's conception of divine freedom is related to Barth's conception of human freedom. I sketch an answer to that question in this essay.

In doing so, I am not primarily interested in resolving questions about the manner in which divine and human action are related; I am mainly interested in clarifying how Barth's concepts of divine and human freedom are related. To rephrase my question as sharply as I can, I am asking this: Might it be the case that when Barth speaks of divine "freedom" he means something quite different than what he has in mind when he speaks of human "freedom"? And might there not therefore be significant ways in which Barth's theology implies that divine and human freedom are not properly considered analogous at all?[2] I

---

1. *CD* III/2, p. 220.

2. Ideas of analogy are, of course, quite slippery, and as a result, one possible response to my query is to shrug and note that of course there are differences between divine and human freedom. To be clear, then, my question is whether human and divine freedom differ in kind, for Barth. A related way of pressing this question would be to ask

---

I am indebted to William Werpehowski for a helpful discussion of the contents of this paper.

am not presupposing that any particular answer to these questions is right or wrong, but it is worth noting that Barth himself appears to want to speak of an analogy between human and divine freedom.[3]

Discussion of Barth's conceptions of freedom must deal with his apparent lack of interest in what he may have considered the philosophical task of expounding theories and definitions of freedom, and the challenges that poses for ascertaining what he means when he invokes "freedom." As Nimmo's discussion implies, Barth was not concerned with theoretically resolving questions about divine and human freedom. Nimmo takes Barth as his model in focusing not on defining terms or providing a theoretical resolution to questions about the nature of freedom but on a descriptive task: both authors speak of freedom, and also of obedience, and even of determination.[4] These concepts are placed in relationship, in that they are set alongside one another, but neither theologian explains how they are related. I find such treatments of the idea of freedom somewhat frustrating, but some theologians might defend the ambiguity of Barth's discussion of freedom.[5] They might argue, for instance, that the dogmatic theologian's task is not to speculate about obscure questions of divine and human freedom — which are mysterious by their nature — but to expound what we have been given to know by God in and through the incarnate Son.

The body of this essay is my main response to these issues, but I want to begin by explaining my motivations for pressing Barth for more conceptual clarity. Though both science and the arts treat subjects of great complexity and mystery, that has never been a good reason for them not to seek as much understanding as they can; without doing so, we have no way of knowing what insights the subject matter allows. And while I agree that theologians should be wary of speculation, it is not enough for us to simply say that both we and God are free, any more than it is enough to simply say that both we and God love. The specific contours of our concepts of love matter — as Barth,

---

whether the correspondence of relationship between divine and human love is quite different from the correspondence Barth sees between divine and human freedom.

3. Cf. *CD* III/2, pp. 193-95; *CD* III/3, pp. 188-89; *CD* IV/2, p. 356.

4. Paul T. Nimmo, "Barth and the Christian as Ethical Agent: An Ontological Study of the Shape of Christian Ethics," pp. 216-38 above.

5. Cf. John Webster, *Barth's Moral Theology: Human Action in Barth's Thought* (Grand Rapids: Eerdmans, 1998), pp. 91-92, 101-2; George Hunsinger, *How to Read Karl Barth: The Shape of His Theology* (New York: Oxford University Press, 1991), pp. 197-98.

who was not eager to blow on the flames of eros, would certainly agree — as does the nature of the relationship between divine and human loves, and the same is true when it comes to speaking of freedom.

Happily, in spite of his lack of clarity at important points, Barth nevertheless does much to flesh out the concepts of freedom he wished to dispute and to defend, and how he does so is worth considering at length. I find Barth less ambiguous in his discussions of the nature of human freedom than in his discussions of divine freedom. As a result, I propose in this essay that Barth's interpreters would do well to use his account of human freedom to limit the ambiguities of his account of divine freedom. This is not to claim that human freedom has an onto-logical or even an epistemic priority, but only that it may be helpful for Barth's readers to give hermeneutical priority to his discussion of the concept of human freedom. Thus, in an effort to read Barth's theology of freedom as sympathetically as possible, I hope to offer a clarification of Barth — *by Barth*.[6]

Barth's Conception of Divine Freedom: An Initial Look

The suggestion that Barth's theology of freedom might require some assistance to maintain its consistency implies, of course, that Barth's concepts of divine and human freedom are in at least prima facie tension with one another. Eberhard Busch has argued that Barth under-stands the freedom of the triune God as unique.[7] The question before us is whether divine freedom is unique in kind, or in degree. If Barth maintains that divine freedom is unlike human freedom in being much greater in every way, there remains a role for some sort of analogy between the two. But if divine freedom differs from human freedom in kind, then it is difficult to see how it would be proper to speak of an analogy between them. To engage this question, let us turn to Barth's discussion of divine freedom.

George Hendry rightly argued some time ago that Barth's discus-sions of divine freedom in the *Church Dogmatics* evoke at least five distin-

---

6. Cf. Bruce McCormack, "Seek God Where He May Be Found: A Response to Edwin Chr. van Driel," *Scottish Journal of Theology* 60, no. 1 (2007): 66.

7. Eberhard Busch, *The Great Passion: An Introduction to Karl Barth's Theology*, trans. Geoffrey W. Bromiley (Grand Rapids: Eerdmans, 2004), p. 121.

guishable conceptions of freedom.[8] Let us begin by discussing three important and relatively uncontroversial connotations of divine "freedom" in Barth, ideas that he seems to consider not only mutually compatible but also mutually implicating. First, Barth speaks of freedom when he has in mind the idea that God has precedence over humanity, and takes the initiative: "We cannot over-emphasise God's freedom and sovereignty in this act. We cannot assert too strongly that in the election of grace it is a matter of the decision and initiative of the divine good-pleasure."[9]

Second, in a closely related sense of the term, Barth speaks of freedom when he has the gratuity of divine grace in mind: "[T]he covenant is a covenant of grace. This concept implies three things. The first is the freedom in which it is determined and established by God, and therefore the undeservedness with which man can receive and respond to the fact that God has chosen and determined and made Himself his God."[10] Both of these connotations of the term "freedom" are relational, in that they are ways in which God is free in relation to human beings, and to the entirety of creation, more generally. But divine freedom does not depend on God being in relation to a creation; God is free in the immanent as well as the economic Trinity (God does not need the world in order to be free or to express that freedom). Thus, the conceptions of divine freedom just mentioned are backed by a third. Barth speaks of freedom when he wants to emphasize that, far from being compelled or coerced by some sort of external necessity, God is self-determining:

> Freedom is, of course, more than the absence of limits, restrictions, or conditions. This is only its negative and to that extent improper aspect — improper to the extent that from this point of view it requires another, at least in so far as its freedom lies in its independence of this other. But freedom in its positive and proper qualities means to be grounded in one's own being, to be determined and moved by oneself. This is the freedom of the divine life and love. In this positive freedom of His, God is also unlimited, unrestricted and unconditioned from without.[11]

8. George Hendry, "The Freedom of God in the Theology of Karl Barth," *Scottish Journal of Theology* 31 (1978): 233-36.

9. *CD* II/2, p. 177; cf. p. 44; *CD* I/1, p. 306.

10. *CD* IV/1, p. 39.

11. *CD* II/1, p. 301. See also p. 302, where Barth indicates that his emphasis on divine freedom is a way of speaking about the traditional concept of aseity.

The reality of divine self-determination makes it possible for God's grace to be unforced and uncompelled, and thus free both in the sense that it is gracious and in the sense that it has priority.

The main difficulty in Barth's doctrine of freedom comes in understanding more completely what it means for God to be self-determined, for God's grace to be uncompelled, and how these things take place. The most common interpretation of Barth's understanding of divine self-determination is in terms of what philosophers call an "incompatibilist" sense, meaning that God determines himself via a choice that is itself undetermined (a fourth idea of "freedom").[12] Barth leaves himself open to such interpretation when he writes of God as the "One who wills Himself,"[13] whose "being is decision";[14] when he asserts that God is unique in that "No other being is absolutely its own, conscious, willed and executed decision";[15] and when he speaks of "God . . . in Himself, in the primal and basic decision in which He wills to be and actually is God."[16] Picking up on such cues, Robert Jenson has argued that, for Barth, "God is the free event, independent even of his own nature yet nonetheless having a nature, because he decides to be and to be what he is."[17] Like Jenson, Bruce McCormack reads Barth as claiming that God's essence is self-determined in that it is subject to his undetermined choice.[18]

Nimmo notes that this reading of Barth has proven controver-

---

12. What I mean in this paper by "incompatibilism" is the belief that free will requires a power to determine one's own path by choosing between alternate possibilities in the absence of deterministic factors. In God's case, unlike our own, this choice presumably takes place in eternity.

13. *CD* II/1, p. 550.

14. *CD* II/2, p. 175.

15. *CD* II/1, p. 271.

16. *CD* II/2, p. 76; cf. *CD* IV/1, p. 39.

17. Robert W. Jenson, *God after God: The God of the Past and the God of the Future, Seen in the Work of Karl Barth* (New York: Bobbs-Merrill, 1969), p. 127.

18. Bruce McCormack, "Grace and Being: The Role of God's Gracious Election in Karl Barth's Theological Ontology," in *The Cambridge Companion to Karl Barth*, ed. John Webster (New York: Cambridge University Press, 2000), p. 104; McCormack, "Seek God," p. 74. For readings of Barth's understanding of divine freedom that have some similarities (though also important differences), see John Macken, *The Autonomy Theme in the "Church Dogmatics": Karl Barth and His Critics* (New York: Cambridge University Press, 1990), p. 155, and Kevin W. Hector, "God's Triunity and Self-Determination: A Conversation with Karl Barth, Bruce McCormack and Paul Molnar," *International Journal of Systematic Theology* 7, no. 3 (2005): 246-61.

sial.[19] Summarizing the arguments of the theologians who have opposed what Hunsinger calls the "revisionist" view of Barth on election is beyond the scope of this paper, but it is notable that while they have found problematic the idea that God's decision to be with us is the basis of the Trinity, they have not turned away from the incompatibilist understanding of divine freedom that provides much of the motivation for the revisionist reading of Barth, and that makes that reading of Barth appear to be a way of making Barth more consistent with his own theology.

To be sure, Paul Molnar has indicated that McCormack's reading of Barth leaves the Trinity determined by God's eternal choice to be God for us, and thus limits its freedom. It would be better, Molnar indicates, if the incarnation is a new choice, and therefore an expression of God's freedom "to be God in a new way as God for us."[20] However, both he and McCormack appear to conceptualize freedom in fundamentally the same incompatibilist manner, as based on nondetermined choice.[21] On the topic of freedom, the main difference between them is that Molnar insists that God is unfree unless God currently has alternative possibilities — when God decides to create and to redeem in Jesus Christ, God is free only if God could have done otherwise. McCormack, on the other hand, implicitly agrees with the philosopher Robert Kane's idea that the connection between freedom and choice among alternatives is indirect, and historical: for an agent to be free is not simply for that agent to have options, but for that agent to be ultimately responsible for who that agent is and what that agent does. As a result, nondetermined choice matters because it is the condition of the possibility of such freedom, but once a self-determining choice is made (Kane calls this "will-setting"),

---

19. See Paul Molnar, *Divine Freedom and the Doctrine of the Immanent Trinity* (New York: T. & T. Clark, 2002), chapter 3; Jay Wesley Richards, *The Untamed God: A Philosophical Exploration of Divine Perfection, Immutability, and Simplicity* (Downers Grove, Ill.: InterVarsity, 2003), chapters 4-5; Edwin Chr. van Driel, "Karl Barth on the Eternal Existence of Jesus Christ," *Scottish Journal of Theology* 60, no. 1 (2007): 45-61; George Hunsinger, "Election and the Trinity: Twenty-five Theses on the Theology of Karl Barth," *Modern Theology* 24, no. 2 (2008): 179-98.

20. Molnar, *Divine Freedom*, p. 63.

21. Richards, in his book, and van Driel, in personal conversation, take similar positions, emphasizing that God is able to be free and gracious in creating only if God makes an undetermined choice among options in doing so. For what appear to be sympathetic views, see Hendry, "The Freedom of God," pp. 237-38, and Busch, *The Great Passion*, p. 114.

further choices between alternatives are not necessary for freedom.[22] Thus, for McCormack (as for Kane) the freedom of God's later actions — even if they flow necessarily from a self-determining choice — is based in and can be traced back to that prior and primal free self-determination.

This narrative conception of incompatibilist freedom strikes me as deeper and more theologically and philosophically adequate than one that simply puts a premium on having alternatives, because it appreciates that the essence of incompatibilist freedom involves more than branching pathways — it involves being the ultimate ground of one's agency.[23] It also has the virtue of explaining that and how God is free in and with regard to the immanent Trinity and divine perfections; on Molnar's view, God's lack of options with respect to being triune, loving, and so on seems to imply that God is free in relation to creation, but not with respect to God's own being.[24]

At the same time, the idea that God chooses the divine nature is confusing. An initial problem is why we should consider the triune God revealed to us in Jesus Christ one with the being of whom the revisionists speak as willing to be gracious, triune, and so on; how is a being without the divine perfections (other than this hyperbolic freedom) the same as a being that does have them? A closely related puzzle is why Christians should call a being without the divine perfection of love-in-relationship God at all; a huge gap opens up between the economic Trinity and the immanent "God." A third problem with speaking of God as choosing the divine perfections is that this god before God appears to be incapable of making a nonarbitrary choice — a being of sheer will, without a nature, seems incapable of having a basis for finding some options more appealing than others. Finally, if Barth's conception of divine freedom is as radically self-determining as the revisionists have suggested, this divine perfection (which turns out not to

---

22. Cf. Robert Kane, "Some Neglected Pathways in the Free Will Labyrinth," in *The Oxford Handbook of Free Will,* ed. Robert Kane (New York: Oxford University Press, 2002), pp. 407-13. In using terms like "prior" or "later" in this discussion, I do not, of course, mean to imply that these decisions are made in time, but that there are logical priorities and distinctions between them.

23. For a relevant discussion, see James F. Sennett, "Is There Freedom in Heaven?" *Faith and Philosophy* 16, no. 1 (1999): 69-82.

24. It would be possible to argue that God has multiple kinds of freedom, some of which apply to the immanent Trinity and some of which do not, but none of the theologians mentioned above has explored, much less endorsed, this view.

be coequal with the divine perfection of loving, but prior to it) has so little in common with Barth's conception of human freedom that it makes little sense to speak of an analogy between the two.

The fact that Barth's conception of human freedom is so radically different from the incompatibilist conception of divine freedom held by some of Barth's leading interpreters suggests that Barth himself is capable of showing us another way to understand the idea of free self-determination — Barth has at his disposal a "compatibilist" understanding of these terms. This conception of freedom is not only central to Barth's views concerning human freedom, but can be used to provide another reading of his understanding of divine freedom — one that makes sense of the idea of freedom in the immanent Trinity without leading to the metaphysical confusions of the revisionist view — but here I am getting ahead of myself. Let us focus, for now, on Barth's conception of human freedom.

Barth's Compatibilist Conception of Human Freedom

In *Karl Barth's Table Talk* a student poses a question about the nature of human freedom: Does freedom mean that we can say yes or no to God? Barth answers:

> The decisive point is whether freedom in the Christian sense is identical with the freedom of Hercules: choice between two ways at a crossroad. This is a heathen notion of freedom. Is it freedom to decide for the devil? The only freedom that means something is freedom to be myself as I am created by God. God did not create a neutral creature, but *His* creature. He placed him in a garden that he might build it up; his freedom is to do that. When man began to discern good and evil, this knowledge was the beginning of sin. Man should not have asked this question about good and evil, but should have remained in true created freedom. We are confused by the political idea of freedom. What is the light in the Statue of Liberty? Freedom to choose good and evil? What light that would be! Light is light and not darkness. If it shines, *darkness is done away with,* not proposed for choice. Being a slave of Christ means being free.[25]

25. *Karl Barth's Table Talk,* ed. John Godsey (Richmond: John Knox, 1963), p. 37.

This answer highlights a number of Barth's central commitments about human freedom, to which he holds consistently in works that span from 1929 to the end of his writing career in 1960. Barth helpfully implies that it is important to distinguish a political conception of freedom — which thinks of freedom as a lack of boundedness — from the Christian concept of liberty. Barth also decisively rejects the idea that Christian freedom depends on choice between alternatives — that, he says, is a heathen conception of freedom.[26] These negative points about what Christian freedom is not are immediately connected to and based on a positive argument: it is not freedom to choose evil, and grace does not make us free by giving us more choices, or a greater power for choice, but rather makes us "a slave of Christ." In speaking of the truly free person as Christ's slave, Barth is, of course, appropriating a metaphor from Luther and Saint Paul that is meant to suggest that freedom depends not on having alternatives but being in the marvelous light of Christ. Only those who are not blind but can see have freedom worthy of the name, rather than the false "power" to fall into *das Nichtige*.[27] Indeed, Barth clarifies that in the fall "The freedom for which God has ordained man is not used."[28] And Barth's rhetorical flourish in speaking of freedom as bondage should not mislead: where the Holy Spirit is present, there is not servitude, compulsion, or coercion, but liberty.[29] Divine grace liberates human beings for our own proper action, and therefore spontaneous and faithful human life. Correspondingly, Barth often adds, human freedom has a very definite form: for us to be free is to live in love, to enjoy God — to live eccentrically.[30]

Human agents are free, Barth says throughout his career, "because they are freed by God for God."[31] Freedom, then, is liberation, be-

---

26. In speaking of Hercules at the crossroads, Barth is presumably referring to the classical theme immortalized in paintings and engravings of Hercules, accosted by female figures representing Virtue and Vice, and faced with a choice concerning which path to follow. He is, of course, literally correct that this is a pagan theme; clearly, however, he is making more than a historical observation.·

27. Cf. Karl Barth, "The Gift of Freedom: Foundation of Evangelical Ethics," in *The Humanity of God*, trans. Thomas Wieser (Richmond: John Knox, 1960), p. 77.

28. *CD* IV/1, p. 485; cf. *CD* III/2, p. 356; *CD* IV/2, p. 367.

29. *CD* IV/2, p. 785; *CL*, p. 93.

30. Karl Barth, *The Holy Spirit and the Christian Life*, ed. Robin W. Lovin, trans. R. Birch Hoyle (Louisville: Westminster John Knox, 1993), p. 66; Barth, "The Gift of Freedom," p. 78; *CL*, p. 94; *CD* III/2, p. 197; cf. Webster, *Barth's Moral Theology*, p. 111.

31. *CL*, p. 88; cf. Barth, *The Holy Spirit*, pp. 6, 11, 19-20.

stowed upon us; it is not something we have in or by ourselves.[32] This implies that human freedom is not a power for self-making analogous to the power the "revisionists" mentioned above think of God as having. Rather, freedom is being and doing what we are called by God to be and do. It is possible for Barth to speak in this manner because what he has in mind amounts to a kind of compatibilist conception of freedom: the deepest conception of human freedom is not as independence, a self-initiated self-making, but a being in activity in line with God's own goodness.

Thus, in speaking of human freedom, Barth speaks of freedom in a fifth sense, in addition to those already mentioned. This conception of freedom is "normative," meaning that it is an asymmetrical way of speaking about freedom, as good — the power to live truly and fully. When freedom is thought of as a power, conceptualizing freedom in normative terms makes sense, especially given Barth's Augustinian conception of evil as nothingness. For freedom to really be a kind of power — an ability, not a disability — it must take a particular shape and point in a definite direction. To be otherwise than loving, obedient, faithful — to be proud, slothful, or false, or to choose such — is not an ability, skill, or power, but a lack thereof, not an expression of the true humanity disclosed in Christ, but a retreat from it.[33]

Normative conceptions of freedom have fallen upon rocky soil in recent times, because they engender fears of heteronomy. But Barth undermines that fear by rejecting the idea that human action is ours only if it is self-initiated in an incompatibilist sense.[34] Barth insists that while Christian freedom is a gift of obedience that cannot be chosen or avoided, it is nevertheless ours, and we are not puppets.[35] To make this

---

32. *CD* III/3, pp. 248-52.

33. See Jesse Couenhoven, "Augustine's Rejection of the Free Will Defence: An Overview of the Late Augustine's Theodicy," *Religious Studies* 43 (2007): 279-98, for some suggestions about how Augustine's privation view of evil relates to Barth's depiction of evil as nothingness. The Augustinian view of the fall discussed in that paper has many similarities to Barth's discussion in *CD* III/3, pp. 355ff., and *CD* IV/1, pp. 484-85. Perhaps partially because Barth often fails to carefully nuance his use of the term "freedom," he does not explicitly connect his understanding of true human freedom to Augustine's notion of *libertas,* but there are important similarities between that idea and Barth's discussion as well.

34. Cf. Webster, *Barth's Moral Theology,* p. 90.

35. Cf. Barth, "The Gift of Freedom," pp. 74-75; Barth, *The Holy Spirit,* pp. 32, 68; *CD* III/3, pp. 254, 260-61.

point as strongly as he can, Barth is even willing to speak of redeemed human beings as having "a simple but comprehensive autonomy," an autonomy possessed not "outside Him, let alone against Him, but for Him, and within His kingdom."[36]

Using the term "autonomy" this loosely strikes me as odd, at best; it stretches the meaning of the term too far. However, it is important to see what Barth is up to in arguing (in this case, as so often, via rhetorical question) "How can there be any question of a conflict between theonomy and autonomy?"[37] He is suggesting that we are not simply passive before divine grace. Crucial to Barth's willingness to speak of human freedom, and even autonomy, as such, is the idea that there is a difference between being coerced, mechanically forced, or otherwise moved from without by some externally imposed necessity, and having a lack of options.[38] Having been determined by a new existence in Christ, a person can be active in taking the one option available, whereas a person is not active in being forced. Barth never puts this point especially clearly, but he does hint at it when he insists (as he often does) that while grace leaves us with only one option (obedience), it is not a fatalistic ruling and disposing, because it does not take away the importance of human deciding. Barth is suggesting that even if God makes a "decision for Christ" a volitional necessity, we "can do no other" in a manner that does not undermine the import and reality of our own human action.[39] This does not leave us with free will in the incompatibilist sense: we do not determine our wills in a manner that is solely up to us, such that we are the originators of our choices and actions. No, God moves in our wills, such that we choose him. But Barth's view is that our choosing God is nevertheless free and in some sense autonomous, because we really do that, of our own wills and with our own minds.[40] The fact that in doing so we cannot do otherwise than ratify what the Spirit is working in us is not a fact that Barth sees as detracting from our freedom; rather, he sees it as the basis of the normative Christian freedom discussed above.[41]

For Barth, then, we are free in ratifying through our own decision

---

36. *CD* II/2, pp. 177, 178.
37. *CD* II/2, p. 179.
38. *CD* II/2, p. 178; *CD* III/2, p. 181; *CD* IV/2, pp. 309-10, 318.
39. *CD* IV/2, p. 309.
40. *CL*, p. 102; *CD* III/2, pp. 180f.; *CD* III/3, p. 247.
41. *CD* IV/1, p. 467.

and activity what God begins in us. Barth avoids developing this idea philosophically — and, in particular, he does not offer a moral psychology that would illuminate how it is possible for God to work in us such that when we are left with only one option we are not forced to take that option. However, he appears to view human beings as free subjects insofar as we will the good given in Jesus Christ through the Spirit: "Man is, of course, purely receptive as regards the movement from God, but he is also purely spontaneous in the movement to God. . . . He is not a mere function at all. In this matter, God is Subject, but over and against God and in relation to Him man is also subject. I imply that I am subject by saying: 'I will.'"[42] Barth is not worried about whether we are independently in charge of willing what we will; it is enough that God calls us to be involved in our own right, by affirming and grasping our being "in the determination which it has not given itself but with which it was created."[43] Thus, we do not need to be the ultimate source of our being in activity to be free in our being and activity. More radically, Barth's discussion also implies that whatever we do voluntarily, or whatever we will, we are responsible for, whether or not we are free in doing so, and whether or not we could have willed otherwise.[44] Christian freedom goes beyond responsibility, in that it is normative, of the Spirit. And though all human persons are responsible for their goods and evils insofar as they voluntarily will them, Barth speaks of sinners as lacking freedom, while he considers those who are in Christ free indeed. Thus, Barth implicitly questions the presumption that only those who are free are accountable; at least in the Christian sense of the term, freedom is valued not mainly as a condition for responsibility, praise, or blame, but as a good in itself.

The fact that Barth appeals to the idea of "wholeheartedness" in his discussion of Christ's freedom suggests that it might be helpful to explore his understanding of Christian freedom in relation to Harry Frankfurt's discussion of wholeheartedness.[45] Frankfurt shares with

---

42. *CD* III/2, p. 180.

43. *CD* III/2, p. 180; cf. *CD* III/3, pp. 232-36.

44. Cf. *CD* IV/2, pp. 367-68.

45. *CD* II/2, pp. 177f. Eleonore Stump and others argue persuasively that these ideas are as old as Augustine, and important to Aquinas, as well; see Eleonore Stump, "Persons: Identification and Freedom," *Philosophical Topics* 24, no. 2 (1996): 183-213; Eleonore Stump, "Augustine on Free Will," in *Cambridge Companion to Augustine,* ed. Eleonore Stump and Norman Kretzman (New York: Cambridge University Press, 2001), pp. 124-47.

Kierkegaard and others a reflexive view of what it means to be a person, on which to be a personal self is to be in relation to oneself. Persons not only have first-order beliefs and desires such as "I would like to eat something with butter in it," but can also identify with or reject those inclinations via such higher-order reflections as "I'd prefer not to want to eat things that are fattening," or "I think it is good that I do not like to eat animal products." With this moral psychology in place, Frankfurt suggests that an important feature of the highest kind of freedom is wholeheartedness — being not internally divided but fully behind and unified in one's desires and decisions.[46]

Barth's understanding of wholeheartedness has implicit parallels with Frankfurt's. Among the reasons sinners lack true freedom is that sinners are always fractured and divided, at odds with themselves, and therefore not fully in the right. Only in Christ is it possible to be wholehearted, to live without self-contradiction, like Christ himself.[47]

The Freedom Proper to and
Characteristic of God: A Second Pass

The fact that Barth's conception of human freedom is most easily and consistently interpreted in compatibilist terms reintroduces the question of the relationship between his conceptions of human and divine freedom. Barth's conception of divine self-determination can sound incompatibilist — but if so, it has a number of drawbacks, on Barth's own terms. First, as we saw above, an incompatibilist conception of divine freedom seems to require an unsatisfying choice between (A) speaking of the immanent Trinity as free in itself at the cost of a dubious conception of divine choice, and (B) not speaking of the freedom of God with regard to the immanent Trinity. Second, it is hard to see how Barth's rejection of the ideas of Herculean freedom, or a neutral or arbitrary freedom, squares with incompatibilist conceptions of divine freedom; at the very least, those who read Barth in incompatibilist terms need to explain more clearly how the freedom they attribute to

46. Harry Frankfurt, *The Importance of What We Care About* (New York: Cambridge University Press, 1988); Harry Frankfurt, *Necessity, Volition, and Love* (New York: Cambridge University Press, 1999).

47. Cf. *CL*, pp. 184, 213-14; *CD* II/2, p. 179; *CD* IV/1, p. 403.

God differs from that which Barth rejects as non-Christian.[48] Third, incompatibilist readings of Barth on divine freedom fail to give an account of how the normative freedom human beings have relates to divine freedom. How does human freedom find its basis in divine freedom if the two kinds of freedom are of such different sorts?

A rereading of Barth's conception of divine freedom as compatibilist has none of these drawbacks. Moreover, such a reading is plausible. While some of Barth's individual statements about divine freedom can certainly be interpreted in incompatibilist terms, Barth never clearly says that God chooses triune being in love as a choice among alternatives.[49] And the fact that Barth has and relies on a normative compatibilist conception of freedom opens up the interpretive possibility that he has this idea not only in his treatment of human freedom, but also in his discussion of divine freedom. Such an interpretation makes sense in the context of his Trinitarian theology: since Barth indicates that Jesus' freedom is the normative freedom of goodness in relation to which he can speak of the "inner necessity of the freedom of God" and that this freedom is found in and given by the Holy Spirit, it makes sense that both the economic and the immanent Trinity should have this freedom.[50] It also seems unlikely that Barth would have supposed that human beings have a freedom that God does not. And in fact, Barth does speak in normative terms concerning the freedom of the immanent Trinity.[51] As Clifford Green has noted, Barth believes that ecclesial theology must speak of freedom as more than formal, and "life" is the normative term Barth chooses to illumine the connection between divine love and God's holy and righteous freedom, in which the Trinity both has and gives life abundantly.[52]

It is also significant that Barth's focus in his discussion of God as one who loves in freedom is on the ideas of divine commitment, limitation, binding, and determination — he downplays the idea of autonomy and rejects that of a *decretum absolutum*. A compatibilist interpreta-

48. *CD* II/2, pp. 60ff.; cf. Busch, *The Great Passion*, pp. 37-38, 112.
49. Richards, *The Untamed God*, p. 137; Hunsinger, "Election and the Trinity," pp. 181, 195.
50. *CD* IV/1, p. 195; cf. Webster, *Barth's Moral Theology*, p. 110.
51. See the excursus on *CD* III/3, p. 255.
52. George Hunsinger, ed., *For the Sake of the World: Karl Barth and the Future of Ecclesial Theology* (Grand Rapids: Eerdmans, 2004), pp. 91-93; cf. *CD* II/1, pp. 257, 263; Barth, "The Gift of Freedom," p. 71.

tion of what Barth means when he speaks of divine self-determination illuminates this trajectory. A compatibilist account of divine self-determination means being determined by God's self as Trinity, and thus not undetermined choice, but rather a primal and eternal self-affirming decision that is shaped by and congruent with who God is.[53] This idea accords with Barth's statement that "we do not say that God creates, produces or originates Himself. On the contrary, we say that (as manifest and eternally actual in the relationship of Father, Son and Holy Ghost) He is the One who already has and is in Himself everything which would have to be the object of His creation and causation if He were not He, God. . . . He cannot 'need' His own being because He affirms it in being who He is. It is not, of course, that His being needs this affirmation. But He does actually affirm it in this way."[54]

This passage suggests that when Barth speaks of God deciding or willing to be loving he has in mind something quite similar to what he has in mind when he writes that "Freedom is the joy whereby man acknowledges and confesses this divine election by willing, deciding, and determining himself to be the echo and mirror of the divine act."[55] Barth is not afraid to speak, in a compatibilist vein, of human spontaneity, willing, deciding, and self-determination, and when he uses the same language with respect to God, it is reasonable to suppose that he means something analogous.[56] Free divine self-determination, therefore, is not a matter of a preexisting will selecting among possible divine perfections, but rather the triune God's wholehearted good pleasure in and affirmation of the life in love that God is. It does not make sense to speak of God as having alternatives to such perfection, because all we are given to know about divine perfection is revealed in Jesus Christ. At the same time, Barth emphasizes that "He does not have to choose and do this" because such goodness is not forced on God;[57]

---

53. Cf. Hunsinger, "Election and the Trinity," p. 181.

54. *CD* II/1, p. 306.

55. Barth, "The Gift of Freedom," p. 79.

56. Cf. Hendry, "The Freedom of God," p. 237. In quoting texts Barth wrote prior to *CD* II/2, I am not ignoring McCormack's thesis that Barth's views on election mature only in *CD* II/2. I am suggesting, rather, that whatever the truth about other aspects of Barth's doctrine of election may be, there is no need to read Barth's treatment of divine freedom in *CD* II/2 as discontinuous with his treatment of divine freedom in earlier parts of the *Dogmatics*.

57. *CD* IV/1, p. 193.

such activity simply is God, God being true to and delighting in himself — and God is free in what Barth calls the Christian sense in being thus. The gracious and loving God manifest in Jesus does not require other possibilities or counterfactual paths not taken in order to be free in this sense, and Barth is able to say all that he wants to say about the unconditioned and sovereign nature of divine freedom by speaking of divine freedom in this sense.[58]

Conclusion

It would be anachronistic to call Barth a philosophical compatibilist, both because Barth's theology antedates that term, and some of the debates it invokes, and because of Barth's disinterest in offering a philo-

---

58. Cf. *CD* I/1, p. 319; *CD* II/1, pp. 305-6; Busch, *The Great Passion*, p. 124; Webster, *Barth's Moral Theology*, pp. 104-5. Nimmo argues that when Barth indicates, in his discussion of Christ's freedom in *CD* IV/1, pp. 193-95, "that the divine nature may or might have had other possibilities than obedience and incarnation," Barth means that God has a variety of possibilities that God limits by a divine choice that makes God "Lord over God's own Being" (Nimmo, "Barth and the Christian as Ethical Agent," p. 226 above). I have no idea what it would mean to be sovereign in such a manner; when Barth speaks of God being his own master, all I take him to mean is that God is not mastered by any power or law other than his triune being in activity (though he would have advanced his rejection of the idea of an arbitrary freedom better if he had been clearer about this). See, for instance, *CD* II/2, p. 100, where Barth associates God's having "lordship over everything else" with God's being independent "of all outward constraint, conditioning, or compulsion." The passage Nimmo quotes is ambiguous about whether divine self-determination requires choice among alternate possibilities in order to be free. All Barth says is that because of a prior decision (presumably, that regarding election) the Son necessarily makes obedient use of the possibilities of his divine nature. Barth does not say what those possibilities are, or how they relate to divine freedom, nor does he say anything about the nature of the decision of which he speaks. He does not, for instance, state that this decision is the basis of divine freedom. Finally, it may be important to note that a compatibilist reading of Barth's view of divine freedom does not imply that the divine nature is without possibilities. Compatibilism does not, for instance, necessarily indicate that God could not have created a world other than this one, or that Jesus could not have testified to the Father in other ways. All a compatibilist, normative freedom implies is that God can be free with regard to perfections and actions regarding which God does not have alternatives if God has the right relationship to those matters (e.g., God is free with regard to having true life in love even if God could not have chosen not to have such life, and have it abundantly, because God wills to have such perfection).

sophical treatment of the idea of freedom. What I propose in this essay is the plausibility of a compatibilist reading of some of Barth's key terms in his discussions of divine and human freedom. I have also argued that such a reading has a number of advantages. Reading Barth in the manner I propose will undoubtedly be controversial, and I am aware that this essay, interpretive as it is, offers little in the way of assessment of Barth's views, let alone a defense of compatibilism. But a final attraction of reading Barth in a compatibilist light is that it places him in continuity with a venerable host of theologians who defend related views, including Augustine, Aquinas, and Calvin.[59]

59. On Augustine, see Couenhoven, "Augustine's Rejection," pp. 279-98, and Jesse Couenhoven, "Dreams of Responsibility," in *Augustine and Philosophy*, ed. Phillip Cary, John Doody, and Kim Paffenroth (Lanham, Md.: Lexington Books, 2010), pp. 103-23; on Aquinas, see John Bowlin, "Contemporary Protestant Thomism," in *Aquinas as Authority*, ed. Harm Goris, Paul van Geest, and Carlo Leget (Leuven: Peeters, 2002), pp. 235-51; Robert Pasnau, *Thomas Aquinas on Human Nature* (New York: Cambridge University Press, 2002); on Calvin, see Paul Helm, *John Calvin's Ideas* (New York: Oxford University Press, 2004), chapter 6.